SECRET SURVIVORS

SECRET SURVIVORS

Uncovering Incest and Its Aftereffects in Women

E. Sue Blume

WILEY

JOHN WILEY AND SONS

New York • Chichester • Brisbane • Toronto • Singapore

Library of Congress Cataloging-in-Publication Data:

Blume, E. Sue.
    Secret survivors: uncovering incest and its aftereffects in women /
    E. Sue Blume.
      p. cm.
    Bibliography: p.
    ISBN 0–471–61843–8
    1. Incest victims—United States. 2. Adult child sexual abuse
victims—United States. I. Title.
HQ72.U53B58 1989
362.7'6—dc20   89–34113

Credits:

"Hey Good Lookin' ", written by: Hank Williams © 1951, renewed 1971, Acuff-Rose
Music, Inc., PO Box 121900, Nashville, Tn. 37212–1900, and Hiriam Music c/o
Warner/Chapell Music Group. Made in USA. International Copyright Secured. All
Rights Secured.

From "Aldonza", from the play, "Man of LaMancha." Used by permission © 1965.
Publishers Helena Music Company, Andrew Scott, Inc. Words by Joe Darion,
music—Mitch Leigh.

"Hail! Hail!" © 1987 by Robin R. Devino. Used with permission of the author.

"Child Abuse Prevention," by Maire MacLachlan, P.O. Box 475, E. Millinockett, ME
04430. Used with permission of the author.

"The 14 Stages" by Karen Lison, MA. Used with permission of the author.

"Flashbacks," by Laurieann Chutis, BCDCSW; © 1987 by Laurieann Chutis. Reprinted
by permission. For reprints, contact Laurieann Chutis, 4500 N. Winchester, Chicago, IL
60640.

Herman, Judith Lewis, *Father-Daughter Incest*. Copyright © 1981 by the President and
Fellows of Harvard College. Reprinted by permission of Harvard University Press.

Printed in the United States of America

10 9 8 7 6 5

Printed and bound by Courier Companies, Inc.

To my friend, Dorit Wolffberg, who died too soon, and my grandfather, Bernard Gottfurcht, who died in his time. Both were lost just before this book was accepted for publication. I share it with them now.

And to the women whose openness about their experiences and whose support of the Aftereffects Checklist led to the birth of this project.

Preface

*T*his book is about the aftereffects of incest. It is not about what incest is, but what incest does.

Sexual abuse victims are found among both men and women, but most are women. This book is partly for women who know they have been abused. It will help them understand how this early experience may have affected the person they became. But countless women *do not remember* their incest experience. This book is also for them. They may be dealing with depression, addictions, anxiety, or problems with intimacy and sexuality, wondering why they can't gain headway toward recovery. These survivors need to break through the secret of hidden incest. Only then can they know what those lost years contained and understand the effects of incest.

Too many research findings describing "people" are actually studies of men. I have worked with women and studied women's experience. The aftereffects I describe are inextricably intertwined with the social experience and psychological training of women—and indirectly with the training of men in domination, which has resulted in the skewing of power called incest. I refer to the survivor as "she" and, because most of those who commit incest are male, I refer to the perpetrator as "he." Two points are important here. I do not wish to imply that all men are abusers. And my book is not about the weakness and victimization of women. It is about their struggle to survive.

To help you understand the aftereffects of incest, I could not write about incest alone. I have had to deal with relationships, social rules, and the gender role training of women and men. My book is about power, and honesty, and healthy selfishness; about how the wrong rules of personhood are taught and the healthy rules are neglected or guessed at.

My book unveils a consistent pattern of emotional and behavioral aftereffects, evidence that incest has more complex and far-reaching consequences than other works have recognized. I call this pattern Post-Incest Syndrome. I offer it as a category for understanding—not a new psychiatric diagnosis and not a damning label that communicates a life detail to people who have no business knowing it. Post-Incest Syndrome profiles survivors' life issues, a response and a struggle. Too many have been mislabeled "promiscuous," "disturbed," "psychotic," "suffering from a biochemical imbalance," "borderline." Too many have been misjudged, disbelieved, hospitalized, blamed, and neglected. Incest survivors need an accurate characterization.

My tool for tracing Post-Incest Syndrome is the Incest Survivors' Aftereffects Checklist. The source of the concept for the checklist was an article by Janet O'Hare and Katie Taylor, "The Reality of Incest," which contained a dozen indicators of incest.* New York Women Against Rape (NYWAR) originally published the article and used it in NYWAR rape and incest counselors' training. Haworth Press later included it in an anthology called *Women Changing Therapy*. The article coincided with the beginning of serious attention to the prevalence of incest and with my own recognition of sexual violence as a common theme in the lives of women I was treating in therapy. Having originally thought that recovery came from discussing the details of the abuse, I shifted my focus and began helping them identify and deal with its consequences.

Simultaneously, I began sharing the NYWAR list with the few clients who were acknowledging histories of childhood sexual abuse. They in turn began to offer other experiences to add to the list. Although some characteristics individually could be seen in most women seeking therapy and some represented the consequences of other childhood traumas, when taken together they formed a definite pattern. The clusters of feelings and behaviors that emerged were, together, unique and constant for incest survivors.

---

*The items incorporated into the checklist are used with the permission of New York Women Against Rape (NYWAR), the original publisher.

The Incest Survivors' Aftereffects Checklist has spread from its downstate New York origins to international distribution among incest survivors, professionals, conference attendees, participants in self-help and recovery groups for sexual and substance abuse, and adult children of alcoholics. The feedback I have received from these diverse and un-related survivors and therapists has validated the universality of the profile.

I stated earlier that my book is not about incest alone. As you read it, you will learn, and perhaps face for the first time, some of the truths I have learned about the human experience. I hope you will learn also how the truth can be strong enough to overcome and repair the damage of destructive lies.

E. SUE BLUME

Freeport, New York
December 1989

———

Note about names: Most names of incest survivors in my book have been changed. A few women, however, asked me to use their given name, as their way of breaking their secret. I have respected their wishes. Real names are indicated with an asterisk.—E. S. B.

———

To the reader: The Author welcomes your comments and reactions, or the sharing of personal experiences which relate to your reading of *Secret Survivors,* although she regrets that she is not able to respond personally to such correspondence. If you would like to share your thoughts, or contact Ms. Blume for professional purposes, write to Box 7167, Garden City, New York 11530.

Acknowledgments

*T*he acknowledgments in a book are in many ways a private correspondence between an author and a variety of people whose names have no meaning to the reader. Who cares, really, if Esther Hossendorf patiently and faithfully read the original manuscript? Why not just write her a private thank-you note? Who reads the acknowledgments section of a book, anyway?

Since you are—and since most of the people cited will indeed be strangers to you—do not focus on the names. Instead, read this as testimony to human generosity. In these harsh and selfish times, in this book on the evils men do, it may be refreshing to remember the kindness of which we are capable as well.

My most sincere appreciation, of course, goes to those incest survivors, female and male, clients and workshop participants and strangers, who shared with me their stories, their anguish, and their victories. From their truths was borne the checklist, and this book; their encouragement, which came to me through letters and unsolicited, often anonymous calls on the telephone ("Just to let you know how much the checklist has helped me. . .") energized and reinforced me.

Thank you also to those researchers and authors who lay the groundwork for our revised understanding of the subject of child sexual abuse. I have quoted a number of you in this work. Thanks especially to Dr. Judith Herman, for saying so powerfully in *Father-Daughter Incest* what I could never have argued as well. Many thanks as well to my network of "telephone friends" (some of whom it has been my great joy to actually meet!), therapists and survivors (and sometimes one in the same) whose enthusiasm and insight kept my attitude positive and my brain working. I especially thank Marybeth Williams, LCSW, whose expertise in trauma theory (and everything else, it seems!) and boundless energy are an inspiration.

My special appreciation goes to those women who have kindly allowed me to borrow their work in this book: Karen Conterio, Program Developer and Consultant for the National Program for the Treatment of Self Injury at Hartgrove Hospital in Chicago, for her article, and for her friendship as well (also, her co-author, MaryJo Bever, RN); Laurieann Chutis, BCDCSW, Director of Consultation and Education services at Ravenswood Hospital Community Mental Health Center in Chicago, and developer of the "rap group" for incest recovery, for her allowing me to pass along her valuable article on Flashbacks. Much gratitude to Karen Lison, co-author of *Reclaiming Our Lives,* who shared not only her clear assessment of the "14 Stages" but also offered herself as an "advance person" for the slings and arrows of authordom.

My thanks as well to Robin R. Devino and Maire MacLachlan, whose eloquent and moving poems appear on these pages.

Thanks also to those who read my early manuscript, wading through the repetitions and typos and wordiness and repetitions; especially Marilyn Stromsness, M.A., Clinical Psychology Doctoral Candidate and founder of Minnesota Survivors' SAA (now SIA), who dared to be honest; and Alan Rosenfeld, Attorney at Law and founder of the Vermont Children's Rights Center, who constantly provokes me to look at things in a new way. Alan's dedication and persistence on behalf of women and children, his quiet insistence on living by the values he espouses, and his courage in taking on the "bad guys" even against the retaliations of those who are threatened or embarrassed by the truths he reveals, put those of us who proclaim our opinions more loudly, but make lesser sacrifices, to shame.

And of course thanks to Barbara and Suzanne and Laura and Lillian and Teri and "Jessica" and all the other survivors, both named and pseudonymed, who are quoted herein. Your words and experiences gave a voice and feeling and truth to this book.

Thanks to my parents, Toby and Alan Blume, for their pride in my accomplishments (and for never ever even suggesting that I should alter my goals because I am female); to RO-Z, for gifts too numerous to mention; and to the Sandersons (especially Brandy!) for their enthusiasm.

Thanks to Vicki Metz, whose New York Times article helped to launch the Checklist; and Malaga Baldi, my doggedly persistent agent, for not giving up—even after I did! And my editor at Wiley, Herb Reich, whose openness, responsiveness, and flexibility were a relief in the face of the "publisher horror stories" I had heard.

Thanks to Diane Conti, for her wisdom, constant willingness to listen to my ideas, and—not the least for typing the manuscript.

And thank you, David Satz, for your computer skills, typing, ideas, editing assistance, and the *countless* hours you devoted to this project. We often disagreed, and I learned a lot about the pitfalls of mixing business with friendship, but your time and effort made this a much more focused and well-written book than it ever would have been otherwise.

Finally, as for my own demons and doubters (many of whom I left back in Albany)—HA! I'm published! Living well is, indeed, the best revenge.

E. S. B.

Contents

Introduction

Among women, incest is so common as to be epidemic.

Incest is easily the greatest single underlying reason why women seek therapy or other treatment. At any given time *more than three quarters of my clients* are women who were molested in childhood by someone they knew. Yet virtually none of these women has identified child sexual abuse as the reason for her problems. Many, if not most, incest survivors *do not know* that the abuse has even occurred! Even if asked, they say—quite sincerely—No, nothing happened. Or, if they know that something happened, they cannot remember exactly what. This surprising phenomenon is the rule, not the exception, of the post-incest experience. Most survivors need many years, and often many therapists, before they can face the truths of their past.

Every day I encounter women who were sexually molested in childhood. When I was growing up, my neighbor was molesting his daughters. (I did not know what his behavior meant until twenty years later.) Recently, I had ambulatory surgery. Another woman and I waited to be wheeled into the operating room. Too sedated to be nervous, we ran through the standard polite queries.

"What do you do?"

I told her about my book.

"Oh!" she said, "That happened to me. . . ."

A national talk show host admits being molested in childhood. So does a senator, and a famous movie star—and more of my clients than I ever would have expected, before I knew what I now know.

Incest is not something that happens only to "those people, over there," the ones across town who don't wash very often. It happens in all strata of society, at all economic levels, and in all ethnic groups. It happened to Elizabeth Barrett Browning and to Bessie Smith, to name only a couple of notables. It happened to a president's son, and to Lana Turner's daughter.

The statistics are disturbing; the most commonly cited is that 25% of all American women have been sexually molested in childhood, most by someone they knew and trusted. Newer research, done more carefully and accurately, indicates that as many as 38% of women were molested in childhood. There are many acknowledged problems with even this research, but the greatest is this: what is not remembered cannot be reported. It is my experience that fewer than half of the women who experienced this trauma later remember or identify it as abuse. Therefore it is not unlikely that *more than half of all women* are survivors of childhood sexual trauma.

If you are one of these women you may not be able to identify what really has been causing the apparently disconnected clusters of problems and pains from which you have suffered most of your life. Nor, if you are in therapy, may your therapist know how to help you, for therapists have been as much in the dark about incest as other people. This blindness may well be a manifestation of a deeper reluctance to face the truth. There are many kinds of denial; not remembering is only one.

Incest is possibly the most crippling experience that a child can endure. It is a violation of body, boundaries, and trust. Unless identified and dealt with, the emotional and behavioral aftereffects can stay with the victim. The very defenses that initially protect the incest survivor later lock these problems into place, interfering with adult functioning and preventing healing or change.

Literally tens of millions of "secret survivors" carry the weight of their hidden history of abuse. The incest survivor may appear to be—and may actually be, in many ways—successful, talented, appealing, even happy. Yet underneath, she may feel as if she were rotting. She may see herself as crazy or unreal. The confusing behaviors and feelings that she endures could make sense if she knew her incest past. Instead she feels trapped, confused, irrational, sick, and weak. This is Post-Incest Syndrome.

To wonder whether you or a loved one might have endured sexual abuse is, itself, accompanied by difficult emotions. If you are reading this and looking at your own life, you may be experiencing uneasiness, even sudden fear. You may suddenly begin to cry. The intensity of your reaction may confuse you, especially if it is accompanied by a strong denial—"No! This couldn't have happened to *me!*" You might even find yourself saying these words aloud, or shaking your head as if to throw the question off. Indeed, the mere *asking* of such a question is bound to create anxiety.

But if your level of tension is extreme, if the mere *possibility* that it happened is very upsetting, then it is important to ask yourself what this intensity means. Please know, however, that you don't have to do it now. If, at this point, your feelings seem too raw, if you are scared or overwhelmed, *you can stop.* If you want to, you can put this book down and shut the subject away and not think about it until you are ready, whether in five minutes or two weeks or a year. You can take as much time as you need. If you were molested in childhood, you may not have been in control of what happened to you then, but you are now. Today you are much more in control of your experience, of what you deal with, how much you feel, and for how long you experience it. The process of your recovery is slow, *should be slow,* as you struggle between needing to know and being afraid to see.

Through the Incest Survivors' Aftereffects Checklist, numerous incest survivors have finally been able to piece together the disjointed fragments of their lives: difficult though it is to face that one is an incest survivor, this is the first step in ending confusion and finding a direction for healing. Using the checklist, incest survivors can understand the feelings and experiences that interfere with their lives and the reason for each characteristic, its basis in the natural drive for survival and self-protection. From this can come the opportunity to convert these maladaptive efforts into healthy and productive feelings and behaviors.

I have written this book for survivors (both those who remember and those who do not), for those who care about them, and for the professionals who serve them. This book addresses the concepts behind the Aftereffects Checklist. After introducing the broadened definition of incest upon which my work is based and discussing incest research, I explore the basic themes of incest—powerlessness, boundary violation, and the secret. Next I discuss the tactics commonly used (and misunderstood) to protect against awareness of a reality that cannot be faced: amnesia, blocking, splitting (depersonalization), shutdown, and others. Subsequent chapters focus on particular clusters of aftereffects:

the ways in which memories "tap" at the survivor's consciousness (flashes, flashbacks, dreams, and nightmares); the survivor's inner reality—shame, guilt, self-esteem, fear, and anger; addictions and compulsions; "self-destructiveness" versus victimization; physical aftereffects (the body and sexuality); interpersonal issues, including intimacy. The last chapter looks at issues in recovery.

THE INCEST SURVIVORS' AFTEREFFECTS CHECKLIST

The Incest Survivors' Aftereffects Checklist (pp. xviii–xxi) is an inventory of 34 items developed through interviews with clients who identified a history of sexual abuse in their lives. As we explored the growing list of characteristics, an unexpected—and very significant—application began to emerge. Among women who had not been aware of childhood sexual abuse but who recognized characteristics in themselves on the checklist, a surprising number began to uncover previously repressed incest. Thus we found that the Aftereffects Checklist can serve as a diagnostic device for suggesting childhood sexual victimization when none is remembered. It also serves as a roadmap for a therapist treating someone whose amnesia or denial is total. Whether or not actual memories are uncovered, the checklist then presents a structure for identifying and addressing the consequences of incest.

The power of the list is in the power of the incest experience and the openness of the incest survivors who helped develop the list. Current research studies are validating the observations in the checklist.

As often as the truth of this checklist has been validated, however, I am aware that the information it contains is "skewed": it is based on the experience of incest survivors whose problems drove them to seek help, be it professional or peer-related. That is not to say that these women are "sicker" than others. Indeed, these women were strong enough to face their trauma and its pain. Those who continue their denial are not included; neither are those whose lives are untroubled. Also missing, however, are women who were so traumatized that they could not function in the "real" world: active addicts, women in mental institutions or jail, homeless women, women who committed suicide. But when I read about such women I see many of these aftereffects in their lives.

In recent months I have come across other lists of the consequences of incest that are notably similar to each other, and overlap with this one. For me, this similarity reinforces the accuracy of the observations they contain. The common focus for those who develop such lists must be the incest survivor herself. She provides the information for a researcher who is willing to listen—who is less interested in imposing realities than in discovering them. Professionals are letting go of the tendency to tell incest survivors about themselves, and are letting the survivors have their own voice. In this regard, I, like my colleagues, am a conduit, not an originator.

APPLICATIONS

The Incest Survivors' Aftereffects Checklist is a starting point from which to explore the development of each aftereffect, from the original abuse experience through its consequences in the incest survivor's adult life. We must view each aftereffect as a survival tactic rather than as a problem to be overcome. Even the inability to remember abuse serves to protect the incest survivor. Incest that has been buried has been buried for a reason. The checklist makes it possible to see both how this repression is accomplished, and what has been repressed.

The checklist describes the many ways that incest affects its victims. We cannot necessarily understand these effects through traditional criteria, which attempt only to measure "damage." No one characteristic applies to all survivors. We must view the consequences of incest in clusters. Most incest survivors whom I have interviewed or who have contacted me find that of the 34 categories of emotional/behavioral items, more than 25 apply to their lives.

Not all aftereffects fall into recognized categories of dysfunction such as phobias, depression, or anxiety. They often describe patterns of behavior or feelings, such as the way the survivor wears clothes, how she interacts, or what "protections" she requires. Incest alters personality in ways that therapists, researchers, society—or survivors themselves—have failed to identify. It does not affect everyone in the same way, nor does it affect everyone equally as destructively, but it changes the survivor into someone she would otherwise not have been.

By illustrating how completely incest affects all aspects of survivors' lives, the checklist reinforces that sexual activity between a child and someone who is more powerful can *never* be benign.

The Incest Survivors' Aftereffects Checklist

Do you find many characteristics of yourself on this list? If so, you could be a survivor of incest.

_____ 1. Fear of being alone in the dark, of sleeping alone; nightmares, night terrors (especially of pursuit, threat, entrapment)

_____ 2. Swallowing and gagging sensitivity; repugnance to water on one's face when bathing or swimming (suffocation feelings)

_____ 3. Alienation from the body—not at home in own body; failure to heed body signals or take care of one's body; poor body image; manipulating body size to avoid sexual attention

_____ 4. Gastrointestinal problems; gynecological disorders (including spontaneous vaginal infections); headaches; arthritis or joint pain

_____ 5. Wearing a lot of clothing, even in summer; baggy clothes; failure to remove clothing even when appropriate to do so (while swimming, bathing, sleeping); extreme requirement for privacy when using bathroom

_____ 6. Eating disorders, drug or alcohol abuse (or total abstinence); other addictions; compulsive behaviors

_____ 7. Self-destructiveness; skin carving, self-abuse

_____ 8. Phobias

_____ 9. Need to be invisible, perfect, or perfectly bad

_____ 10. Suicidal thoughts, attempts, obsession (including "passive suicide")

_____ 11. Depression (sometimes paralyzing); seemingly baseless crying

_____ 12. Anger issues: inability to recognize, own, or express anger; fear of actual or imagined rage; constant anger; intense hostility toward entire gender or ethnic group of the perpetrator

_____ 13. Splitting (depersonalization); going into shock, shutdown in crisis; a stressful situation always is a crisis; psychic numbing; physical pain or numbness associated with a particular memory, emotion (e.g., anger), or situation (e.g., sex)

_____ 14. Rigid control of one's thought process; humorlessness or extreme solemnity

_____ 15. Childhood hiding, hanging on, cowering in corners (security-seeking behaviors); adult nervousness over being watched or surprised; feeling watched; startle response

_____ 16. Trust issues: inability to trust (trust is not safe); total trust; trusting indiscriminately

_____ 17. High risk taking ("daring the fates"); inability to take risks

_____ 18. Boundary issues; control, power, territoriality issues; fear of losing control; obsessive/compulsive behaviors (attempts to control things that don't matter, just to control something)

_____ 19. Guilt, shame; low self-esteem, feeling worthless; high appreciation of small favors by others

_____ 20. Pattern of being a victim (victimizing oneself after being victimized by others), especially sexually; no sense of own power or right to set limits or say no; pattern of relationships with much older persons (onset in adolescence)

_____ 21. Feeling demand to "produce and be loved"; instinctively knowing and doing what the other person needs or wants; relationships mean big tradeoffs (love was taken, not given)

_____ 22. Abandonment issues

_____ 23. Blocking out some period of early years (especially 1–12), or a specific person or place

_____ 24. Feeling of carrying an awful secret; urge to tell, fear of its being revealed; certainty that no one will listen; being generally secretive; feeling "marked" (the "scarlet letter")

_____ 25. Feeling crazy; feeling different; feeling oneself to be unreal and everyone else to be real, or vice versa; creating fantasy worlds, relationships, or identities (especially for women: imagining or wishing self to be male, i.e., not a victim)

_____ 26. Denial: no awareness at all; repression of memories; pretending; minimizing ("it wasn't that bad"); having dreams or memories ("maybe it's my imagination"); strong, deep, "inappropriate" negative reactions to a person, place, or event; "sensory flashes" (a light, a place, a physical feeling) without a sense of their meaning; remembering the surroundings but not the event

_____ 27. Sexual issues: sex feels "dirty"; aversion to being touched, especially in gynecological exam; strong aversion to (or need for) particular sex acts; feeling betrayed by one's body; trouble integrating sexuality and emotionality; confusion or overlapping of affection, sex, dominance, aggression, and violence; having to pursue power in sexual arena which is actually sexual acting out (self-abuse and manipulation, especially among women; abuse of others, especially among men); compulsively "seductive" or compulsively asexual; must be sexual aggressor or cannot be; impersonal, "promiscuous" sex with strangers concurrent with inability to have sex in intimate relationship (conflict between sex and caring); prostitute, stripper, "sex symbol," porn actress; sexual acting out to meet anger or revenge needs; "sexaholism"; avoidance; shutdown; crying after orgasm; all pursuit feels like violation; sexualizing of meaningful relationships; erotic response to abuse or anger, sexual fantasies of dominance or rape (Note: Homosexuality is not an aftereffect)

_____ 28. Pattern of ambivalent or intensely conflictive relationships (intimacy is a problem; also focus shifted from incest issues)

_____ 29. Avoidance of mirrors (connected with invisibility, shame/
self-esteem issues, distrust of perceived body image)

_____ 30. Desire to change one's name (to disassociate from the perpetrator or to take control through self-labeling)

_____ 31. Limited tolerance for happiness; active withdrawal from
happiness, reluctance to trust happiness ("ice=thin")

_____ 32. Aversion to making noise (including during sex, crying,
laughing, or other body functions); verbal hypervigi-
lance (careful monitoring of one's words); quiet-voiced,
especially when needing to be heard

_____ 33. Stealing (adults); stealing and starting fires (children)

_____ 34. Multiple personality

The Incest Survivors' Aftereffects Checklist is not complete—never
will be. As awareness increases, it will grow and be further refined.
Ultimately, this list will combine with such bodies of knowledge as
trauma theory, feminist power analysis, and bereavement theory, to enhance our understanding of the total experience of the incest survivor—described by Post-Incest Syndrome.

SPOILED LOVE: An Overview

*I*ncest may not be what you think it is.

The term *incest* has been taken to mean sexual relations between siblings, the marriage of first cousins, the seduction by fathers of their teenage daughters. People refer to "incestuous relationships," as if there were a relationship, as if there were reciprocity. Society tries to hold anyone responsible for incest other than the man who commits it. Therapists themselves have operated on the belief that "cold," nonsexual mothers or "seductive" daughters are responsible for a father's sexual abuse of his child. People think that incest is done only by scruffy men with day-old beards who can't resist their sexual urges.

This is not a true picture of incest.

WHAT IS INCEST?

The literal, traditional definition of incest is "sexual intercourse between two persons too closely related to marry legally." What incest is really is nowhere acknowledged in the traditional application of the word. Actually, it is the most serious and most common form of child sexual abuse. Arguably, it is also the most serious of all types of child abuse.

Relationship Between Child and Perpetrator

Even those who understand the word *incest* in the context of child welfare have generally applied the rigid and literal qualifier of blood relationship. In the eyes of the law and the mental health profession, incest has meant sexual activity between a child and a parent, sibling, cousin, uncle, aunt, or grandparent. All other sexual abuses of the child were seen as not significantly different from abuse by strangers.

Blood relationship alone, however, does not represent an accurate qualifier. If we are to understand incest, we must look not at the blood bond, but at the emotional bond between the victim and the perpetrator.

Incest survivors first articulated this distinction, in the literature generated by a number of support groups. Therapists who specialized in incest and who were open to learning from their clients soon adjusted their understanding. The new definition took into consideration that incest—unlike abuse by a stranger or acquaintance—*violates an ongoing bond of trust between a child and a caretaker.*

Because the perpetrator of incest derives authority through a dependency relationship, incest has more serious emotional consequences than does abuse by a stranger. Not only is the body violated, but the child's trust and love as well.

In this regard, it must be noted that abuse at the hands of biological fathers is often experienced as the most painful of all. Supporting this theory are a number of respondents in Diana Russell's book, *The Secret Trauma: Incest in the Lives of Women and Girls.* One survivor's story from her book makes the case very powerfully: Olga experienced genital fondling by a doctor when she was 17, rape by a male partner when she was 41, forced oral sex the following year, and rape by an ex-lover at 47. Yet, in her report, a one-time fondling of her breasts by her father was the most upsetting of all. She shared this reaction with a number of other survivors interviewed, who had experienced multiple abuses, some with battering, but virtually all of whom reported that abuse by their fathers was the most traumatizing.

In incest, the very person or persons whom the child most relies on and needs take advantage of her dependence. Therein lies both the real damage of this abuse and the domination that allows it to happen: the child has no choice, not merely because the perpetrator is bigger, or older, or more socially dominant, but because her emotional and physical survival depends on her acquiescence. Even when a child is molested by a trusted coach, teacher, regular babysitter, mother's non-residential boyfriend, she still experiences both levels of the abuse: the sexual trauma, by virtue of the power imbalance, and the violation of trust and boundaries.

A child may be molested by a kid down the street; this is not incest. A little girl may be raped by a stranger; the proverbial schoolyard bum in a trenchcoat is actually a rarity, and this abuse is not incest. A runaway kid, living in the streets (having probably run away from some form of family abuse, often incest) may be picked up and prostituted by a middle-aged businessman; this form of sexual abuse may not be incest either, but once the man takes the child in and becomes a surrogate parent for the child, it becomes incest.

Depending on the relationship, a perpetrator may be a father, mother, stepparent (or parent's lover), grandmother, grandfather, uncle, aunt, cousin, babysitter, doctor, dentist, teacher, principal, priest, minister, rabbi, foster parent, neighbor, family friend, coach, therapist, worker in a residential facility, nurse, or anyone else in long-term contact with the child. In the life of a child, six months is a long time.

Can a child's softball coach, for example, be seen as a relation? The important criterion is whether there is a real relationship in the experience of the child.

An Imbalance of Power

Can sex play between same-age siblings or cousins be incest, although it is presumed not to involve abuse? What term can we use for this activity, if not incest?

What distinguishes abuse is a power imbalance. Such an imbalance may exist even between two children of the same age if one (usually male) is physically larger or has more status or more power in the eyes of the victim and/or her family or society. For instance, a devalued daughter, if approached by a favored son, feels unable to say no even if they are the same age and size. She might be the daughter who can't do anything right; he, the son who can do no wrong. She might not receive approval or nurturing from her parents; he, her only ally, gives what little attention and protection there is to be gotten at home. But at what price? What would she have to sacrifice to end the abuse? Where can she go to complain? Who would support her? Who would believe her? He might tyrannize her, abusing her emotionally and physically as well as sexually. Where is there protection from this chosen son? Indeed, what is to be done if his family is as dominated and fearful of him as she is? In no way can this sexual activity be called harmless experimentation.

"Incestuous play," as I use the term, applies to sexual experimentation that is equal, cooperative, and voluntary, and therefore not likely to yield negative consequences. This meaning is quite different, however, from the meaning I am using for incest itself.

The findings of such researchers as Diana Russell, author of *The Secret Trauma: Incest in the Lives of Girls and Women,* reveal that these equal and nondestructive experiences are much less prevalent than some suggest. More commonly, someone is taking what he wants, and someone else is going along with it. In other words, much of what we perhaps have been calling "sex play" is incest after all.

Incest, as both sexual abuse and an abuse of power, is violence that does not require force. The victim is being used by another, treated in a way that is not wanted or not appropriate by a person with whom a different relationship is required. It is abuse because it does not take into consideration the needs or wishes of the child, rather meeting the needs of the "caretaker" at the child's expense. If the experience has sexual meaning for a caretaker, in lieu of a nurturing purpose for the benefit of the child, it is abuse. If it is unwanted or inappropriate for her age or the relationship, it is abuse.

Incest, a New Definition

Given these realities about the *true* consequences of sexual violation of the dependency bond, *incest* can be seen as *the imposition of sexually inappropriate acts, or acts with sexual overtones, by—or any use of a minor child to meet the sexual or sexual/emotional needs of— one or more persons who derive authority through ongoing emotional bonding with that child.*

This redefinition has far-reaching implications. To adopt it is to broaden the scope of this word's narrow traditional meaning, taking it out of the hands of therapists, lawyers, and sociologists and reframing it through the real experience of the victim. As a result, the institutions of law and therapy can truly begin to see the real consequences of this form of child abuse.

Rape without Intercourse

Must incest involve intercourse? Must incest be overtly genital? Must it involve touch at all?

The answer is no.

Let us again turn to the experience of the incest survivor. By what acts did she feel violated? What acts influenced her sexual frame of reference? What act did damage? In this framework, we can understand that incest is not necessarily intercourse. In fact, it does not have to involve touch. There are many other ways that the child's space or senses can be sexually violated. Incest can occur through words, sounds, or even exposure of the child to sights or acts that are sexual but do not involve her. If she is forced to see what she does not want to see, for instance, by an exhibitionist, that is abuse. If a child is forced into an experience that is sexual in content or overtones, that is abuse. As long as the child is induced into sexual activity with someone who is in a position of greater power, whether that power is derived through the perpetrator's age, size, status, or relationship, the act is abusive. A child who cannot refuse, or who believes that she cannot refuse, is a child who has been violated.

Certainly our attitude, for both children and adults, is that forced intercourse is a more serious crime than fondling. However, this distinction often makes no difference to the child; once touch has moved from safe, nondemanding affection to confusing, inappropriate sexuality, the damage is done. Not that penetration doesn't provide added risks: it can cause serious internal injuries, and may be experienced as more traumatic by the victim. But we are talking about a category of abuse, not degrees of damage. The courts and therapists alike have minimized the pain of too many incest survivors. Survivors themselves have learned to dismiss their own complaints when met with, "Oh, it was 'only' touching."

Abuse is sexual when it has sexual overtones or content, such as when a sexual "attitude" comes over the molester. Although the victim may be too young to understand or have a label for his changed breathing or husky voice, these are strange and uncomfortable experiences for her.

In some cases, the parent elevates the child to spouse-confidant. This may occur when the perpetrator's partner has died, or is sick, or "fails" the perpetrator in some way. In a troubled marriage, the abuser, instead of facing the problem with his or her mate, may turn to the child, with whom an interaction is not intimidating. The child, then, becomes a companion for one parent while she must suffer through repeated litanies of the failings, including sexual, of the other parent.

This type of incest, which is often nonphysical, sometimes is called "covert" or "emotional" incest or seduction. It is the second most common type of incest reported to me about female perpetrators, with whom overt sexuality may not occur, although touching is frequent. It is not exclusive to women, however.

In such quasi-spousal abuse, the abuser shares with the confused child information of a deeply personal or sexual nature about her parent, putting her in the center of a controversy where she is forced to be disloyal to one parent and bear the pain of the other, often being expected to provide physical, if not sexual, comfort. At the same time, she may be bestowed with special attentions or gifts. Having been made betrayer of one parent and mate and "kept woman" of the other, she is filled with ambivalence and robbed of both her parents and her childhood. Survivors of this kind of incest may struggle even more with identifying that they have been abused, for the abuse is less obvious than more directly physical or sexual abuse.

Force, Resistance, and Secrecy

Force is not necessary in incest, and is rarely used. The child's natural dependence and powerlessness are used against her. The closer the relationship, the less necessary force is and the less likely the perpetrator is to use violence. Fathers are least likely to resort to violence: the child's need, as well as the power of his guardianship role, virtually guarantee access. More distant relationships may necessitate some threat of force, or, more rarely, some actual violence. The younger the child, the less there is even a question of tactics; a one-year-old does not do—she gets done to. As Andrew Vachss, children's attorney and author of novels concerning incest, says, incest is "rape by extortion." Thus the child's very childhood becomes a weapon used to control her.

Should the child manage a weak resistance, a whimpered protest, she is ignored. Despite our current attempts to teach children to shout an emphatic "NO!", this truly revolutionary no-longer-obedient-child is still a rarity. When such a protest occurs within the context of an incest-bound relationship, it carries little weight. And so there is truly no choice. The child either has no means of defense, or her refusal carries no impact. As much as he might be hurting her, she loves him and needs her family. So she decides not to decide and lets it go on. In the confused loyalty of the victim, she protects her abuser, holds his secret, and now even carries his shame, for she has "cooperated." She blames herself, as if there were really choices.

Secrecy, a necessary component of control, is imposed on the victim of incest. The secrecy surrounding the abuse validates what her guts have been telling her—that there is something wrong—but renders her even more incapable of doing anything about it.

In many ways the secret may be more damaging than the incest, with its resulting confusion, self-doubt, and feelings of craziness and powerlessness. Later, if the truth finally comes out, they will say, "No, that can't be true! She never said anything at the time!" That is what the relatives of Long Island high school student Cheryl Pierson said when, in 1987, at age 17, she was brought to trial for the "contract killing" of her father. But then they said as well, "He was a fine man. We wouldn't have believed her if she had told us, either."

Women as Perpetrators

Incest often manifests itself in a manner consistent with gender socialization: for a man, the abuse is generally overtly and directly sexual; for a woman, it may be more emotional, more focused on relationship and bonding, or perhaps manifested through care of the child's body, her primary domain. Although certainly abuse, this activity may be without a sexual intent on the part of the abuser. In my experience, when mothers, grandmothers, or aunts are abusers, they are often recalled as being obsessed with forcing frequent, ritualistic, unwanted and unneeded enemas, genital exams, and similar, if more perverse, procedures on the child. Whatever intentions the actors in these dramas may have had (and certainly there are many occasions when the care of children legitimately requires touching them), these occurrences are often experienced as sexual abuse by the victim.

Let us be careful to use the same standards to define what is incestuous abuse by women and men. There is a tendency to see men as committing identifiable incest but, in expanding the category of incest, to include acts that might not truly be abusive. Russell points out that we define incest as sexual until we want to look for women perpetrators, at which point the definition is broadened considerably—and broadened into areas that are not then applied to male behavior. Further, there are acts—such as commenting about their daughters' breasts—that men do, and women virtually never do. True, a mother might call her son "big and handsome;" to some, this represents incest. But does she ever comment about his penis size?

So that the behaviors of women can be included, I have, for instance, seen "seduction" used to describe a situation where mothers cry on the shoulders of their children. Although this role reversal is inappropriate, it is not incest (unless she's explicitly crying about her husband's lack of sexual attention to her, or how he isn't gentle with her the way the son is). I have also seen studies of "seductive behavior" that focus exclusively on mothers, with fathers' behavior not investigated at all. (Even so, in one such study, only 10% of the mothers were found to be seductive.) With regard to the "body function abuse" that some women commit, there may not be exactly a "sexual" purpose for the abuser, but some gratification that is harder to categorize, almost certainly coming out of the distorted response patterns induced by the abuser's own early abuses.

Given women's constant involvement as mothers with the intimate physical functions of children, what is striking is how infrequently such abuses occur. Often when women are perpetrators "more often than not it is at the instigation and encouragement of men," as family violence researcher David Finkelhor states. For a more comprehensive analysis of female and male perpetrators, see recent books by Finkelhor and Russell.

The Many Faces of Incest

Incest has many subtle faces. Incest can be an uncle showing pornographic pictures to a 4-year-old. It can be a father masturbating as he hovers outside the bathroom where the child is, or one who barges in without knocking. It can be the way a babysitter handles a child when he bathes her. It can be a school bus driver forcing a student to sit with him, fondling her under her skirt at traffic lights. It can be an older brother forcing his sister to undress, or a cousin and his friends cornering the little child in the basement and forcing that child to touch them "there."

It can be the way a father stares at his daughter's developing body, and the comments he makes. It can be the way an aunt caresses her niece when she visits. It can be forced exposure to the sounds or sights of one or both parents' sexual acts. It can occur through a father and mother forcing their child to touch or be touched by other children while pictures are being taken, or by a father "pimping" his daughter to his best friend, or passing her around to his buddies in the bar. Per-haps she must look at, read, or perform in pornography alone or with others (children, adults). That, too, is abuse. It can be the way a priest kisses a child goodbye. Or it can be a father's jealous possessiveness and suspicion of the boys his daughter associates with, his inquisitorial insistence on knowing the details of her sexual encounters. And it need not restrict itself to victims who are "children" in the literal sense. The disabled, always more vulnerable, are particularly at risk, and those who are incapacitated can be said to be victimized by "child abuse" throughout their lives, due to their neverending helplessness and dependency.

It can be abuse perpetrated by many family members, one at a time or in groups. Horribly, increasingly, it can occur as part of a cult ritual activity engaged in by a network of adults and involving many children—violence and abuse of animals as well.

Incest does not contain itself. It usually does not stop at one act, but becomes an ongoing part of the child's life experience. It generally does not stop with one child either; it may pass from daughter to daughter, or child to child, as each outgrows her or his availability or "desirability." (There are different types of child molesters. Many do not discriminate on the basis of sex.) The molester will violate anyone to whom he has access; the family may provide him with his victims, or he may pursue activities, such as coaching, that offer access.

Incest is not the consequence of one sole family member gone rene-gade. It often passes through the generations from victimizer to victim-become-victimizer or from victimizer to victim-become-mother-of-victim. From grandfather to father to uncle to children, and. . . . My clients frequently voice concern for their children's visits to grandpa, or nieces and nephews to the brothers who once molested them.

Other Experiences that Can Feel Like Incest

Several types of experience are not actually incest but may feel like sexual abuse to the child. They may be associated with violation of a relationship because of the role parents are seen as playing, although they may not occur for the sexual benefit of the adults. For example, a child may have to undergo medical procedures on her genital or pelvic region at an early age; a doctor or a team of white-coated strangers may hold her down, put a mask over her face, and touch her body in embarrassing places, without consideration for her feelings, or with barely any acknowledgement of her. Whether this occurs in the presence of a parent, which makes it feel like a betrayal, or with the parents absent, which then feels like abandonment, it is still experienced as a violation of trust.

Alan Rosenfeld, a Vermont attorney who is the founder and director of the Vermont Children's Rights Association, offers this ironic example of another such experience. The child may feel sexually violated if, after reporting incest, she is forced to undergo verbal and physical examinations by staff assigned to verify her complaint. "Sent" by her mother, too young and overwhelmed to understand why she must repeatedly go over the details of her trauma for no therapeutic purpose, she will often feel violated again and again. One child told her mother, "The Child Protective man raped me!" Rosenfeld thinks she got confused; it was probably a gynecologist doing a court-ordered, "legitimate" examination, but that part hardly matters.

"INNOCENT" BEGINNINGS

Incest does not start with puberty. Those who may first reveal the existence of abuse in their teens have probably been enduring it for years.

- In 1988, 35% of all reported child sex abuse cases were of girls under 6.
- According to the FBI, most rape victims are between ages 10 and 19. One quarter are under 12.
- Dr. Michael Durfee, of the Los Angeles Department of Health Services, reported in 1984 that more sexual abuse was reported on 2-year-olds than any other age group. Three- and four-year-olds were next.
- In 1985, Dr. Arthur Green, director of Columbia Presbyterian Medical Center's Family Center, was quoted in a United States Government public affairs pamphlet on incest as saying that the hospital was "horror struck" by the number of babies and preschool children brought in with genital injuries, gonorrheal infections of the throat, venereal warts, and syphilis.
- In March 1988, Long Island *Newsday* published a report about a man accused of molesting a 1-month-old baby, who suffered permanent injury to her bowel.

Incest often starts as seemingly innocuous touching, wrestling, tickling, playing. Lilly* describes this scene: "My uncle would teach me how to dance. I was 11 or 12, he was 23. I can remember the day it changed. One day, and forever after that, his hand would rub up and down my back. I didn't like it. The cold, sweaty feeling of his skin. His funny breathing. The way his voice sounded. God, his hands felt—awful. One time my aunt walked in on us. I can remember how he pushed me away from him and jumped back. And his body got all tight. I had always felt something was wrong; now I knew."

As much as she was uncomfortable with the situation, Lilly was unable to describe exactly what the problem was. Sometimes, incest is even more obscure for the child. The older the child, the more intrusive and overt the sexual act, the more able she will be to understand that there is a real reason for her discomfort. Unfortunately, however, incest rarely begins when the child's ego or sexual awareness are that well developed. It often begins when she does not yet have the verbal or cognitive capacities to describe to herself or others what she is experiencing. Before she has even heard of rape, or learned about lovemaking, she has this introduction to the world of sexuality, but "sexuality" that is tainted by violation and, by its nature as abuse, violence.

More confusing, it is abuse that often occurs under the guise of love, or of more acceptable forms of physical contact. (When the molester is a woman, the denial and isolation can be even more extreme.) The victim is left doubting her own perceptions and feelings. This is compounded when everyone around her acts as if nothing is wrong. She is left feeling crazy, as if she is the one with the problem. Having no "corroboration," the victim is once again victimized.

Incest and the Victim's Age

Many professionals who work with adult incest survivors believe that the child's emotional, cognitive, and other age-related development is arrested at the time the incest begins. For instance, a child whose victimization begins in infancy is said to remain a one-year-old emotionally while her body and brain grow into adulthood, whereas a woman who was first molested at 14 will be much more mature in her functioning.

One problem with this theory is that there are many psychological schools of thought about these so-called developmental stages, and some are in serious disagreement. Some of the more well-known theories are recognized as exploring male development only. Women's development has rarely been studied, as Carol Gilligan points out in her outstanding exploration of the invisible psychology of women, *In a Different Voice*. Psychoanalysts believe that developmental stages include an oral stage, an anal stage, and an Oedipal stage, while other therapists do not see any evidence that this is reality, and in fact criticize this view as fostering some of the most serious abuses that incest survivors have suffered at the hands of therapists and society.

Yet some things can be agreed upon. Certainly the work that a developing child must do on issues such as bonding, trust, self-esteem, identity development, intimacy, and tolerance for distance, are different at different ages. A 10-year-old child is different from a 14-year-old child, and both are different from an adult. Certainly a child who is sexually abused will be affected differently than an adult woman who is raped. An adult is fully formed (although not finished growing and changing). Her sense of herself as a separate yet interrelated individual, as well as her sexuality, are more advanced than that of the child; a child victim of incest, however, experiences a course of development (emotional, interpersonal, sexual) that is shared, every day, with premature sexuality, lack of safety (even terror), and deformities of many life skills. The child victim's entire view of herself and the world will be clouded by the effects of her abuse.

Although recognizing and applying these factors in assessing the influences of the abuse on the functioning of my incest survivor clients, I am not sure I fully agree that a survivor's development stops when she is molested. I have seen many incest survivors who are emotionally well developed in many areas of their lives, who have strengths on which we both rely as therapy progresses. More than their growth being totally, universally retarded, I have found that there are gaps and distortions in individual areas, related to specific tasks.

THE IMPACT OF THE INCEST EXPERIENCE

Incest ravages childhood.

For the child victim and the woman she will become, incest is more than rape of her body. Because of her dependence on her abuser, incest is a rape of her trust as well. In this sense, the sexual aspect of incest is secondary. Someone the victim trusted, instead of giving her love, took what he wanted from her, terrorized her, hurt her, humiliated her, controlled her, disgraced her, and shattered the separateness of her. Although he called it love, he raped her, robbing her of the opportunity to develop into a healthy, intact adult, abrogating his responsibility to care for and protect her.

Children are always at the bottom of the social pecking order—all adults have power over all children. Children do not have the status to impose their will on adults, and they lack the ability to be allowed to control their own lives. This gives those around them a special responsibility: although we are never responsible for the lives of other adults, we are always responsible for children. The younger children are, the more dependent they are; the more dependent they are, the greater our obligation to protect them. As much as we can protect them, we can abuse them, thereby putting them especially at risk.

In the eyes of the law, children are totally unable to make decisions regarding sex with adults. By definition, sex between children and adults is rape—statutory rape—which means that even a child who appears to consent is not seen as consenting, for she has not the power to refuse. If her no has no power, her yes has no meaning.

Basic Human Needs

Incest affects the fundamentals of human development.

Love At the core is the distortion incest represents to the primary human need for love. Love is a verb. Love honors the other person. It manifests itself when we treat other people with consideration for their feelings and concern for what is best for them.

It is the parents' job to serve the needs of the child. A parent expresses love for a child through attention to what the child needs. In the beginning, the child's needs are put first; the younger and more dependent the child, the more her needs take precedence.

It is enough of a trauma for an adult, who has already developed ego strengths, to be held captive—as, for instance, a prisoner of war—and to be raped besides, but for a child to be virtually born into this situation, before she is fully developed psychologically, is to damage her to the very core. To be lacking in these at the time when they need to be integrated into the formation of the personality often results in a lifelong quest—a quest either to get them, or to compensate for not getting them by trying not to need them.

Validation   Validation is support and reinforcement of the child's feelings, perceptions, and ideas, her selfhood, and her right to be who she is. It is affirmation of her very existence. When a child's needs are responded to, she learns to understand herself, to understand that she exists. When a child's needs are met, she learns that they have worth, and therefore she has worth.

The antithesis of validation is negation. By ignoring the child's needs, incest nullifies her right to her needs. The victim learns that what she needs is so unimportant that she has no value at all. She might as well not exist.

Mastery   Mastery is impact. It gives the child a sense that she makes a difference, that her efforts count. A child develops a sense of mastery when what she tries, she succeeds at; when she reaches out into the world around her and something changes; when she asks for something, or asks for something to stop, and it happens, as she wanted.

The lack of mastery results in passivity and resignation. The incest victim learns that she has no power; her efforts don't matter at all. No matter what she says, what she does, she is not heard, and the abuse continues. Someone else can always have his way with her. She learns from this that she is not in control of her own life, that she has no control over her environment.

Unconditional Acceptance   This is really one definition of pure love. It means that the child is loved just as she is, not for living up to someone else's standards; loved not for what she achieves, but for sitting in a chair, for just being there, for messing in her diapers, spilling her milk, sleeping. She can expect love even when she's not perfect. The child victim of incest, however, is loved not for herself, but for how well she serves another person. "Love" is used to justify certain expectations of her. Incest teaches her that she does not deserve acceptance merely for who she is, and that she should never expect it.

Nonpossessive Love   Nonpossessive love is freely given, without expectations or strings; there is no "ownership" attached to attachment. The gift of love, like any other, is a gift only if the giver lets go of it. Incest, however, gives with one hand and takes back with the other even more than was imparted. The victim is precisely a possession. She learns to equate love with indebtedness. The message is "produce and be loved." To be loved is to be owned, and to owe.

There is, of course, no love in this equation at all, no opportunity to develop a sense of self-worth when she is treated as if she has no worth. And yet it comes in a package called love, from the people whose job it is to love her. Thus is she taught the meaning of these terms, and comes to believe that "love" always requires sacrifice—that it is something taken, not given.

Ego and Body Integrity The child must learn boundaries— where she ends, both psychologically and physically, and where the other person begins. She must learn that she is, and is entitled to be, a separate self, distinct in identity, needs, desires, feelings. With boundaries defined, she is able to set limits, and to determine, for example, when, how, and by whom her body is to be touched. Incest obliterates all of this, teaching her that she is an extension of everyone with whom she is close. It is as if she does not exist as a separate self.

Long-Term Effects

Time does not cure the effects of incest. Although the memories go underground, the consequences of the abuse flourish. Sometimes they are buried under other problems—substance abuse, relentless rage, self-destructive behavior. But they lie waiting, waiting for the clarity that sobriety brings; waiting for release from thought-confusion and phobias, the lifting of depression, the opening that comes through therapy or intimacy. They also may erupt on their own. Untreated, they can lead to suicide, or even murder. And, in the saddest paradox of all, the aftereffects that comprise Post-Incest Syndrome usually spell continuing victimization—for the survivor herself, for her lovers, even for her children.

Some who were molested rally their strengths and survive their abuse relatively unscathed. Some stubbornly refuse to surrender, and live lives of satisfaction. Some are so damaged and endure such repeated horrors that they must rebuild themselves almost from scratch. Unarrested, untreated, this confusion of sex, love, guardianship, and violence infests families and can fester in the individual for life.

OTHER CONSIDERATIONS

In addition to the intrinsic harm of incest, there are other circumstances that affect the impact of the abuse on the victim. Some concern the incest itself, and some concern the context of the child victim's life. These include:

1. *How close was the relationship of the perpetrator to the child?* Was he a primary caretaker such as a parent or stepparent? Was she strongly emotionally bonded to the abuser? This is a key factor—the severity of the physical violation may not be as destructive as the emotional violation.

2. *At what age or developmental stage was she?* The younger she was, probably the more severe the effects and also the more difficult to root out.

3. *What types of acts were perpetrated on the child?* There is no "not bad" incest. Many survivors find that the severity of the damage is not directly related to the nature of the actual act. For others, however, there is a correlation.

   Diana Russell found that there was a correlation. She suggested that the more severe the trauma, the greater the need—and the tendency—to minimize the consequences.

4. *Was the incest itself violent? What other abuses occurred?* If the incest occurred within the family, were there emotional or physical abuses, apart from the incest, perpetrated against either her or her siblings? Was there an overall feeling of fear or danger in the family? Was the child forced to witness rituals of violence?

5. *How many abusers were there?* What impact did it have on a child for more than one abuser to have molested her? The number of perpetrators may or may not be as significant as their relationship to the victim.

6. *How long did the abuse go on?* Many incest survivors report being as traumatized by short-term abuse as others do by a lifetime of abuse. However, owing to the repression that often surrounds these memories, it is difficult to know exactly when

abuse started or stopped. It must also be noted that even a single incident can cause lifelong scars.

7. *Did she tell? What happened if she did?* Failed attempts at getting someone to understand could leave her feeling more hopeless, totally defeated. The fact that she told somebody then, however, can help her now to locate the abuse in time and place and help her overcome the feeling that she "let it happen."

8. *Were there outside resources available to the child?* These might be adults, other children, pets, emotional outlets or "safe places." Perhaps they could not stop the abuse, but they could care about and support her.

9. *What internal resources did she tap?* What she "does" with the event is influenced by her history, attitudes, and areas of deficits. The impact of an event is also affected by her inner strengths: her capacity to rationalize, or intellectually understand and assess, her ability not to blame herself (which is part of self-esteem), her ability to hope for change—and, not least, her sense of humor.

There is no formula that can be applied to any of these influences. For every individual, different aspects will carry different weight. Researchers have attempted to measure the impact of various factors, but, humans cannot and should not be reduced to statistics. Every woman's story is important, whether her experience is "statistically significant" or not. Many incest survivors, already crippled by a tendency toward self-blame and dismissal of their own feelings and pain, feel even more unimportant when the research tells them that their experience rarely (or never!) happens.

Let us avoid the tendency to attempt to decide whether incest is "bad" by its consequences. Are enough survivors depressed in their later life? Are they depressed enough? David Finkelhor, author of several books on child sexual abuse, reminds us that incest, like rape, is bad in and of itself: no matter whether there is resulting trauma, or how much there might be, it is still a violation. We do not need to measure the degree of trauma caused by a burglary, for instance, to bring it to legal judgment; the act is evaluated on its own terms. So, too, should we view sexual robbery.

ADULT CHILDREN OF ALCOHOLICS

There is an enormous overlap between incest and family alcoholism. As Finkelhor reports, one researcher found that incest perpetrators are more likely to use alcohol than any other type of sex offender. So correlated are these two experiences, both in occurrence and consequences, that it may be difficult to know where one begins and one ends.

Incest frequently coincides with an alcohol-filled environment. Some perpetrators have the disease of alcoholism. A large percentage of children of alcoholic homes, called adult children of alcoholics (ACOAs), have experienced sexual abuse by a parent. Some perpetrators use alcohol to disinhibit them and facilitate their abuse of a child, or to serve as an excuse for their loss of control. For others, both the alcohol abuse and child sexual abuse serve the same function, in that they provide a false sense of control and relief of tension, but one does not rely on the other.

Many of my clients are both ACOAs and incest survivors. Specialists in Adult Children's issues have in recent years begun to stress the prevalence of incest histories among ACOAs; Claudia Black, renowned ACOA expert and author of such books as *It Will Never Happen To Me,* routinely addresses incest issues. Many incest survivor support groups began as offshoots of ACOA meetings. To help many ACOAs— and their therapists—see the significance of a family history of alcoholism, many people have developed "lists" of ACOA characteristics. Similarities with Post-Incest Syndrome are striking: control, boundary, trust, self-esteem issues, depression, anxiety, a general inability to modulate feelings, high risk taking, co-dependence, assertiveness problems, a need for excitement, and a deep sense of responsibility for everything that happens are all found in both groups. In addition, gender roles are extremely exaggerated in alcoholic families, as they are in families or relationships where incest exists.

Yet even more interesting is the omission of this factor from recent books and research on incest, even those that are accurate and comprehensive in many other respects.

Because of the overlaps of the characteristics, I am concerned about the validity of any analysis of incest that does not address ACOA issues. If an incest survivor comes from an alcoholic family, as many do, and the effects are so similar, as many are, how can we know which aspect of her history yields what consequences? Indeed, although the aftereffects cited here are clearly, for me, associated with incest, there are times I wonder which I have written a book about. Some characteristics are exclusive to Post-Incest Syndrome and do not apply to ACOAs or the survivors of other types of childhood deprivation (such as "simple" abandonment) or trauma (such as "simple" emotional or physical abuse). However, incest and these other experiences all overlap and thus share aftereffects in the experience of the person who endures them.

CHILD VICTIM, ADULT SURVIVOR

Incest combines all the forms of abuse that can happen to a child. It contains the violence and violation of physical abuse, the self-esteem consequences of emotional abuse, and often the actual or perceived abandonment of the nonperpetrating parent or parents as well as the confusion and chaos of family alcoholism. Incest is the most devastating form of abuse that a child can endure. It robs her of her childhood, her innocence, her ownership of her body, and her sexuality. It damages trust and disrupts bonding. It isolates her in an unpredictable, emotionally confusing bond with her abuser, secured with secrecy and threats.

In short, incest kills. Not all at once, not totally, but one way or another, sooner or later, piece by piece. The whole child, or just a piece of her. Just her body or just her soul.

Children should be able to expect to be loved. Period. They are entitled to be loved without having everything taken from them—without having anything taken from them. They deserve to learn that it is safe to be dependent. And they should experience having their needs met without tradeoffs or payback.

The child victim of incest has had none of this. She is a child without a childhood, forced to choose between violation, violence, and abandonment. She was a victim in every sense of the word; yet, as an adult, even as she endures the impairments of Post-Incest Syndrome, she is not a victim, but a "survivor."

Why do we call her a survivor?

When she was a captive child, her immersion in the inevitability of the abuse made her a victim. As a true description of her experience, the term serves as a reminder that *she* was not the wrongdoer.

But now it is over, and she has endured; she is a survivor. On one level, that term can be applied simply because she is still here: after a childhood of horror, she has kept on going. On a deeper level, she is a "survivor" because a "victim" is characterized by passive helplessness and is seen with pity. But in survivors of the Holocaust, POW camps, or natural disasters, as well as incest, there is strength, dignity, resilience, and entitlement of respect. To continue to call her a "victim" is to insult her by overlooking the victory of her survival.

And now, having survived, she can begin again. She can go beyond surviving and work for the quality of life that she deserves. She can unlock and break the secret, take her power back, shed the guilt and self-blame of the experience and learn, finally, to be angry at what was done to her—instead of at herself. She can refuse to accept a life that feels confused and out of control. It is not enough to get up each morning and suffer through the day. When she faces her past and reclaims herself, she will not just have survived; she will have triumphed.

SUPPOSITION AND RESEARCH:
What We Know, What We Think We Know

*I*n her powerful book *Father-Daughter Incest,* psychiatrist Judith Herman writes that a therapist who had turned to a supervisor for help regarding a client's newly revealed incest was advised "not to open that can of worms!"

Therapists were not the first or only group to legitimize incest or disregard its victims. Several of the books cited in the list of Recommended Readings present the historical context that has tacitly approved the sexual abuse of children. The responsibility for seduction is placed on the children in Genesis 19:30–36: "And the first born said to the younger . . . 'Come, let us make our father drink wine, and we will lie with him that we may preserve the seed of our father. . . . ' " This passage has been notably absent from commentaries by fundamentalists, who insist that the Bible speaks literal truths. How likely is it that this alleged seduction was planned by the children? Just whose fantasy does this sound like?

FREUD'S LEGACY

In the late 1800's Sigmund Freud invented psychoanalysis, a theoretical approach to therapy. He took many risks and revolutionized thought about sexuality, the existence of an unconscious and psychological defenses, the value of talking about feelings and the consequences of not

21

doing so. He also developed many theories that were inaccurate, especially regarding women, but which are passed on by graduate schools today.

Freud asserted that certain inevitable, natural, internal conflicts cause emotional disturbance later. These struggles, he said, take different forms during certain developmental stages, such as the oral stage, the anal stage, and the Oedipal stage. Freud proposed that out of these stages arose "castration anxiety," a common experience for boys, and "penis envy," a universal source of distress among girls.

Both theories presume that much of human experience centers around the value of the male sexual organ. By this measure, boys are innately gifted whereas girls are innately deficient. (Actually, I have never met a woman who wished she had a penis, except when she went camping. Mostly I hear women express relief at not having that fragile organ that might reveal their sexual longings.)

Carol Tavris, in her *Ms.* article called "The Hundred Year Cover-Up: How Freud Betrayed Women," relays a wonderful story that puts this view in perspective. The four-year-old daughter of a friend had recently seen a little boy's penis for the first time. "Mommy!" she exclaimed, "Isn't it a blessing that he doesn't have it on his face!"

Initially, Sigmund Freud acknowledged the presence of incest among most of his early female patients. Later he renounced his "seduction theory," attributing the problems of his patients to what he called an Oedipal fantasy—the desire of a child for the parent of the opposite sex and desire to get rid of the same-sex parent.

As Freudian scholar Jeffrey Masson points out, the abandonment of the truth of incest had a social consequence: it helped conceal the frequency with which men allowed themselves to sexually molest children.

Subsequent generations of researchers and therapists continued the lie. Even analyst Helen Deutsch, in her book *The Psychology of Women,* never mentioned incest, but this betrayal was not exclusive to psychoanalytically oriented therapists. Some who perpetuated this attitude were surprising. Some were not.

CHALLENGES TO FREUD

Alice Miller, a Swiss psychoanalyst and child advocate, challenges many of Freud's theories in her book *Thou Shalt Not Be Aware: Soci-*

ety's Betrayal of the Child. She suggests that a child may be traumatized to the point of pathology by outside events, and needs to repress childhood trauma such as incest (as Freud initially suggested). This analysis is different from the "failure to resolve" the oral, anal, or phallic stages of development. She challenges especially the last of these stages.

Miller says in *Thou Shalt Not Be Aware*, ". . . the Oedipus complex does not owe its survival to experimental data but to the entrenched power of the psychoanalytic societies, whose goal is to uphold the defense mechanisms of generations of fathers." In addition to the various critiques of Freud's theories and those of his followers, is this factual one: because the "Oedipal period" occurs between ages 3 and 6, how could it serve as the explanation for a child's complaint of incest that began when she was 8, 10, or 12—or 6 months old?

Miller (like Florence Rush, Judith Herman, Jeffrey Masson, and a number of other recent authors) discusses Freud's now notorious betrayal of his women clients, and all incest survivors. Various authors try to explain why Freud initially acknowledged the existence of incest and later proclaimed that his patients must have made up or wished for the alleged abuse. Some 30 years later, according to Miller, he claimed that he had overvalued reality and undervalued fantasy.

To the misfortune of many, this attitude has been carried on. In the foreword to the German edition of Florence Rush's *The Best-Kept Secret*, Alice Miller states that when she presented her view that children had been betrayed by the therapists' need to ally themselves with parents, she was criticized for not focusing enough on the child's fantasy, and for believing her clients too much!

The literature is full of frightening stories of analysts and their supervisors focusing not on the trauma endured by the victim, but on her supposed enjoyment of the event, if not her outright invention of it. Miller's book relates a number of these stories. When she first presented her ideas to a group of about 300 analysts, they were relieved and surprised that the experience and pain of the child were finally being validated. Many—including male audience members with tears in their eyes—told her that it was their lives that she had been describing. Later, however, when she submitted her ideas to psychoanalytic journals, the editors refused to publish them.

Children of both genders were sacrificed to what Miller describes as a bias in favor of the authority of parents, but women especially so.

Several authors observe that the Oedipal theory is "so obviously tailored to fit male development" (Miller) that Freud, as Harvard psychiatrist Judith Herman says, "forfeited his ambition to understand the female neurosis [and went on to develop what was really] a psychology of men." Due to his refusal, or inability, to stand by the truth of women's victimization through incest, what Herman calls a "common and central female experience," it is not surprising that he could never answer the question, "What do women want?" It's simple, Sigmund: they want to be believed. And they want to be seen as whole persons, with value in their own right rather than imitation men with missing pieces.

THE DAMAGE CONTINUES

In addition to traditional psychoanalysts, other sex educators seem to have been more a part of the problem than a part of the solution. Some have promoted incest as a right of men and a benefit to children. Most notable of these was the Kinsey organization, which as Herman describes it, "demonstrated a keen sensitivity toward the adult offender. As scientists and leaders in the struggle for enlightened sexual attitudes, they felt it incumbent upon themselves to plead the offender's case." They protested that "heterosexual incest occurred more frequently in the thinking of clinicians and social workers than it does in actual performance." The problem, they said, was not in the incest, but in the reaction of parents and society, who were getting too upset! "We have only one clear-cut case of physical injury done to the child, *and* [my emphasis] a very few instances of vaginal bleeding which, however, *did not appear to do appreciable damage*" [emphasis mine].

In 1976, *Forum* (an offshoot of *Penthouse* that pretends to be about sexology) ran this statement: "Incest between adults and younger children can also prove to be a satisfying and enriching experience" (except, the author goes on to say, when it involves "force, violence, or coercion"!). Who was the author? Was it some sleazy pornographer? It was Wardell Pomeroy, one of the co-authors of the famous, well-respected, and scientific Kinsey report.

As recently as 1979, under the guise of shattering repressive attitudes, what Herman calls a "pro-incest manifesto" was written in a nonpornographic sexuality-education journal. It identified the problem as "a fear of incest, similar to the fear of masturbation." The journal was from the Sex Information and Education Council of the United States (SIECUS), a nationally known and respected institution for sex education. A decade later SIECUS published my first article on the Aftereffects Checklist!

Other researchers continue to study why there is a taboo against incest, as if the problem is in the taboo (and as if the taboo really existed). Or they devote their energies to attempting to validate incest, studying the times that it supposedly does no damage. Herman cites two researchers who sought subjects whose incest experiences were positive; they heard from a whole lot of fathers who thought this was so, but very few daughters who were enthusiastic.

Research on sibling incest has generally remained blind to the difference between abuse and experimentation, even when an imbalance of power and the resulting coercion are clearly evident. The message has traveled down to the victims themselves. "It was only my brother," they tell me.

In 1972, sibling incest was studied from outpatient clinics in Ireland. The author of the study, psychiatrist Narcyz Lukianowicz, said that virtually all were "far from being innocent victims: on the contrary, they were willing partners and, often, provocative seductresses." He concluded that this incest "did not result in any bad effects." As Russell, who presents this information, points out, one wonders then what these people were doing in outpatient clinics.

Research perpetuates lies about the incest that society condones. One of the best-selling books of all time is Nabokov's *Lolita*—accepted by scholars as a literary classic. The book is about a stepfather's "fascination with" (actually, rape of) a 12-year-old and other evils he commits before and after he entraps her. The book presents the view that the child seduces him. This is one of the myths that we as a society continue to support: the victim wants it to happen and is the likely seductress.

We use another myth to discount the complaint of the child victim: children lie. But when children make up lies, they are creating a safer, more acceptable reality than the one they know. Who of us has ever retreated into a fantasy that offers us less than reality? All of us who work with incest have seen how hard the survivor works to deny, forget, minimize, or avoid the painful reality of her past. Why, Alice Miller asks, would they "work so hard to discredit . . . something . . . they themselves have invented?" "Sometimes," she says, "I have to ask myself how many children's corpses psychoanalysts require as proof before they will stop ignoring their patient's childhood suffering. . . ."

You might protest that our awareness is changing. In some circles, it is. But not nearly enough. In the McMartin case, many of the children at the Manhattan Beach preschool were treated for vaginal and anal infections and internal damage. Yet no medical professionals suggested that the source was sexual abuse until one mother was told that her son's anal bleeding was probably from a rape—the second time the physician saw him for the same problem.

I have something to tell you about those children who society claimed were lying, who fantasized the abuse, who wanted the abuse. They are the women who I see as adults trying to repair their shredded souls, struggling to survive, trying (still) to protect the abuser's image by ignoring what he did, or blaming themselves, believing they're crazy so it won't be true. They come to therapy, week after week after week, crying, struggling, denying, and finally, with a combination of relief and sadness, admitting to the truth of their pasts: "Yes, it happened; yes, I was hurt!" And finally the wounded child is free of the lies and the "research" and the silences, and her voice is heard. *She* is the confirmation of the truth that these children are forbidden to tell.

DIFFICULTIES IN CONDUCTING RESEARCH ON INCEST

A book by David Finkelhor, *Child Sexual Abuse: New Theory and Research,* helped usher in a new era of accurate research on incest. A later book, *A Sourcebook on Child Sexual Abuse,* consists of an exhaustive team review of studies about incest survivors and perpetrators, addressing the errors and contradictions found.

Diana Russell, in *The Secret Trauma: Incest in the Lives of Girls and Women* published in 1986, offers the results of her own study, which was done in 1977. In this book she also critiques existing research and offers an analysis of the biases found therein.

These books are especially useful due to the enormous contradictions found in even contemporary research about incest.

Defining Incest

Major discrepancies show up in estimations of the prevalence of incest. According to Finkelhor, estimates of female victims of incest range from 6% to 62%, while estimates for males vary from 3% to 31%. In Diana Russell's study of 930 women in San Francisco, 38% revealed that they had been physically molested (e.g., touched) before age 18. When non-physical abuse was considered, *over half* of her subjects reported that they had been victimized. What is responsible for these differences?

A significant issue is definition: how is incest defined? Some studies restrict incest to sexual abuse by a father, some include stepfathers, and some include all relatives. Admittedly, no study to date has defined incest as broadly as this book does. What act comprises incest? For most, it requires touch. Russell, for instance, did not include noncontact abuse in her research. Yet what impact does it have on a child to be forced to watch her father masturbate? (At one point Russell acknowledges that this does yield similar results, and says that maybe she should have included it after all.)

What age difference is the threshold of abuse? Russell and Finkelhor required significant age differences in order to consider an act abusive—at least 5 years (unless trauma was reported to be associated). Yet Finkelhor recommends that peer abuse be included in what is investigated as abuse, and non-contact abuse as well; and Russell acknowledges that "the possibility of true consent recedes as the age gap increases." Why, then, require a certain number of years? And what effect would the altering of this requirement have had on the results?

A number of more technical factors influenced the results, including how the questions were asked and how the sample of women was selected for the study. All these factors must be taken into consideration before the results of any research about incest are incorporated into the body of accepted truths.

Repression, Self-Reporting, and Time

There is another factor that is likely to distort the results of any research (especially findings on frequency) but is generally overlooked or minimized: the techniques that incest survivors use to survive the abuse. These include denial, repression of memories, blocking out a period of childhood or a person or place, and blocking out the more painful aspects of the abuses (e.g., abuses by one person but not another, or certain portions of the abuse). Also, self-blame might result in a survivor's not acknowledging her victimization. Furthermore, much abuse occurs when the child is so young that she might not have the words or the awareness to describe what happened to her; with incest that begins in infancy, as much of it does, the victim is totally nonverbal. If, as many clinicians believe, more than half of all incest survivors are likely to be affected by one of these situations, what consequence will there be on research findings?

Russell's study reflects many examples of the possible impact of repression on the findings of researchers:

- When all types of child sexual abuse (incestuous and extrafamilial) were reviewed, the majority of perpetrators were not family members. But what if only the less traumatic events—which would generally be those from less intimate relationships—were remembered?

- Conclusions were drawn on the number of incidents that occurred; however, virtually none of my clients remember every event.

- Respondents were asked to evaluate which event was "most severe." What if the real "most severe" were least remembered or acknowledged?

- She obtained information regarding prevalence of perpetrators who were fathers, stepfathers, uncles, siblings, cousins, and so on. If the most traumatic is least remembered, wouldn't these results be almost the opposite of the truth?

- 47% of the women who were molested by fathers said they were molested only one time. Yet the authors of "The Reality of Incest" say that in their experience on staff at New York Women Against Rape, incest virtually never occurs only once.

One basic problem that I see in any attempt to do research about incest is that of self-reporting. Can an incest survivor—can anyone—accurately assess the impact of a trauma? Russell's interviewers often saw discrepancies between how an interviewee said she felt and how she acted; for instance, many claimed not to be upset by what had happened, but acted very distressed. Unbelievably, only 12% of Russell's respondents reported that the incest had a negative effect on relationships, and 14% saw a negative effect on sexuality.

Finkelhor points out a related concern: "It is well established . . . that the validity of reports declines with distance from the event." In fact, "investigators are reluctant to research what occurred over one year in the past." This would seem to put a cloud over any attempt at research of a trauma from a person's distant past, as researching adults about childhood sexual abuse must be.

Other Traumas

One clear gap in even the most reliable research on incest is the failure to include the other childhood and family traumas that so often overlap with incest. For instance, alcoholic families are never mentioned; neither are other forms of family violence, all of which can have consequences similar to those of incest. (Russell asks about violence as a part of the incest, but not apart from it.) Thus it is hard to know to what one can attribute the respondents' complaints. The consequence of these aspects of a child's early life must be separated from those of incest before we can see a true picture of the consequences of sexual abuse. Or if it turns out that they *cannot* be separated, then no research can hope to encompass the problem unless it takes all these parts into account.

MALE AND FEMALE VICTIMS AND PERPETRATORS

Are there really only a few male incest survivors and a few female perpetrators? Both Russell and Finkelhor endorse the overwhelming body of research findings that the vast majority of victims of incest are female, and the vast majority of perpetrators, male.

Although we are finding that more boys are abused than were previously thought, the ratio is not shifting significantly. Both Russell and Finkelhor project that, when those that abuse boys are taken into consideration, about 20% of perpetrators of incest are women. (Actually, Russell's respondents reported that only 5% of their female relatives were perpetrators—a figure she calls "strikingly low"—but she acknowledges that the inclusion of male victims would alter this number. And while Finkelhor found 19% female perpetrators, he defined incest to include sexual experimentation. He also found that more females were likely to experiment than violate.) Women also committed fewer acts of abuse, and their acts were found to be much less "severe" and totally devoid of violence.

These findings on male victims and female perpetrators bring to light an intrinsic problem related to quantifying these life experiences. Lately some have suggested that as many women molest as men, and as many boys are victimized. Some of those who are suggesting this are male incest survivors, or survivors who were abused by women, who perhaps feel that their experience is not perceived to be as valid as the experience of those who belong to a majority. Their message seems to be "what happened to me is what happened to all those other people; just as important, because it is just as common." Of course, one's pain is just as important—whether one is abused by a woman or when the one who is abused is male. This problem underlies all statistical analyses on incest survivors.

Sadly, many survivors are so self-doubting, their sense of entitlement so fragile, that they feel their problems are somehow "not good enough." If research reveals that their experience is shared by a minority, their feeling of insecurity or insignificance may increase. It is hard enough for any of us to feel we are "the only one" of anything (how often my clients—incest survivor and nonsurvivor alike—say: "Do other people feel this way?"). But to feel like a member of a stigmatized minority (although they might actually represent a majority) and to be different *even from them* is very difficult to deal with indeed.

However, from all indications, neither the abuse of males nor abuse by females occurs as frequently as the abuse of females by males. Abuse becomes oppression when one group (men) is generally the victimizer of the other (women). This is more than an individual problem.

And that is a point that some groups have a vested interest in minimizing, leading to a strange partnership in this stance, regarding male and female victims and perpetrators. There is today an assault against the truths that are finally coming out about incest (as well as battery, rape, and other sexual violations, which almost exclusively are perpetrated by men—usually, in fact, the *same* men)—a backlash against the recognition that women are often the targets of abuse by men. Unfortunately, those who take this stance, men who minimize the true abuses experienced by women, often disguise themselves by pretending advocacy for victimized children.

Balance and accuracy are both necessary. For instance, with regard to the question of abusers who are women, between the anti-feminists who claim that women are just as abusive as men, and those who claim that no woman would ever hurt anyone, are the voices of the incest survivors, once again silenced. This is not acceptable, but neither is the sacrifice of women or the excusing of men through our refusal to acknowledge the realities of imbalanced and abused power. There really is a gender gap in abuse: men are much more often perpetrators than women are. And women are more often victimized, by this as well as all other forms of sexual violence. But no one's experience is unimportant.

In my work with incest survivor clients I have known only a handful who were molested by women. Several of these women were multiply abused, one by only women in an all-woman household, and the others by both women and men. In all my correspondence with incest survivors and incest survivors' groups, I have known of only a few more. That is what I know of "numbers." As to the consequences, when female perpetrated abuse occurs, one survivor described this: "It's so much more complicated for me to deal with my mother's abuse of me. After all, she was *mom;* I expected more from her—like nurturing. My father, well, hell, I can accept distance, even face abuse. But *she* was the one I turned to . . . she's *like* me. We're both *women.* How could she do this to me?"

The struggle of these survivors is complicated by the uniqueness of their situation. Their feelings of alienation, isolation, self-doubt and low self-esteem are likely to be exacerbated by the discomfort of others. Even among their "allies" these problems can occur, as exemplified by an experience that Terri had when she went to her first support group. It was a therapist-run group that she had waited months to be admitted to. When she told the women who her abuser had been, she heard one of the other women catch her breath. She left feeling as if there was no place on earth where she really fit. Even in a group of incest survivors, there was something "wrong" with her.

Fortunately, at this writing, there are several anthologies being prepared of experiences with female perpetrators. Also, male incest survivors are slowly beginning to devote as much energy to taking care of themselves as they have seen female survivors do.

IN SUM

Incest research has been used to hide truths and support lies; like the Bible and your daily horoscope, some research findings somewhere can be found to support almost any premise. Although recent research has tended to take into consideration such issues as bias and has been evaluated from a more educated position regarding incest, there are still serious gaps and omissions.

In the end, as Finkelhor points out, any conclusions from incest research "must be tempered by the fact that they are based on a body of research that is still in its infancy . . . [and that still has] sample, design, and measurement problems that could invalidate their findings." And perhaps the entire premise of this research must be approached with caution. Herman puts it this way: "The insight of a skilled clinician cannot be matched by any questionnaire or survey instrument presently available. Subtle forms of emotional damage, which may not be detected in broader sociological studies, are apparent in clinical reports." In quantifying human experience, we may lose its richness, if not its truth.

In reality, probably many incest survivors struggle alone, uncounted and unrecorded. Russell acknowledges that her study does not include a cross-section of incest survivors. Missing are survivors who are in brothels, in prisons, in mental hospitals, the retarded and disabled, women who are living in the streets—and those who have died. In that sense, it is the most seriously damaged whose voices cannot be heard.

3

IN SOMEBODY ELSE'S HANDS:
Control, Power, and Boundary Issues

*I*n incest, an omnipotent person imposes his or her will on a child. Already powerless and weaker because of her age, developmental level, and size, the molested child must deal with those vulnerabilities; in addition, her emotional need for her caretaker(s) is used against her. Thus she is robbed of control over her life, her body, her choices, her right to protection against unwanted events. The abuser's absolute access to her shatters her sense of power and her ability to develop control over her destiny. *"You have no say,"* incest declares. *"If I want it to happen, it will happen. It doesn't matter what you want."* She learns that to survive, she must surrender. Eventually, she learns that she has no self.

HOME AS HIS CASTLE

When incest occurs within a nuclear family, the family is already characterized by a socially prescribed imbalance of power: father is the "head," his home is "his castle," and his castle is protected under the guise of protecting "the sanctity of the family" (so championed by religious and political fundamentalists). Society joins with already powerful parents, and the already powerless child is betrayed. (Alice Miller describes this betrayal in several of her books.) The Old Testament Commandment dictates that the child honor its father and its mother, who already are the beneficiaries of status and power. But who protects the powerless? Who honors the child?

Power, in this society, is seen as the birthright and the domain of men. Words that describe power are all referenced to maleness: a courageous person has "balls," and a powerless person feels "impotent," or "emasculated," "castrated." In this view, the feminine condition is inherently weak and powerless. A threat to power is a threat to manliness.

Authoritarian Perpetrator

The incest experience represents abuses of power and loss of control. Families where paternal incest occurs are generally characterized by a power imbalance wherein a father wields absolute authority over a relatively powerless wife and children. He asks no one's permission or approval for anything he does. He takes what he wants, expecting others to accommodate him. Often, he exercises his power in abusive, violent ways. What passes for order is really frozen chaos. A well-known example of this type of family that commanded much media attention in the '80s is the Cheryl Pierson case, mentioned in Chapter 1. Cheryl's attorney was quoted by Ellen Mitchell in her *New York Times* article to express the concern that, had Cheryl reported her abuse to authorities, her father might have killed her: "I don't think Mr. Pierson's machismo could have withstood the shame of such an allegation. I don't know if he could have lived with it, and I don't know if he would have let Cheryl live with it."

In this kind of family, the father exerts authority through threat and fear. There is no climate of respect. The situation is similar in alcoholic families, where incest often takes place. Alcohol abuse makes life in these families internally unmanageable, although the outside world often sees them as model families. Father may be a respected teacher or community leader. Behind closed doors, however, the family lives on constant guard for the next explosion, for the next period of cold silence, for the next broken promise, broken plate, the next incident of abuse. Family members share the private horror and embarrassment, protecting the secret through their isolation and public facade, and privately blame themselves.

Timid Perpetrator

In another type of family the paternal perpetrator is timid and unassertive, weak and ineffectual. He is often intimidated by adult relationships, especially if his partner is strong, or, as she is often described, "demanding." (He is not, however, physically or financially in jeopardy as a battered wife in the previous situation would be.) Yet both he and his spouse still believe in a birthright where he is supposed to be "the man of the family." But he does not state his case respectfully, *asserting* his needs. He cannot stand up to another adult. Instead, he takes what he wants from the only person in the family by whom he does not feel intimidated, the only person in the family from whom he *can* derive a sense of power: the child. So he abuses or molests his daughter, the one weaker organism in the system.

This family too teaches all the wrong lessons about power and powerlessness, control and loss of control. This father also acts on a sense of entitlement at the expense of others. He does not ask for what he wants; he simply takes. If assertiveness can be seen as a respectful, healthy pursuit of one's needs, he is no more *assertive* than the dominant, abusing father. He simply focuses his domination only on his children, for he does not have the capacity to face his adult partner with his complaints or emotional needs. In the outside world, where he must compete for his rights with other men, he is often seen as a wimp. In Judith Herman's *Father-Daughter Incest,* Nicholas Groth, the often-quoted director of the Sex Offender's Program of the Connecticut Department of Corrections, describes these men as "generally ingratiating, deferential, even meek," in the face of authority, "inadequate," or "weak" as described by their peers. "[M]any sexually abusive fathers were described as tyrants in the home . . . yet professionals often find this 'tyrant' to be 5'7", 150 pounds . . . [an] anxious, harassed, and overburdened man."

The incest perpetrator who is unable to have—or to take—his share of power in the real world or in his adult relationships is a man whose self-esteem is threatened and who feels cheated of his "rights." But he knows that in his family his absolute authority is a given. There, he competes with no one. He remembers that in his family of origin, power was clearly located in the husband. He knows this, and he knows that others know it. Yet even in the family he may feel unable to conduct himself with another adult (his spouse). As a man, he sees power as his birthright. But power is only available at the expense of an innocent child. Groth says this: child molesters, "threatened by adult sexuality . . . feel inadequate and unable to manage their own lives or meet the needs and expectations of other adults. . . . It is through sexual activity that the child molester seeks to meet needs that relate to acceptance and approval and enhance his sense of personal worth and esteem. Thus . . . he obtains a sense of power and control through involvement with the child."

Whether he is a "powerful" or an "ineffectual" tyrant, the incestuous abuser feels fully justified and entitled to use his daughter, for she is seen as his property. This right has been endorsed by society through history, and may have been modeled by his own family (as well as his spouse's). In his eyes, it is not some failure that has led to his turning to his daughter: he is simply not obligated to consider the other person.

These are not "needs" that he should have pursued with an adult partner, either. To take what one wants, when another human being is involved, is always wrong. To have "taken" from an adult would have been no less a crime. The fact that he simply chose a smaller, more compliant victim is, in a sense, incidental.

EARLY ABUSE AND LATER ABUSIVENESS

Many or most incest perpetrators (statistics vary widely) were themselves molested as children. Some attribute the later abusiveness entirely to early victimization. Groth, who subscribes to this view, describes victimization so broadly that he includes circumcision among the traumas that can lead a man later to hurt children.

Some object on principle to this emphasis on the perpetrator's early life. In *Conspiracy of Silence* Sandra Butler complains that such exploration of the abuser's past and social skills "provides the sex offender with a safety net of psychological excuses . . . when a man breaks into a store and steals from it, the response of the criminal justice system is clear and unequivocal. When the offense however is to break into the body of a small child and steal [her] childhood, . . . we grow confused about the nature of the behavior [and do not see it as] criminal. . . ."

Florence Rush, writing in "Give the Abuser Jail Instead of Therapy," a *USA Today* article that followed the airing of the TV show "Something About Amelia," also criticized these attempts to "understand" instead of punish: "Once he is designated as 'sick' [or plagued by] poor impulse control, we are no longer expected to hold him fully accountable for his behavior. . . . [He] is now also classified as a victim. . . . [W]hile we are ostensibly outraged by adult-child sex, we continue to tolerate the Lolita Syndrome, whereby little girls are projected as a source of sexual delight and molesting men are accepted as being only human.

"Understanding" the Abuser

The sad truth is that when men victimize their family members through physical or sexual abuse, they are treated far more lightly by the system than men who commit similar crimes with strangers. This is an outgrowth of the attitude I described earlier: society honors a man's access to and absolute authority over "his" family. They are his to use and abuse. If he hurts someone in his family, we want to "understand" him. As Cheryl McCall, in her 1977 *Life* cover story, quotes FBI special agent Kenneth Lanning, "The incest offender is after all just a child molester who stays home."

Prevention of abuse and treatment of abusers *can* benefit from understanding what leads to abuse. However, many people use these explanations as rationalizations: it was because he himself was victimized that he "had to" (rather than "chose to" or "allowed himself to") victimize another; isn't it sad? This rationalizing feeds the social tendency to see child molesters as "sick men" rather than as "criminals" or "perpetrators," to resist the notion that they should be brought to the same justice as a man who rapes a woman.

This application of "understanding" is unwise. Whatever happens in one's childhood, one is responsible for one's adult acts; one's past does not *cause* one to do violence to another. Allowing oneself to hurt another is an active behavioral choice. Although it may be true that most child molesters were molested in childhood, it is not true that most people who were sexually abused as kids grow up to abuse others sexually. After all, most incest survivors are female, yet there is, as David Finkelhor says, a "male monopoly on child molesting." And even among men, childhood victimization does not automatically result in the victim later going on to abuse others.

Perhaps only 30% of male incest victims grow up to incestuously victimize children (statistics on other forms of violent behavior, within or outside the family, are not available). Many such men are affected in the same way as women: they grow up with a sense of powerlessness and then victimize themselves but not others.

Incest and Power Needs

What factors determine whether someone will molest children? The fact that women and men are trained to view power and sex differently cannot be overlooked. As Butler says, men "are socialized to sexualize power, intimacy, and affection, *and sometimes hatred and contempt as well*" [emphasis mine]. Conquest, rather than sexual fulfillment, is the primary goal of rape; evidence of this is found in the "rape and murder" of 80-year-old women who resist robbers, and in the fact that to "rape and pillage" is considered one of the "spoils of war."

Incest is first an abuse of power, with sexuality the manner in which the power is taken. It arises out of these factors, not sexual deprivation, with certain other contributing factors, such as a history of abuse. It is not a product of loneliness or sexual unfulfillment any more than adult rape is. Does the perpetrator achieve sexual gratification in spite of the humiliation, fear, and protests of his victim, or because of them? What does it say about a man that he would be excited by imposing terror and sex on a whimpering, breastless, hairless, smooth-skinned sweet trusting child? What does it mean that he would feel this for *his* whimpering child?

In the case where the abuse occurs outside the family, the perpetrator's abuse of his power, failure to control his acts, and attitude of unquestioned access are the same. The victim may be driven to his company by the same distortions of power in her own family.

Through incest, *power* is seen as a limited, not a shared, commodity: the more I (you) have, the less you (I) can have. If you try to take your share, you threaten mine. Thus the child's development is inhibited, for part of growing up necessitates growing more powerful.

In addition to these distortions regarding power and ownership, molesters lack empathy (the appreciation of the other person's feelings). McCall, in her *Life* story, cites "Joe" as an example. Joe's "big worry" was that his nine-year-old stepdaughter's screams would wake his wife. "When it was over, she was crying," he complained, "using her guilt trip on me." Another chilling characteristic of perpetrators is revealed by Finkelhor in their attitude toward women, sex, and violence. When these men were tested psychologically by being shown pictures of nude women, about 85% said that they saw scenes of women being sick, dead, or dying!

CONSEQUENCES FOR THE VICTIM

Whether it includes or does not touch, and irrespective of the exact relationship between the abuser and the child victim, the violation of incest affects the foundation of human security in the developing child, as well as her relationship with the world around her.

Mastery

Whether control is sacrificed to angry outbursts, alcoholic unreliability, or episodes of abuse, the experience of childhood incest teaches guardedness and manipulation of reality—a reality that is seen as ever-changing without reason or order. The child learns not to make choices, not to reason, and not to assess and understand. She learns how to survive in a war zone, how power can be abused and robbed by others, how powerlessness feels, and how women are helpless.

Without a relation between her acts and the responses of her environment, the child cannot develop a sense of mastery. Growing to believe she has no power, she is trained to see herself as a victim. Without a sense of cause and effect—the association between her actions and their consequences—she experiences the world not as a place of order, but of chaos, with herself spinning helplessly inside.

Boundaries

In a healthy family, the boundaries between members and around the family are strong but permeable, with movement and communication across them. Within the family or in other healthy relationships, members maintain separate identities, balancing contact among themselves with their dealings with the world.

In families or individual relationships where incest or alcoholism take place, a fortress of shame and secrecy isolates the unit from the outside world, which is threatening. The family protects itself from the negative judgments that would accompany the prying eyes of outsiders. Nonalcoholic or nonabusive family members often share the same experience, the same pain, but are isolated from each other, driven apart by threat and deprivation. Their denial prevents openness both within and without the family. This is distinctly different from a healthy family or early caretaking alliance, where the child slowly outgrows the bonds of security that the relationship provides, as she ventures into the newness of the world and learns to maneuver on her own.

Instead, the child victim of incest is held too closely into the pathology of the system, yet deprived of security—unable to develop independence, not permitted (or often able) to leave, yet given nothing. She is kept close at the side of the abusing parent or perpetrator, as his companion and mate, when she should be leaving such dependencies and finding her place in the world. The perpetrator acts as captor, isolating her from the influences of society as cults do: controlling her thought process and belief system, humiliating and embarrassing her, while giving her attention and in many cases necessities such as food and shelter. Often such fathers act like jealous, possessive lovers: they criticize her dress as "sluttish," tell her boys are "only out for one thing," are critical of everyone she dates and suspicious of (or invasively curious about) her sexual activities. These attitudes are a significant indicator of sexually abusive behavior.

When incest occurs in the extended family, with grandfathers or uncles (although it is my experience that this often occurs in the context of a "family chain" of incest, where father is a perpetrator as well) or outside the family, many of the same themes are played out. The issues of boundaries then manifest themselves less directly, because no one outside the nuclear family controls the victim's world so completely. But whether in the immediate, extended, or extrafamilial form, what always accompanies incest is this: the abuser loses (or fails to properly exercise) control. The abuser also takes control: he steals across the child's boundaries—in effect, *negating* her boundaries—and steals all of her control over her own body, her own life.

In isolating the victim from the rest of the family and the outside world, the abuser creates with her an enmeshment, a state where she has no sense of herself as separate from *his* agenda, *his* needs and wishes. She loses her own feelings, desires, thoughts, and opinions. Incest does not require permission to approach. The message of this abuse is, "I can touch, I can take, I can enter." It does not merely violate boundaries, it annihilates them. She has no separate self. She does not separate from the identity of the family to form her own identity in the outside world. She becomes an extension of him. She *becomes* him. Her growth is suffocated, for she not only cannot leave—she cannot move at all.

Reality Testing/Judgment

Because the incest victim is robbed of the power to determine who touches her, where, and in what way, incest is similar to the more simple form of child abuse, battering: violence is done to the body of the child. But incest is not simply physical abuse. It usually begins in a deceptively innocuous way and remains confusing. At first, it often does not look like violence or even violation. It may begin as tickling or caressing, or even kissing. Kissing that is too intimate, yes, but the victim may not have a framework for objecting to that. Nor can the unsophisticated child see the violence it represents.

The child finds much of what takes place in the early and middle stages of incest confusing because, while it makes her uncomfortable, she cannot be sure just *what* is wrong with it, *why* it should feel so bad. Seeing her trusted parent, sibling, babysitter or friend as choosing to hurt her is threatening to the core of her existence. Lacking a framework through which she can define the action as harmful, she chooses the safer route: she doubts herself. "There must be something wrong with me," she decides, "for thinking there is something wrong." Thus, incest violates the child's capacity to validate her own feelings and experiences. It contaminates her perceptions and renders her incapable of trusting her own judgment.

Further confusing the child are the overt lies that the abuser tells her about the abuse: he calls it love. When child abuse takes the form of battering, no one attempts to tell the child that the act of being thrown against a wall is love. The abuser may call it discipline, or say it is being done for her own good, or even (later, in the calm) say the action was an angry outburst for which he or she is sorry. But no one pretends that a punch is a kiss. And even a kiss can take many forms. The incestuous abuser often tells her that rape is love, that taking is giving, that "sex" is affection, and that kissing her on the mouth, like *that,* is fatherly.

She is bound by her confusion, robbed not only of the ability to control her boundaries, but of a chance to know what kind of control to exert. She has lost the chance to develop the conceptual framework through which to determine her likes and dislikes—the proper labels to attach to things so that she can know what choices she would make *if she could make choices*. In her guts she knows that a certain act feels awful, but she doesn't exactly have words for what's wrong with it, and anyway, *he* says it's all right. He says it's the way parents, or uncles, or priests, are *supposed* to act. So it must be true: the fault must lie in her judgment.

Without judgment, she is a shell. She cannot learn to depend on what her senses tell her about her inner world or her outer environment. She cannot trust her perceptions, her assessments, her reactions—her understanding of reality or its meaning in her life. These abilities are the foundation that a fully functioning, healthy human being develops, and they are necessary for adult functioning.

Differentiation

In an ideal world, the child develops certain conceptual understandings of her existence. She begins to see that she and the people around her are different and separate. She learns that other people (however beloved) can do things that are different from what she does—can have different tastes, reactions, behaviors—and still be OK people. Likewise, she learns that she can be different than her parents want her to be and still deserve their love: for instance, she can excel at sports and not get the grades they want for her, or she can be unique and creative rather than nice and sweet and still be worthy and lovable. Professionals call this "differentiation": understanding that one is not simply an extension of one's parents or other loved ones, but a person who owns—and is entitled to—her own characteristics and choices.

Incest robs her of the ability to differentiate. This is the lesson we hear today about saying no to "bad touch." When we casually tell our children to "go kiss Uncle Walter," we interfere with this lesson, for we are telling the child, "You are not allowed to decide whom you kiss or who touches you. You must do it because I say so." On the other hand, healthy development helps an individual decide how close she wishes to stand or sit with others, whom she wishes to touch and in what way, when she wishes to share or give something away, what information she wishes to reveal. Respecting the child's privacy by not reading her mail or diary, and respecting her personal space by letting her close the door of her room, are examples of positive ways to show respect for those boundaries.

A child molester does not abuse his victim because she is desirable. He does not do it to hurt her necessarily, although he may do it to satisfy his anger at others (his ex-wife, for example). He does not have (or perhaps he chooses not to have) any awareness of *her* pain, *her* needs, *her* desires. He has a fantasy image of her that he has constructed as part of the defense system that allows him to justify his abuse of her: she wants it; she needs the education about sex; this is love.

In short, she does not exist for him as a separate self. This is what many incest survivors, at some point in reconstructing their memories, are forced to face as one of the most painful pieces of the picture. Loving, trusting, innocent, she was invisible to this man who was so important to her. The faraway look on his face as his sexual excitement mounts is not only arousal, but an absorption in his own world and his total disregard for her presence. She is an extension of his craving, the playing out of his impulses, an object for the satisfaction of his need for control and power through sexual dominance. Her whimpers, cries of emotional and physical pain, her pleadings, her terror do not matter to him; *he does not see them,* because *he does not see her.*

The child's body is the core of her world, the center of her personal space, the essence of her separateness. But she does not end with her skin. If we force her to live in a climate over which she has no influence, we teach her that she has no control, no impact, no power over life. Not only her sense of boundaries and her sense of control are violated, but her existence as a separate self.

The caretaker who commits incest puts his needs ahead of those of the dependent child, in fact using the child's natural dependent state as a weapon against her. Try to imagine the humiliation and violation of a rape. Then imagine it as constant, unpredictable but inevitable. Now place it in the context of imprisonment. And finally, put it at the hands of a beloved caretaker—while he says it's for you that he's doing it. What sense of control over your life would you be able to salvage? The lesson is—why try? What does it matter? Why even use your voice if it is never heard? The child's life becomes like the nightmare that many of us have had: we're in danger, we open our mouths to scream for help, and—nothing comes out. Try as we might, we cannot scream, cannot manage more than a useless squeak.

To some degree, whether there is an escape is not as important as whether the child believes there is; she is as powerless as she believes herself to be. Diana Russell heard many stories of child victims who were able to halt their abuse. Indeed, according to her research, in about three-fifths of the cases where incest was stopped, the child was able to stop it—by pretending to sleep or be sick or by avoiding the abuser. Russell calls these "successful resistance strategies."

Many factors influence whether a victim is able to defend herself: the threat of violence, actual violence, economic dependence, her capacity at the time she is approached (e.g., is she sleeping when the abuser creeps up on her?), whether she is "disarmed by deception" (e.g., does he pretend to be playing), her ability to understand what is happening to her, the authority of the perpetrator, her fear of her mother or other nonabusing caretaker, her level of self-blame (or fear of blame), the conflict experienced over her love for her abuser, her neediness, her powerlessness.

Force is, however, rarely used; the closer the dependence relationship, the less force is necessary. Generally, his power is derived from her need for him and, often, her love. What is left is coercion. There are several different tactics that the abuser may use to coerce the child into tolerating what he wants to do to her. (I intentionally use the word "tolerating" rather than "permitting," because the latter implies that the child has the power to make a choice, which presupposes the ability to stop the abuse. This is not the case, so the word really cannot be used.)

She may be beaten, or at least threatened with further physical abuse if she resists or protests. So her fear is, "I won't be heard, and I'll probably be punished anyway. The best I can hope for is to close my eyes, clench my teeth, and get through it." Although direct threats often occur, frequently they address not "what will happen if you don't obey" (for the small and powerless child really has no choice but to cooperate at the moment of the abuse), but "what will happen if you tell." Threats are not necessary to commit the abuse, but to ensure the keeping of the secret that protects it.

The perpetrator's choice of victim is a primary tactic. Is she a particularly needy child? Or is she independent—even rebellious? Do they have a close relationship? Does she have a closer relationship with anyone else? If he is not a primary caretaker, is she alienated from those caretakers—thereby making her more responsive to the attentions in which he shrouds the abuse?

In situations where there is no emotional currency with which to blackmail the child, there is still the entrapment that occurs when powerful people and powerless people reside together. The powerful individual controls access to the outside, and all that occurs inside. Home becomes like a prison. Life-sustaining necessities—food, shelter, warmth, clothing—are subject to the will of the jailer. The emotional climate (abuse, attention, nurturing) are all within his control. Survival depends on his whims and decisions. Even if it were possible, it would not be wise to rebel against his wishes.

It is easy to understand why abusers do not need to resort to force. The child victim knows—or believes—that her life is at stake if she refuses. (This fear appears to be endemic to sexual abuse; many adult rape survivors report that even without the presence of a weapon, their rape left them afraid for their lives.) Actual verbal statements are not necessary, for the threat is implied: "I am in control of your existence. I have made clear what I want. What do you think would happen if you didn't keep me happy?" The threat is to her survival.

And on into adulthood. She learns she has no control over anything. She learns she might as well give up trying to exercise her will. She learns that she is not a person, but an extension of everyone around her.

THE AFTEREFFECTS: LIFE OUT OF BALANCE, LIFE OUT OF CONTROL

Post-Incest Syndrome describes a life out of balance—a life of emotional, behavioral, and attitudinal extremes. Some of these extremes are mutually exclusive (for example, an individual may be verbal or nonverbal, but not both); some (such as unassertiveness and control) can occur simultaneously; some shift over time (from overly sexual to totally asexual, for instance). These extremes are not a matter of the incest survivor's current, conscious choice; they were largely determined in her past, created by a combination of the abuse she suffered and her early life responses. She does not respond cleanly, in the here-and-now, to current events; she responds with the mighty weight of her past.

Love can threaten; touch can burn; caring can seem to violate. Is it any wonder that the adult incest survivor feels out of control? Her reactions may come as a surprise, even to her; they may be the opposite of what she wants them to be, or of what reason and sanity say they ought to be.

In childhood, the victim had no say. No one listened. Or they turned her words of pain against her, blaming her, telling her she was crazy. What can she do with this? She can live in rage or give up. The aftereffects are the survivor's attempt to find something between these extremes.

For many survivors, the only way to control these unexpected and unmanageable responses is to control their feelings—to eliminate, or numb them. This is a way of denying power to an abuser: "You cannot hurt me." Often this response continues into adulthood when others hurt them. This response is not limited to incest survivors. I see it frequently as a response to conflicts with parents and then other persons perceived as threatening or competitive. Assuming that the offending party knew he or she was hurting us and wanted to do so, we often suppress our pain because we "don't want to give them the satisfaction." But we deny ourselves the satisfaction of venting our pain. We may feel as if we have won some power, but what price do we pay for a victory that requires denying our own feelings?

This denial affects particularly the ability to ask for help. Some incest survivors must believe they are "just fine." Their self-esteem is based on how well they're doing, how unaffected they are by their abuse. Although their struggles are obvious to everyone around them, they deny that they have any problem. This denial is not, of course, exclusive to incest. It is usually the stronger people who seek help; the weaker, needing to act strong, avoid it.

Boundaries: "Personal Space"

Because, on the most simple and concrete level, incest is a violation of the child victim's *physical* boundaries, in later life, the incest survivor is sensitive to any crossing of the invisible wall with which we surround ourselves. She is frightened or enraged when someone touches her by surprise, or when someone hugs her without asking, or when someone playfully grabs her from behind. She is overwhelmed when her movement is contained or she is trapped. Her gut reaction may be to snap at you or even punch you if you do this, or she may become paralyzed and terrorized. There are three simple and universal rules to apply here: NEVER *touch an incest survivor without her permission. NEVER come up from behind to surprise her. NEVER impede her movement.* If you do one of these things and get an unfavorable reaction, NEVER criticize her for her reaction or tell her to lighten up.

Physical and Emotional Boundaries

Once, an incest survivor client of mine decided to sit on the floor of my office. Priding myself on my egalitarian practices, I said, "Well, OK! I'll sit on the floor too!" I was only half out of my seat when she jumped about five feet back, yelling NO! The boundaries of an incest survivor can extend so far that what seems to be respectful behavior appears to her to be a threat. Even though we were at least eight feet apart, she reacted as if I were about to jump on her. Attempts at exploration were futile. At the time, I had no checklist to apply to her behavior and, even though I knew she had been molested, the connection did not occur to me. This behavior represents the boundary distance maintained by incest survivors. Now I don't even lean forward in my chair or move an inch toward them without asking permission.

The incest survivor may manifest either extreme with regard to boundaries: she may be *extremely protective of her boundaries,* establishing her invisible wall at a far greater distance away from her body than most of us do, or she may be extremely *indifferent* to boundaries; even if she feels the need to maintain boundaries, she may be totally unassertive, tolerating whatever another person wishes to do with her. She may try to make a career out of this aftereffect: prostitutes, strippers, and actresses in pornography are generally incest survivors, many of whom have tried to "take control" of their lives by taking the reins of their own exploitation.

The incest survivor may also keep people at a great distance, never revealing feelings or personal information—never allowing herself to be touched emotionally. Incest survivors who are casual about their bodies may be totally inaccessible emotionally: "You can touch me, but you can't *touch* me." An incest survivor who experiences this may flirt, talk, react, even seem to share generously about her life, but none of this has meaning for her. Her response to you is well rehearsed, not unlike the sexual sharing of the prostitute: it does not indicate that you, or what she has told you, are important to her. On the contrary, she almost seems to try to see how much she can give without sharing or taking. She has not let you in, although it might appear that she has.

At the same time, the incest survivor's ability to understand the boundaries of others is often skewed. She may be *extraordinarily sensitive to your boundaries,* almost never asking intrusive, prying questions (indeed, sometimes never even asking questions that would express appropriate levels of interest). She may be the least likely to listen when you're on the phone in the other room. She is a great person to share a secret with!

At the other extreme, she may be *incredibly intrusive and pressuring*. Unable to pick up social cues, she may insist on being around when you do not want her to be. She may tell you things you do not want to know about her, and question you on the most personal issues. She demands, at those times, that you assert yourself directly and firmly. Sometimes her own rudeness puts you in a position of having to take an uncomfortably strong stand.

Emotionally it is as if the incest survivor's whole surface is a raw nerve, at risk for pain, unprotected against further abuse, any movement in its proximity is a threat. Yet asking is not possible for many incest survivors; for others, it is not enough. Often unable to tell me honestly what they do not want, some become paralyzed, and some flail out in fury. When I ask, I listen not only to words, but to body language that might express the no she cannot say, and I try to hear the fear behind the aggressiveness, while assertiveness is pursued in treatment as a better way to take care of establishing boundaries. It is tricky to maneuver in this kind of relationship, and no one can read another's mind.

Territoriality

Our boundaries are not limited to our physical or emotional selves; they extend into the space around us. They also concern our time, attention, personal disclosure, and living space. Therefore, boundary issues manifest themselves as territoriality as well. Some incest survivors are comfortable socializing only in their own homes. They feel in command of this space; when they want to be alone, they know they have the power to ask a guest to leave. Some other incest survivors feel safe only when visiting others because they can walk out! Many incest survivors protect their private space fiercely, choosing carefully whom they allow in their homes—often keeping unlisted phone numbers. Some incest survivors never let most people know where they live—especially family members. For them, any penetration of their territory is an invasion; the only safety they know is in their home.

The absolute access of the perpetrator—who, in fact, the victim might actually have had to live with—resulted in her not having a home, not even knowing what home was. Thus many incest survivors are very aware of turf. They feel safe in their own homes, even if it's twenty years too late. They need to know that, while they cannot correct the past, it is never too late to take power! But they also need to know that safe space around them can only partly compensate for a lack of safety inside themselves. They must face the pain of the past; it cannot be erased by a fortress built today.

One's privacy can feel invaded in many ways. One aftereffect is *sensitivity to being watched*. She often feels watched—senses eyes on her, even when no one is there. Actually being observed (for instance, as part of job training or supervision) causes enormous anxiety. For instance, Gretchen remembers that during nursing school she almost flunked out because of the anxiety she felt over having her work observed. Jessica can't tolerate anyone in the same room when she's cooking or talking on the phone, or anyone looking over her shoulder when she writes. One explanation for this aftereffect concerns the original abuse. Some incest involves pornography; some, the observation of the child being sexual with someone else (or while she masturbates). Or the perpetrator may force the child to watch him masturbate. Her most private functions are not protected. Understandably, when she feels eyes on her, her skin crawls.

Powerlessness and Assertiveness

Like the starving street urchin who fights for food, the incest survivor fights for the few scraps of power she feels she can preserve. At the same time, she often exhibits a marked inability to be assertive due to a depleted sense of (or ability to manifest) her own power.

Her attitude is best described by the following statement: "It never occurred to me that I *could* be assertive."

She may not know how to make choices because she was never entitled to *have* choices. To make a decision when one is demanded of her—which job should she take, should she go to this meeting or that one, what pair of gloves should she buy—can be crippling. Decisions about relationships, ever so much more complicated and threatening, can be impossible. However, she may be extremely capable in all aspects of her life except the emotional. She may, in fact, mobilize her energies and become a powerful fighter for the victims of the world, for justice. Many national children's rights and other activist groups are built by these women.

The issue of power must be put in its psychological and sociological context. Sigmund Freud reduced basic human functions to issues of *sex* and *aggression*. I disagree. Freud's theories were restricted to male experience. He accurately observed sexist male behavior, not general *human* behavior, and certainly not women's behavior. To many men, love equals sex (men sexualize; women "affectionalize," minimizing their sexualities as much as men may overfocus on theirs); also, men are trained to see power as competitive and hierarchical (e.g., aggression, or power over another). The core of human distress should be described, however, not as sex and aggression, but love (or lack of love) and powerlessness.

Powerlessness is an issue for all women, although incest survivors are generally more sensitive to it. Taught that ladies do not demand power but give it away, women who were molested in childhood struggle both against the weight of their pasts and the pressures of society. Sexually, for instance, men are taught to be persons of action, to be the ones who do *to*: they are on top. Women are taught to be the receptacle. Sexual abuse is an extension of this socially indoctrinated imbalance of power. Judith Herman describes the dilemma of some survivors in this way:

> Daughters of seductive fathers thus learned that they had two choices . . . (to) remain their daddy's good little girls, bound in a flirtatious relationship whose sexual aspect was ever-present but never acknowledged, or . . . attempt to become independent women . . . and in the process risk their father's [and all men's] anger or rejection. They reached adulthood schooled in the complicated art of pleasing a man and knowing virtually nothing about how to please themselves.

The incest survivor is the victim of these distortions. The abuser's absolute access to her, shattered her sense of power and the resulting capacity to be in control of her destiny—already diminished by her social role. Affection is contaminated by sex—aggressive sexuality at that. (This is discussed in more detail in Chapter 13.)

High Risk Taking

Many incest survivors—even the most passive and nonassertive—may be inclined toward high-risk behaviors, daring the fates. One example of this behavior is in the movie *Saturday Night Fever,* where the hero and his buddies are climbing on the railings of the Brooklyn Bridge. The guy wires are thin, there is often a wind, and the fall to the water would be almost surely fatal. Yet for these boys with little to lose in life, walking on the edge of death is an adventure—and proof that they're not cowards. Another example is the heroine's behavior in *Looking for Mr. Goodbar.* She picks up strangers in a bar, cavalierly unconcerned about the consequences until she is horribly, sadly, murdered by one of these men.

Hanging out in sleazy bars satisfies this aftereffect for too many incest survivors. So does driving recklessly and too fast—or violating the law. To be in danger is to feel alive and, paradoxically, in control.

To dare the fates is to pretend to have power—"Nothing can touch me." There is the edge of anger to it, an implied "Screw you." The anger is also turned against herself. Although the survivor fails to exhibit assertiveness in her interpersonal affairs, she may skydive or climb mountains. Risking danger of any kind is less threatening to the incest survivor than the risks involved with interpersonal assertiveness—emotional risks.

Control and power problems can also manifest themselves in an adolescent rebelliousness—an "I'll do as I damn well please" attitude. This attitude often occurs in children from alcoholic families. Never having had firm, consistent, caring controls (at the same time that some abuse took their control away), some teenage survivors do not tolerate any attempts to control what their curfew is, their school attendance, or the like. As adults they are likely to have difficulty with schedules, work attendance, and other authority issues. In the extreme, these survivors may be destructive, feeling that hurting and destroying are the only kinds of power possible. Although rare among women, this aftereffect does exist.

Adult incest survivors who attain positions of power and authority in their work are likely to be affected by their incest histories. They may feel ill at ease with their authority, or, being without power for so long, they may let the power go to their heads and abuse it.

An often hidden manifestation of this aspect of the aftereffects is stealing: shoplifting or kleptomania (the compulsive, often unconsciously motivated stealing of useless objects). Betsey, a home health aide, would feel the urge to steal small, inexpensive objects while in her patients' home. Her reasons make sense in the context of Post-Incest

Syndrome. First, stealing is a high-risk behavior. Second, it is the ultimate control: "I wanted it, so I took it. I didn't ask. I didn't have to spend money on it. I just took it." And she felt entitled: "I've suffered a lot, so I deserved it." She knew that this patient really loved her and would probably be thrilled to give her one of these baubles. Why, then, the urge to *take* it—a far more dangerous behavior? "I can't accept gifts from people or feel good about them. I feel like I'll be expected to give something back." And so, psychologically, stealing is *safer* than accepting gifts; the penalty is more tolerable. Besides, she doesn't feel likable enough. Her crippled self-esteem makes her unable to believe that someone might want to give her anything.

Some, of course, can take risks in no area, neither daring nor assertive. These survivors can appear either weak or, like the patriarchal perpetrators described earlier in this section, controlling and demanding. Neither is capable of direct, reasonable assertiveness (as opposed to attempts at conquest); ironically, it makes them feel too vulnerable. The weak must crush or be crushed. Strength—true strength—is required for the shared power of assertiveness.

Fear of Losing Control

The incest survivor's emotional and mental states often are the focus of her fear of "going out of control." This attitude is not exclusive to incest survivors; it characterizes many people who seek therapy. But the incest survivor has darker ghosts awaiting her on the other side of her fear, a fear that occurs as only one among the numerous concerns that comprise Post-Incest Syndrome.

"I'm afraid I'll lose control" means:

- "I'm afraid I'm going crazy (and no one will be able to put me back together)."
- "I'm afraid if I start crying I'll never stop."
- "I'm afraid if I try to stand up for myself I won't be able to talk."
- "I'm afraid if I get angry I'll kill someone."
- "I'm afraid if I say no to someone they'll kill *me*."

- "I'm afraid if I start letting out my memories, they'll all come out and overwhelm me."

Feelings that are "stuffed down" for too long can seem unmanageable. They are like the long string of attached scarves that magicians pull out of their mouths—they seem to go on and on (and on and on)! Each tear that is cried attaches to another and another, and sadness seems never to end. Anger pushes against the dam that holds it back with such force that it threatens to crush the incest survivor and her surroundings. Feelings that are not released or dealt with when they occur, that are stored and added to over time, seem as if they can explode unless forced back—and so the tendency is to continue to force them back, thus compounding, instead of relieving, the resulting emotional overload.

The incest survivor needs to understand three things in relation to her fear of loss of control:

1. Although the child *did* lose control in the beginning to the incest perpetrator and the situation, ever since that time she *has* in fact been in control (of her memories and feelings of whether to face the trauma). She has held back (perhaps too well!) her memories, her tears, her anger. Control over her feelings is in fact the best control she knows.

2. As she will see when she begins to risk experiencing emotion (in a therapy session, for instance), what usually occurs is that she will experience only a brief moment of that emotion (tears, perhaps) before she closes off, putting the feelings away for a while. In fact, she may feel extremely dissatisfied with the natural limits that occur in these moments. She will want to do *more* and not be able to.

3. When an incest survivor's control over the rhythm and speed of remembering is taken from her, there are problems. In other instances, emotions can flood the incest survivor because of circumstances in her life or the work she is doing in her recovery. At those times, it is especially necessary that she make full use of available recovery resources (such as self-help groups). She must take the risk of asking for help, and she must be helped to implement whatever skills she has to con-

tain the explosion and to ground her. Sometimes the flood-
gates *can* open—and crying or anger or flashbacks can seem
as if they will never stop. There are several reasons this might
occur. I have heard of incest survivors pursuing hypnosis with
a hypnotist uneducated about incest, and memories were un-
leashed for which they were not prepared. Or an incest survivor's perpetrator unloads upon her his version of some
incidents before she remembers them.

The available internal and external resources, however, in rare instances, may not be enough. Some incest survivors really are so damaged that they have "nervous breakdowns"—they may become
paralyzed by depression or anxiety, seriously suicidal, overwhelmed by
the pain they feel or memories that flood them, or nonfunctional in
other ways. Sadly, although at this point they often genuinely need residential care, their only options are psychiatric hospitals where the
treatment may feel like more abuse. Psychiatric hospitals are generally
ill-equipped to deal with incest, when what she needs are warm surroundings and women who know the needs that she cannot express.
She is likely to feel victimized by the control taken away by the hospital, the lack of appropriate therapy, the loss of control over her physical
surroundings and over her body. She may feel threatened by the male
staff in positions of power and by male patients, by the hospital atmosphere, by the medications that numb her consciousness. The abuses of
medication in many such institutions compound her problem. The
abuses sometimes committed by staff members—from psychiatrists to
aides—recreate the hell from which she seeks escape.

What is needed for these women, and what regrettably does not
exist, are "safe homes" of the type offered to battered women, and
residential programs such as those offered for the addictions: safe
space, with counselors who have "been there," in a home-type environment where she continues to participate in tasks of the "family" to the
best of her ability—rather than being put in the passive role of
"patient."

Repression, Splitting, Shutdown:
Loss of Control or Attempts to Control?

To feel in control of one's life is perhaps the most important pre-
requisite for a feeling of safety in the world. It is difficult to tolerate

(let alone fully enjoy) life without this sense. The incest survivor does what she can to regain control from the moment the incest begins. Repression or "blocking out" of memories is an initial way to do this, and the development—or perhaps "creation"—of multiple personality disorder is an extreme way to do the same thing. These cognitive coping mechanisms will be explored in detail in Chapter 5.

Hiding

An attempt at protection—one that may have served her well as a child—is hiding. For one who sees herself as powerless, hiding may be the best way she can get some control over her abuse. This tendency to make herself unavailable may be the best way the survivor knows to say she doesn't want something. "The world isn't safe," the hiding survivor feels, "and I'm gonna go where no one will find me."

A Distorted View of Power and Relationships

The original incest experience consists of at least two individuals of vastly different age or status. Many incest survivors perpetuate this pattern by becoming involved with partners who are older or more powerful: a 12-year-old girl may become involved with a 16-year-old; adult women have partners who are old enough to be their fathers, or they become involved with their doctors, lawyers, ministers, therapists. (These professionals are violating their sacred trusts and committing a crime that approximates incest.) One example is Mary Lea Johnson, daughter of J. Seward Johnson, founder of the Johnson & Johnson baby products empire—and child molester. Mary Lea, the model for the company's first and most famous label illustration (the smiling baby powder baby exposed to the world) revealed in her recent book being sexually molested by her father. Later, when he was 76, he married his 34-year-old nursemaid. Mary Lea went on to marry first a very dominant man, then a psychiatrist who became a voyeur to her sexual encounters with men he desired. Johnson & Johnson now funds a domestic violence hot line.

It is a social expectation that older men have younger partners. For example, Bing Crosby, at 53, married a 23-year-old; Pablo Casals' bride was 28 when he was 81; Edgar Allan Poe at 26 "married" a

13-year-old, as did Jerry Lee Lewis (for which he was temporarily cast out of polite society), and Elvis Presley (she was 14). Beloved performer Charlie Chaplin, at age 35, married a 16-year-old girl and years later, when she had a nervous breakdown, a doctor diagnosed her as having "sexual shock" from this experience. But the tendency of these "younger" women to engage in such imbalanced relationships may have a more specific root than gender-role training.

Power-Sex Confusion

Intrinsic to the incest experience is a confusion of power and sex. This confusion is partly responsible for victims' becoming perpetrators, when they do: the adult who was molested in childhood attempts to compensate for his or her feeling of powerlessness through dominance. Absolute dominance, in combination with the inevitable sexualizing of the post-incest experience (sex and aggression) often is accomplished through the sexual subjugation of a child. Or worse. Many mass murderers were incest victims as children. In one of the rare cases of its kind, an incest survivor named Diane Downs attempted to kill all of her children; some survived. The bestseller about this horror, *Small Sacrifices* by Ann Rule, clearly shows the relevance of the aftereffects she experienced.

But this relief is only temporary. The abuser then is faced with feeling even more out of control than before the abuse. Like an alcoholic, the abuser is now faced with more guilt, low self-esteem, and powerlessness—which, in this pathological state, feels as if it can be remedied only with more conquest. This dynamic incorporates the abuser's feelings of entitlement—a little like what the kleptomaniac feels, but what the abuser steals is someone else's childhood.

As the perpetrator (usually male) attempts to regain power and control through the abuse of another, the female survivor is more likely to try to do this through taking charge of exploiting herself. It is not in a woman's socialization to equate sex with dominance. Her power comes from being *wanted*. Many times when a woman makes an avocation out of being wanted (e.g., becomes a "sex symbol"), being wanted means being exploited, being *used*—again.

Name Change

One creative, positive method that incest survivors use to regain control is a name change. The power to self-label is mighty. It is lost in marriage when a woman takes her husband's name. This tradition originates in the legal status of wives and children as possessions of men. Women in positions of power keep their names. Women incest survivors are also challenging this convention by reclaiming the power to name. Some choose new last names to dissociate themselves from their perpetrating fathers, paternal grandfathers, uncles, cousins, or brothers. Some let go of their married names to take power back from perpetrating husbands. Unfortunately, without the same action for their children, these kids carry an abusing father's name.

They also may select new *first* names. This choice says, "I will decide what to call myself. I will give myself a title that reflects who I am, and what I am becoming."

Empowerment

Regaining power over her life—every human's birthright—is the incest survivor's primary task. This is called "empowerment." The first step is for the incest survivor to become aware that she has the right to make choices. This area of her life has been so punished and banished that she has relinquished it in favor of life-preserving passivity (now life-inhibiting passivity). In that sense, the incest survivor might better have been called an "endurer." Because of the incestuous abuse, she stops considering choices and develops the capacity to "adapt to what it is."

To understand that one has choices sounds deceptively simple. Yet it is a turning point. I can still remember the moment when I realized I had the right to have choices. I was in therapy, in my early 20s. I had accepted an invitation for Thanksgiving, but I really did not want to spend that day with these people. I complained to another member of the therapy group I was in that I "had to do" this thing. "Then don't go," she said.

"What?!" I had never considered this possibility. "I said, you can tell them you're not going." But how could I?! I had made a commitment. The thought of taking this power back filled me with a deep sense of anxiety: I couldn't. I just couldn't. I *had* to go.

I didn't go. And nothing happened, except that I learned that I was in control of my own life. Now, when saying what I want comes easily, I try to remember the overwhelming feeling of weakness and fear that I experienced in that moment. It's an important feeling for a therapist to be able to recapture.

The incest survivor must first acknowledge and develop compassion for the bind that the child *really* was in, and stop hating and blaming herself for her powerlessness. Her next task is to understand that she is no longer the powerless, defenseless, dependent child, but a grown, capable adult. Her world is no longer under the control of her parents alone: theirs is not the only roof under which she can live, food she can eat, approval she needs. Her abusing uncle is not the only person to whom she can turn for attention. Her brother can no longer use his status as preferred child to tyrannize her. Threats from the needed teacher/abuser cannot hurt her now. *The abuse can never happen again.* In short, she needs to learn to do "reality testing," and stay in the *now,* seeing her life situation as it really is for an adult.

Next, the incest survivor needs to begin to set limits: "No, I can't come over now." And up to "No, I don't want to tell you that." "No, I don't want to go to bed with you." As you can see, much of limit setting has to do with learning to say no—and understanding that not giving someone else what she or he wants is OK. This intertwines with issues of trust and abandonment, which will be explored later.

However, being healthy means not having to be in control of everything around her, all the time. It means realizing, and accepting, that you cannot be in control of everything. Sometimes trains are late. Sometimes you don't get the answer you want from someone else. Sometimes kids make noise when you want them to be quiet.

Being healthy means also being capable of letting someone else decide what movie to see or what route to take to get there. It means understanding that sometimes you have to compromise, or do things the way someone else wants. It means being able to accept someone else's authority sometimes (like an employer) and questioning authority at other times (when one is being abused by an individual or a law), and it means having the judgment to know what to do when.

When the incest survivor takes control of her life, she can let go of the need to control everyone else's. At the same time the incest survivor learns that with power comes responsibility.

For many, it seems the lesser of two evils to hide behind "Look what was done to me," or "Look what everyone else is doing to me," instead of saying "I am responsible for my life. My messes are of my making: my choices have consequences, and I have to face those consequences. If I make the choice not to go to work when I'm needed, I might be fired. Or someone who is counting on me might be let down.

If I never follow through on my promises, people might not trust or want to know me."

To be responsible means to acknowledge what you feel, to understand that these feelings are yours (no one makes you feel that way, although you may feel it in response to what they did), to go to the source and share what you feel, and to do something about it if it's a problem. It could mean speaking up, changing jobs, or no longer putting your needs on hold while fuming inside. In the beginning these steps are difficult and frightening; in fact they may feel totally impossible. Once taken, however, they add up powerfully and become much easier than staying stuck ever was. What I have seen in my clients is that once they turn this corner, the only thing that feels impossible is going back to being self-sacrificing.

Directly in relation to the incest, the survivor needs to see that, finally, she is in control. Not of what already happened, but of how it is experienced now: now she can learn to protect herself by being aware of her boundaries, her needs, her limits—and making choices that respect these vulnerabilities. Thus she takes back her power.

Note to partners and friends: Painful and difficult as it is, her increasing ability to say no to what *you* want is a statement that she trusts and values you enough to risk these new, healthier behaviors. It is a test, on one level, of your value system to be involved with an incest survivor who is reclaiming her power. Which would you rather have: an intimate who gives you everything you want and hates herself, or one who stands up to you and can grow with you? But it is also a test of your patience. Who wants to sacrifice one's own needs all the time for the other person's benefit? (Now you know what she's had to deal with!) There are no easy answers. But one thing is sure: if either partner in any kind of relationship is always sacrificing, it is bad for both of them—and the relationship is probably doomed.

Don't push an incest survivor to deal with the incest. She's been pushed around enough. She is setting her own pace, even through what you may see as "resistance" (which really means she isn't doing what you would like her to do!). When she doesn't want to face something, when she seems to be blocked emotionally, she is really taking power. She is protecting the child from pain, where no one has ever protected her before. Let her; support her. When her aftereffects scream "stop," though her voice can't speak, give voice to that wish for her: "It looks like you don't wish to go on." And tell her, "That's OK." Endorse her right to say no. Applaud even resistance—it is her ability to assert her control over her own life. For, after incest, this is a victory indeed!

Author's Note: *Ritual abuse—also called cult abuse and Satanic abuse—is a phenomenon whose pervasiveness is only now becoming clear to those who deal with child sexual abuse. The chilling stories told by unrelated victims around the country are virtually identical. The truths of this abuse are so shocking to society that the victimizers are protected by our disbelief.*

Forced by groups of perpetrators to participate in all forms of violence as part of an indoctrination into various ideologies, the victims are often told they have a bond with the devil, which may be enforced through "marriage" or "bridal" ceremonies. The child's ability to connect with positive loving "higher power" is often destroyed. Ceremonies may include sacrifice of animals, human torture, or cannibalism; victims have been forced to participate in the rape or murder of another child.

Mind control is accomplished through brainwashing; for instance, the victim is trained to believe that were she to reveal the truth of her experience she would have to commit suicide. This does not result in the internal self-protective "splitting" that is described elsewhere in this book; rather, she is literally robbed of her ability to remember, and forced to think and act in certain ways. She totally loses control.

Indicators of a history of ritual abuse include night terrors, extreme fear and guilt; images of blood, dead babies, circles of people (often in robes and hoods, with chanting or repeated phrases); fear of God; unexplained scars; extreme negative associations or blocking out of certain places. Survivors will fear death when they begin to remember, and have (justified) paranoia. They often suffer extreme disassociation, self-injury, psychosis, multiple personality disorder, self-hate. They may become sadistic or murder.

Their flashbacks and memories may represent an unwanted truth, but a truth nonetheless. Believe them. Help them to see that they are good and that there is hope. Be careful, and go slowly. Be aware that they struggle with despair, and that suicide is a real risk at certain stages of healing. And seek out the experts. (Some resources are listed in Appendix B.)

THE SECRET AND ITS ENFORCEMENT:
The Emperor's New Clothes

*E*ither the incest perpetrator is emotionally and physically necessary for the victim's survival, or he can influence those who are. Thus he can build walls around her.

The secret completes the trap. In fact, Judith Herman defines child sexual abuse as "any physical contact that had to be kept a secret." That, she says, automatically "corrupts" the bond between the child and parent. By eliminating any possibility of intervention, the secret allows the abuse to continue, protecting the abuser. As she continues to guard this secret into her later years, the incest survivor unintentionally continues to protect him from facing the consequences of his assault on her. Ironically, many of the same aftereffects that protect the incest survivor protect her abuser as well.

THREATS

Although threats may have been only minimally required in allowing the perpetrator to initiate the abuse, they are more necessary (and more often called upon) to enforce the secret. These threats reinforce the powerlessness of the child. Almost exclusively, they concern not the victim but those around her. She has not the power that would require threatening her; it is enough to jeopardize her environment, whose existence she rightfully sees as responsible for her welfare. Without a home, without caretakers to provide the basic necessities, she will die.

The child is often warned that if she doesn't cooperate, she will be removed from her family—sent away, perhaps to foster care or a reform school. This is more than an idle threat: it really happens. In fact, telling the secret can, in the long run, result in her abuser's getting sole custody of her.

Physical Harm

A tactic of some abusers (as in the Manhattan Beach or "McMartin Preschool" case) is the actual or threatened abuse of small animals. In some instances, rabbits and other small creatures were destroyed before the eyes of terrified children. This practice is particularly common in the context of ritual abuse, whose perpetrators often meet in groups to perform ceremonial child abuse. The victim may be told that, should she not cooperate, similar harm will befall her beloved pet—or her family—or herself.

Other threats against her family might include the statement that if anyone found out, Daddy (if her father was the abuser) might be sent away (thereby also putting the family in financial jeopardy), or Mommy and Daddy would divorce. It is an awesome and awful power for a child to bear—this belief that the choices and futures of the adults around her are controlled by her actions.

"No One Would Believe You"

Many perpetrators say, "Do you think anyone is going to take your word over mine?" This statement is virtually unnecessary. There is no reason for a child to believe that anyone would take her word over her father's, or that of any adult. She has experienced the social preference given grownups. What they say is respected and believed, especially when what she says is different.

When the perpetrator is a community leader such as a priest or doctor, bias against believing a child is much worse. In *Conspiracy of Silence* Sandra Butler presents a vivid example. One young incest survivor describes running away from abuse by her father, ending up in juvenile hall. Realizing she must break her silence or be sent home, she pours her heart out, watching the counselors' faces change as her story unfolds.

[Later, another interviewer] . . . asked me if what I said was the truth. I told him yes, and he said he had traced my father and he was the owner of a store and a deacon in our church and an umpire for the Little League. He told me what I had said was a terrible thing to say about "a man like your father" . . . [and that] my parents had been notified and were on their way over to pick me up.

Totally trapped and left to face the consequences of having broken the secret, wanting to destroy the thing that had caused all that trouble and confusion and hurt, she proceeded to find a razor and "tried to cut off her skin."

What If Someone Does Find Out?

Guilty and self-blaming, the child victim is often afraid that someone *will* find out. What if they *do* listen—who will they really think has done something wrong? She is sure they will blame her. Even if she might be believed, she has no reason to trust that any action will be taken. She has seen that her impact is minimal in comparison to that of adults; she eats when adults decide it's mealtime, goes to bed when they think it's best; if they say she must go to school, to the dentist, to the babysitter, then she must. The power that they command that forces her to obey the demand for sex is the same powerlessness that she believes *must* accompany her plea for help. Of course no one will intervene. An interruption of paternal incest would require an invasion of the authority of the family. But what about the defenseless child? Family rights, in this as in other cases, are really father's rights; they have nothing to do with protecting the rights of the abused.

An abuser who is not a parent is likely to tell the victim that her parents know that the abuse is taking place, and that they in fact are permitting it; the abuser may cite a common phrase that parents routinely say as a "sign." A kidnapper may capitalize on problems she has in her family. Or he may even tell her that her parents are dead; thus the abuser robs her of a sense that her family can offer her safety.

COLLUSION—OR ENSLAVEMENT?

How does the child hear these threats? What meaning does she bring to them?

She is terrified by the possible physical harm that can come to herself or others. Beyond that, she is burdened with the task of maintaining the security and sanctity of her family. If the perpetrator and this threat come from within the family, she must "collude" with her abuser to keep the outside world at bay. If the abuser is an outsider, her collusion may feel necessary for preserving what little security he can offer.

This collusion is really further victimization, for there is no possibility of her choosing another path. At risk is not only her physical well-being—and that of her loved ones—but her survival in a broader sense: because a child is dependent upon a particular environment and cannot provide for herself, a threat to that environment amounts to a direct assault on her. A child has a limited understanding of death, but she knows that being lost in the department store leaves her with a deep, dark, overwhelming fear more awful than words can describe. In that sense, *abandonment* may be the most horrifying threat of all for a child. This has practical as well as emotional implications.

Abandonment is perhaps the threat that underlies incest on all levels. If her parents separate, she faces abandonment; if her father is sent away, that's abandonment; to be punished by her family for what she has "allowed" an outsider to do to her (if she believes, indeed, that she still has a family) is also abandonment. In fact, any disruption of the world that surrounds and protects her that offers her a home and the stability of constancy (however abusive that might be) is abandonment. To be faced with the loss of that structure is a disruption that she cannot imagine surviving. After all, her family is her whole world in the early years of childhood, and the safest, most predictable refuge from the world as her development progresses.

Abandonment is also the alternative to incest in terms of the relationship between the child victim and her abuser. For it is her bond with him—real or desired—that is, in her view, at risk. If she does not "give him" what he wants, she risks losing his affection. It is that simple. Simple, but by no means easy. Abuse or abandonment.

Barbara remembers her father molesting her when he took her swimming. Terrified, in great physical and emotional pain, she gave no sign of the horrible reality going on under the water and out of sight of the other swimmers. Her face gave away no sign of distress; her lips pressed together to repress any sound that would give her away. Perhaps the others might have helped; more likely, they would not have.

After all, they would have asked him, wouldn't they, and he would have laughed and dismissed them with, "Why, what are you talking about?"—and who would the stranger have believed? But whether they believed her or not, either would have been equally problematic for the child: if they didn't believe her, she would have been carried home in his arms, to be taught a lesson with—what? A beating? His disapproval of her would have been enough. And if they *did* believe her, then what might that have led to?

So she remained quiet, and he did what he wanted, not three feet from the other swimmers. She kept the secret to protect him, her family structure, *herself*. If she tells, she will lose everything she loves. If she tells, she will be alone. If she tells, perhaps he will not kill her, but she might as well be dead.

And so she protects the secret with all her might. That, in combination with her need to block from her awareness the horror of what she's been through, often results in repression of her entire childhood experience.

THE EMPEROR'S NEW CLOTHES

In 1984, Dr. Herbert Ketterman, a family physician, was arrested for aggravated sodomy and molesting a 14-year-old girl. He was the author, several years earlier, of *The Complete Book of Baby and Child Care for Christian Parents*.

The child victim of incest who wants to cry out is like the child in "The Emperor's New Clothes," the Hans Christian Anderson fairy tale in which the emperor parades down the main street of the village, claiming to display his magnificent suit, when in reality he is naked. The villagers, awed (or intimidated!) by his power, his status, all behave as if he is, indeed, wearing these clothes (or any clothes!): they act as if his word, not what they see, is truth. Only one little girl has the courage to cry out, "But the emperor is naked!" And the people listen to her. But of course, it is a fairy tale.

The child who has been the victim of incest knows that adults have more status than she. All adults (even respected members of the community when they are naked before the child) benefit from this bias. Against them, who will believe the child? The child, without being told, knows this. *Knows* this. She knows that *she* is invisible, that she doesn't matter. She knows that no one asks what's wrong, even if they see bruises, even when they see her haunted eyes. They don't ask because they are afraid of the answer. On one level, she is relieved that they don't ask, because then she doesn't have to tell them. So she tries not to cry out, in any way. She tries not to act upset, ever.

Thus she is trapped with her reality and her pain. Which is worse: if they don't know, or if they know? Like the rat in the learned helplessness experiment, who gets shocked if it pushes the lever, and gets shocked if it doesn't, the child victim curls up in a psychological fetal position and remains very, very quiet and very, very still.

THE AFTEREFFECTS:
KEEPING AND BREAKING THE SECRET

The incest survivor often stays quiet, perhaps for the rest of her life. If she is experiencing denial about her abuse, she is probably also blocking the injunctions that forced her to keep the secret: she will feel compelled to keep the secret, but not know what or why. So she will try not to attract attention. For then they might ask, and if they ask, *she* will have to know.

Repression

The incest survivor develops a repertoire of behaviors designed to preserve the secret, in addition to the cognitive blocks (described in Chapters 5 and 6) that keep her from *remembering* the abuse. Concomitantly, she maintains other behaviors designed to prevent revealing the hidden information—now a secret of which she may no longer be aware. Like other aftereffects, these behaviors are not calculated or even conscious. They become automatic and, over the years, almost part of her personality. She denies that she was abused by repressing the memories of her trauma. This is the primary manifestation of "the secret": incest becomes the secret she keeps even from herself. (Repression in some form is virtually universal among survivors.)

Silences and Secrets

Many incest survivors are extremely quiet, soft-spoken, and nonverbal. They are used to trying not to be heard (even if they forget the reason), and as adults they continue to make it difficult to hear them. Incest survivors who manifest this aftereffect might do this also because they feel worthless and undeserving of attention, nor do they believe that such attention, if received, would be positive. Incest survivors are particularly inclined to be quiet when there is something of emotional urgency that needs to be heard, for the risks are greater if the issue is important, and their bad self-image may be tapped as well.

Their voices are softest when sharing highly personal information—secrets. The incest survivor is not necessarily aware of this; her voice may not seem softer to her. She may feel very put upon when people (for example, at support group meetings) interrupt her at sensitive moments to get her to talk louder. It's not that she doesn't believe them, but that it is so frustrating that both her voice and her ability to gauge its volume fail her at the same time.

She may be silent when she laughs or expresses emotions of other kinds, such as anger. In bed she is silent. She learned long ago not to cry out in pain when sex was imposed on her. Now she does not cry out, even (especially!) with pleasure, for she feels that her sexuality and its pleasures are shameful, and is embarrassed by them. To call out with joy while involved in this activity would make no sense.

When she does talk, she is likely to select her words carefully. After a lifetime of guarding her secret, of monitoring every word to guide the attention of others away from the reality that screams inside her and dominates her thoughts if she lets it, she is used to choosing her words with precision and care. This interferes with her ability to reveal herself in relationships. How can she learn how much to tell, when, to whom? And how superficial, then, must her relationships remain, when she becomes so personally withholding? As holder of the secret, she can also become generally secretive and vague; she may avoid specifics in virtually all her conversations.

On the other hand, she may become a compulsive talker. Desperately lonely, desperately needy, she may be driven to tell her story compulsively, barely taking the breaths necessary for others to interrupt and set a limit. It is easy for others to become so impatient and annoyed that they no longer see her pain.

Between these two extremes is the incest survivor who is working on her recovery. Having finally found someone who believes her and listens, she welcomes this positive attention and uses it to tell her story.

Lies

Lies are harder to keep straight than truth. Telling the truth is uncomplicated: one *remembers* the truth because it was *experienced;* one can tell the truth, can answer questions about it. Honesty is economical, as an old friend used to say. But one must concentrate on a lie. What did I say? What answer did I give last time to that question? If I say *this* or act like *that,* will they know I'm lying? Will they figure out the truth? Absorbed in this obsessive lifestyle of lies, such a person can barely look anyone in the eye.

Often an incest survivor lies out of fear of not being what another person expects or wants. The other person, any other person, is automatically an authority figure brandishing the unspoken threat of an unfavorable judgment.

The lies are not just about whether her homework is done. They are more often and more importantly about whether she loves somebody, whether something hurts, whether things are good enough for her. There is a taboo against disappointing someone who is vulnerable; complaining, not understanding the other person's needs, not being brave enough, and not trying hard enough to overcome the pain; expecting too much, being self-centered and selfish, ruining her one and only chance ever.

The incest survivor shares this problem with the adult child of an alcoholic, who often lies when telling the truth would be easier. In her dangerous childhood lying meant survival, and telling the truth often put her in jeopardy.

Secrets, Denial, and Depression

Although she does not *remember* the truth, she feels that something is "bad" about her. Even though she cannot describe it, she "knows" it is stamped on her forehead where others can read it. Like Hester Prynne, whose "Scarlet Letter A" told the world her sin of adultery, the survivor feels as if she bears a scarlet letter; but she can't figure what the letter is and what it means.

Because her awful secret cannot be identified, it can grow to be totally unmanageable. As horrible as the truth is, her imaginings are more horrible. The secret pushes against her consciousness just as it pushed at her lips as a child, threatening to burst free. Now, without knowing what the secret is, she is afraid it will slip out. ("What if I tell?" From her childhood, there is a feeling of danger associated with telling.) At the same time, she has a great urge to tell this secret she cannot identify. And she believes *no one would believe her anyway.* Or they would blame her or treat her as if *she* were broken and reject her.

As with any lie, the juggling act can become overwhelming. She withdraws and becomes more and more secretive, leaving more and more out, even in her closest relationships.

When memory begins to break through, the old fears surface with a vengeance. After all, there are injunctions against telling, and remembering is telling herself. With it goes a primal sense of danger. As she comes closer to actually *telling*—telling a friend, a therapist, a support group—this feeling heightens and combines with guilt for failing to follow orders.

Yet telling is exactly what she must do to begin to heal.

Imagined Dangers

In holding his secret, she sacrifices herself to the demands of the incest perpetrator. She agrees (however unconsciously) not to tell what he did, while holding the resulting poison inside her body and consciousness. She pays the price every day for his crime—*his price,* the price that he should pay.

Imagined dangers are more powerful than real ones. But she can't know that. To an endangered person, real dangers are always imaginary until they happen; the only distinction that makes sense is which imaginary dangers have come true right now and which ones haven't come true yet. With an actual threat, one can rally one's internal and external resources, explore one's feelings and choices, and face the monster. However, when danger is imagined, it becomes the black hole, spinning out of control, the end of the world. These disasters are beyond anything in reality, and they seem unsurvivable.

Every child is easily conquered. Abandon her, and she will not survive. Lock her out in winter, and she will freeze to death. Refuse to feed her, and she will starve. Take love away, and she will shrivel and die in her heart. The child knows this. The threat on the other side of "don't tell or else—" is that she will be destroyed. Even long after childhood, these threats hold their power. The adult incest survivor feels the child's fears, sees them through her eyes. She is afraid as the child is afraid. She may have emotional support, survival skills, self-sufficiency, cognitive abilities, some degree of emotional development, but she has little confidence in herself and does not feel her fear in this context. She feels it as the defenseless child.

When she begins to admit the secret, it must be received with awareness of the difficulties she feels in telling it. Keeping the secret has given her a sense of control. It gave her the only (illusion of) choice she had: if he said "Don't tell, or else," she, at least, could choose "don't tell" over "or else."

At first the child's fear—long suppressed and silenced—must be encouraged to find a voice, and must be received with calm and caring. Her fears may no longer make sense in the real world, but before she can face the real world, the child's world must be acknowledged.

Then she needs to be reminded that she is not that child, that she is an adult who can cope—who will survive—indeed, one who has coped, has survived. Her therapist and loved ones can tell her this. Her support group can show her that others have survived, can cushion her when she falters, catch her if she falls.

Ultimately, the best way for her to understand that she can survive is to stand up to that threat and to survive: to own the secret and shatter it. She *sees* that it is her secret, her experience, her victimization, and ultimately her triumph!

Reactions to the Truth

The child who proclaims that the emperor is naked may be met with the scorn, rather than the support, of the community. After all, they need to be able to continue to believe in the teacher, the priest, the doctor. Families, too, often turn against the adult incest survivor who breaks the secret. "Daddy wouldn't do that," replies sister, angrily. "My son? How dare you, you little brat," screams grandmother, the perpetrator's mother. They may tell her she's crazy as they rally round him, as an innocent victim, and make *her* the guilty party. "She lies," they tell people. "She's making it up. She's a trouble-maker, too." (This is by no means the only reaction when adults share an incest history with other family members. Others will be discussed in Chapter 16.)

The incest survivor who dares to point out that the emperor has no clothes is *herself* the one who ends up being criticized and ostracized, frozen out with anger or gossip. When she faces others with the truth, it is she who may be cast out, for they need to see the truth cast out. To her face they might extend sympathy, but when they are alone with the perpetrator, they may then, by their support of him, betray the wounded child.

They are protecting themselves. To be married to a man for forty years and suddenly have to face that he hurt your child, or other children, is to question your entire life. And to accept the accusation as truth is to contend with awful guilt: how could I have allowed this to happen? (Society, it must be said, enhances this guilt.) To have your *son* accused of doing such a heinous thing is a direct attack on one's parenting. Enormous conflict accompanies this truth, and the psyche fights it through attacking its messenger.

They are protecting themselves in a more fundamental way. Incest often occurs through the generations. So do secrets, including the secrets we keep from ourselves. If an incest survivor's sister acknowledges that Daddy molested her sister, she may have to face what was done to herself. Or, if mother acknowledges what her husband or son did to her daughter, she may have to face her own hidden past. Or if grandfather faces what his son did, he may have to face what he, the abuser's father, did to his own son.

The incest survivor protects them as well. Several women whose quotes appear in this book at first gave me permission to use their full names, saying, with heads held high, "Yes, use my name, dammit! I have nothing to hide, nothing to be ashamed of!" Later, virtually every one of them changed her mind—to protect her (nonabusing) adult family members. How many of those family members, knowing the situation, perhaps being told that using her name would be empowering to their loved one, would do for the "victim" what she had done for them? Would they say, "We know that this is what is best for you, and so we will do it, hard as it is for us—we will rally round you, *because it is you who have been hurt?*"

If the "closeness" that she risks losing by telling is a closeness that was bought with her silence, it is built on a lie. She cannot trust it. She may live in an illusion of family intimacy, but what she sacrifices for the *label* of "family" is any sense of trust, security, or honesty. This is a pattern that appears in her adult relationships: to survive, to have connections, she must sacrifice herself.

Breaking the Secret

As painful as her family's rejection or abandonment may be ("See," the voice inside her will cackle, "I told you this would happen!" "You're right," she will reply to the voice, "I *must* be bad."), it will be the first time she *has her way*. Once opened, the door to the closet where the secret was hidden cannot be shut. She cannot be stopped from telling. She can finally say no.

In that way, breaking the secret is incredibly freeing and empowering. "I own my life," she proclaims by telling the truth about her pain. "This happened to me, and I can do with it whatever *I* want to. You do not own me, you cannot control me, and you cannot hurt me or destroy me as I used to believe you could." To break the secret is to say, "Somebody hurt me. I was victimized. And I *protest!*"

The survivor can break the secret on many levels. She can tell her story to her friends, lovers, therapist, support group. By telling others she validates herself.

One of my favorite stories in this vein concerns a young woman who had attempted to enlist the help of the legal system to stop her abuser and perhaps even to punish him. The system refused to cooperate. Because this man's job gave him access to other children, telling only his family was not enough. So she had posters made that showed his picture and said, "WANTED FOR CHILD MOLESTING." She hung them around town. Such an action put her at risk of a lawsuit, or worse. It is quite revealing that this man never took action to stop her. A word of caution: I am not advocating this action. A rape crisis center that helped a woman do something much less public was just *successfully* sued for an enormous amount of money by a man who had avoided prosecution and was therefore technically innocent.

When the system abandons the victim, it forces the strong to resort to "guerrilla tactics" to protect themselves and others. Breaking the secret through remembering is the necessary first step. Telling *someone*, the next. Confronting her family, if the abuse was familial, may follow—and then, if she chooses, confronting her abuser. (All of these assaults on the secret will be discussed in Chapter 16.) Finally, the responsibility we all bear to protect the defenseless falls on the shoulders of the recovering incest survivor as well. She must face the reality that she holds information whose withholding keeps others at risk. No perpetrator stops on his own. In breaking the secret, she has, finally, the power to break the chain.

If someone you know seems secretive, there is a good chance she might be protecting something. Create a safe climate for the sharing of safer things, and perhaps the breaking of this much more volatile secret can follow. Know, then, that much of her recovery will be spent uncovering the secrets that have built over the years, until she is free of the fog they have led to, and clear, and real again.

AM I CRAZY?
—No, You're Coping (Part 1)

Some of these aftereffects allow the survivor to avoid facing memories and feelings; those are presented here. Others assist her in remembering; those shall be discussed in the next chapter.

The isolated, disbelieved, threatened child rallies her resources to protect herself from a reality that she cannot tolerate. Early in life, she develops a variety of cognitive adaptations. Many outsiders (including mental health professionals) view these adaptations as "pathological," or as mental disorders, although actually they are creative—even admirable—survival techniques. Because she both endures and denies sexual violation at the hands of someone close to her, she cannot seek emotional resolution, much less escape, and is likely to develop emotional difficulties. These difficulties are not deficits, but normal, natural reactions to an abnormal situation.

The aftereffects of Post-Incest Syndrome are not "problems" to be "overcome," but coping mechanisms that have negative side-effects. By attaching the concept of "disorder" to these consequences, we damn the incest survivor to weakness instead of attributing to her the strength of spirit, creativity, and endurance that she deserves—that she has *earned*. She does not deserve to be seen as weak, after surviving such a trauma! Yet even some incest or therapy professionals call her "victim" instead of "survivor." While some do this to emphasize the fact that victimization has occurred (a fact which the incest survivor herself often ignores) to do this is to ignore the survivor's strengths. Most women who are undertaking the task of healing and who have become involved with a support network call themselves survivors; they do not call themselves victims.

But let us be clear: what saved her may now interfere. Millions of adults who were molested as children are the "walking wounded"—on the outside, functioning the same as anyone else; on the inside, aching with every step. The survivor's responses to the incest are natural and even meritorious, given the reality of her early life. We must comprehend how limited her choices were. *She* is not crazy—incest is crazy. She does not have an "affective disorder"—she is mourning a murdered childhood. But what has saved her may also cripple her.

FEELING CRAZY

When Jessica attended her first incest survivors' self-help group, she said there was one moment when she knew, undeniably, that this was where she belonged. "Someone there said that she'd always felt crazy," she said, eyes filling with tears of relief, "and something inside me woke up, hearing that. '*That's* it,' I thought. 'That's what that feeling is.' . . . I, too had always felt crazy. And I never told anyone, because I was afraid that, if I admitted it, somehow that would make it true."

Later, some months into her treatment, she was able to analyze it this way: "If I, as a child, claim that something awful has happened— that someone has done something terrible to me—and everyone around me acts as if nothing is the matter . . . then either *I* must be crazy, or all of *them* are. And when you're a kid and your life depends on all these people, there is no choice: of course, I must be crazy." Crazy to be upset when "nothing" has been done to you, crazy to feel so uncomfortable around someone who "loves you so much" and "would never do things like that," crazy to see and feel things that "aren't happening" according to everyone around you, and crazy to be so unhappy about what he did to you—for after all, he said it was "love." And of course, she needs to believe that he really did love her. As long as she needs to preserve that image of him, she will lie to herself.

Even the most secure adults doubt their own perceptions if there is enough pressure from others. For example, when adult test subjects are surrounded by people who have been coached to say that two lines of equal length are in fact different, nearly all the test subjects abandon their own perception and agree with the crowd, believing steadfastly that they actually saw what everybody else said they saw. For a child, whose sense of herself is yet so fragile, to be able to maintain her belief in her perceptions when all around her tell her that rape is love, or that what she experienced never happened at all, is virtually unimaginable. Her dependence plays heavily here as well. Her survival depends on continuing to believe that she can count on her caretakers; if her choice is between disbelieving herself or disbelieving them, then there is no choice—she will learn to doubt her own experiences and feelings, to defer to the views and the demands of others. She loses her self. She has little, if any, choice.

The threats that accompany the secret force her to deny her pain and withhold protest. Under these circumstances, where can truth go? Can it continue to press on her consciousness, when there is no release into the outer world, no relief, and no escape? Can it continue to assault her daily awareness, when it and she have nowhere else to go? She cannot dwell on what she cannot escape. Of necessity, the truth of her experience begins to work its way further and further away from her awareness.

The process is partly fueled by hope. In a little girl, hope struggles to survive—"maybe this time he will just take me swimming and not make me sit on his penis under the water;" "maybe this time he will just hug me without touching me 'there';" "maybe this time he will just listen to me, play ball with me, care for me—*just be a daddy!*" Or perhaps she tries to tell, and is not believed; perhaps she cannot communicate in words that grownups understand. Therefore her reality is ignored or denied, further reinforcing her feelings of craziness.

In my experience, women who did not complain to anyone about being molested are more damaged than those who, somewhere during or immediately following their abuse, vented their feelings and were cared for emotionally. The incest survivor who contains her anguish, endures feeling powerless, and continues to be in contact with her abuser, is at risk for worse consequences than rape trauma syndrome: not only are pain, abandonment, and violation her legacy, but her feelings and memories become so buried that her relationship with reality may be jeopardized.

POST-TRAUMATIC STRESS DISORDER (PTSD)
AND OTHER LABELS

Increasingly, therapists who specialize in working with incest survivors assign the diagnosis of "post-traumatic stress disorder" when they are required or committed to assign a diagnosis. This diagnosis recognizes that emotional problems can be predictable consequences of external events, not, as in the "internal" tradition, arising from within the individual. Yet while the use of post-traumatic stress disorder represents an enormous improvement from previous diagnoses, this diagnosis fails to acknowledge the admirable survival spirit and *inevitability* of the emotional and behavioral consequences it describes. It also is not entirely accurate in describing the post-incest experience.

We would be wise, as a society, to appreciate that "mental problems" are a combination of a stressor and a response. Some loss, or trauma (or series of losses or traumas) *combines* with characteristics of the victims (such as their personal histories, coping skills and other strengths, and their perceptions), social factors (which include resources such as loved ones, healthy families, and often "political" issues such as social oppression/powerlessness). *All* of these must be addressed if we are to understand a troubled individual. However, when a trauma is severe enough, it can account for the bulk of the damage.

With the arrival of this diagnosis, psychotherapists were forced to see that the reality of their clients was more important than theory. These men and women shared a trauma so destructive that it must be recognized as the cause of their problems. Once this diagnosis developed, therapists independently began applying it to survivors of incest. Many have extended this application to other traumatized children: those who were physically, verbally, or sexually abused; those whose families were contaminated by alcoholism; those who witnessed the battering of a parent. But trauma theory addresses only part of the problem.

Bereavement theory is necessary to address the other aspect of family trauma: the emotional loss suffered by the child. The abused child has much to mourn. She grieves the loss of the family she would have wanted, and the safe, warm love that a family is supposed to represent. She grieves lost hopes, lost safety, lost innocence. She grieves her childhood. And she grieves the view of the world as a safe place, for that is lost to her forever. Like the cognitive aftereffects, grief is a normal and natural consequence of abuses such as incest. Have not the majority of therapy clients been driven to treatment by trauma or loss? (In her outstanding work, *Living Through Personal Crisis,* Ann Kaiser Stearns discusses the wide application of a loss/bereavement model to the life problems we experience—not just death, or relationship endings, but also many emotional and concrete losses.) The label of Post-Incest Syndrome combines trauma theory and bereavement theory with the specifics of sexual abuse.

As defined in the so-called bible of psychiatry, American Psychiatric Association's *Diagnostic and Statistical Manual* (DSM-III-R), post-traumatic stress disorder concerns reactions to a "traumatic event that is generally outside the range of normal human experience"—emphasizing the serious nature of the precipitating event rather than the inherent weakness of the respondent. DSM-III-R says that some events frequently produce the disorder (e.g., torture) and others produce it only occasionally (e.g., car accidents.) The effects of some traumas are virtually inescapable: incest falls into the category of torture. And what is never mentioned in DSM-III-R?

Incest.

Rape is mentioned among the dozen or so examples of events that can lead to post-traumatic stress disorder. But not incest. Not anywhere. Although incest might easily be understood as rape (even if no penetration occurred), in terms of the violation that even touching can represent, it is not merely rape: it is ongoing, it is entrapment, and it is done to a child—by a person (or persons) on whom she is dependent.

People suffering from PTSD are often misdiagnosed as psychotic or, specifically, schizophrenic. When a person reacts to trauma by hearing or seeing images evoked by the trauma, many psychiatrists hear only the "craziness" and miss the meaning of what the person is doing—the meaning of the hallucination, the meaning of the panic or hysteria. In relation to incest, this misdiagnosis occurs because psychiatrists tend to overvalue "symptoms" and undervalue life, to overemphasize "chemistry" and underplay human feelings. At the same time, they are unwilling to acknowledge sexual abuse of children. These attitudes reinforce the self-blame of the trauma survivor. The diagnosis of post-traumatic stress disorder also fails to describe the post-incest experience because it generally ignores issues of how early trauma affects a child's development. It only generally addresses some issues (the sexual aspect of incest) and ignores others (the violation of the relationship). However, it remains the best available psychiatric framework for understanding the effect of this trauma. Many professionals concerned with trauma theory are attempting to modify it for a more specific application to incest. Toward that end, Mary Beth Williams, a Virginia social worker, has created and used a 39-item scale, which includes many items from the Incest Survivor's Aftereffects Checklist as well as material from other sources.

THE INNER GUIDE

With so many aspects of her life out of control and hidden from her, her emotional development disrupted, unable to connect with trusted caretakers, the child victim grows into adulthood with only the coping mechanisms of Post-Incest Syndrome, which, at best, complicate her life. She basically must "grow herself up," yet she is struggling with numerous internal and external deficits.

Psychiatrist Elisabeth Kübler-Ross, renowned for her work on death and dying, describes the heightened spiritual strength of the otherwise damaged, ill, or deprived child. I have seen this strength over and over in the existence of an "inner guide" in many incest survivors.

The inner guide is not some other-world spirit or "past life" guide, but an aspect of the incest survivor herself. This internal caretaker ensures that no matter how complicated or painful the incest survivor's outer life becomes, she protects herself enough to "keep on keepin' on."

In many instances, she is uncannily wise. How does she so unerringly know what decision to make? This manifestation of the survival spirit is outstanding in many women who endured sexual abuse as children. I do not mean to describe a magic or perfect solution; sadly, not all can be rescued. But many, many incest survivors have within themselves this spot of wisdom—especially survivors who are strong enough to seek help and healing. The inner guide meters out the defenses described in this chapter, guiding the incest survivor by blocking and releasing memories and feelings.

REALITY AND UNREALITY

Considering the sexual abuse of a child, the real question is "Who's *really* crazy?" Incest is, after all, a violation of the natural order, which charges the adults of a species with the care and protection of their young. But facing this is more than many incest survivors can do. Whether crazy, different, or bad, at least they don't have to see the betrayal.

Consequently, the incest survivor often feels as if she is unreal and everyone else real, or vice versa. After all, everyone can't be right at once; it can't be true that it happened and didn't happen. It can't be true that Daddy loved you and hurt you at the same time. Someone must be wrong. One picture must be real, and one not. The simple world view of the child creates two categories and splits them apart.

Because those around her deny the complicated truth that a loved one can hurt you, reality becomes sharply divided into absolutes of good and evil. (In their denial, in fact, they often glorify the abuser: "He would never hurt you! He's such a good man!") Yet these mutually opposite absolutes coexist in the real-life experience of the child. Therefore, life itself takes on an unreal quality, and in adulthood, the incest survivor never really trusts her perceptions or her feelings, forever doubting herself and feeling crazy. This confusion is compounded by the tactics to which she must resort for self-protection.

Amnesia ("Blocking")

Amnesia, or "blocking," is the most common feature of Post-Incest Syndrome. It can take many forms, affecting memory, feelings, or perceptions. It can result from efforts the victim makes to separate from what is happening to her at the time of the abuse, or from techniques that she resorts to after the abuse. It is achieved through dissociation.

The impact of this aftereffect cannot be underestimated. I have found that most incest survivors have limited recall about the abuse. Indeed, so few incest survivors in my experience have identified themselves as abused in the beginning of therapy that I have concluded that *perhaps half of all incest survivors do not remember that the abuse occurred.* These women cannot understand their lives and do not know why things seem so out of control. They therefore cannot seek the help they need. They cannot respond accurately to research questions designed to determine statistical information about this form of child abuse—and yet these research findings have far-reaching effects on our understanding of (and provision of services for) incest. Because of this blocking, therapists, physicians, and other professionals whose relationship with their clients might be affected by incest, must arm themselves with the tools necessary to diagnose a history of hidden incest.

An incest survivor may know she has strong emotional sore spots and other characteristics that suggest incest; she may have intense reactions to people or events in her life that suggest incest. Still, she would rather point to any other explanation. She should be helped to "trust her guts" at the same time that her struggle about doing so is acknowledged. The first step in recovery for the incest survivor is to acknowledge that the abuse has take place. Often this acknowledgment occurs before any specifics have actually been remembered. Naturally, this helps the self-doubting survivor to doubt herself even more!

For many incest survivors, the process of remembering after the initial acknowledgment never feels complete.

Blocking Out Some Period of Childhood To encapsulate and eliminate unwanted memories, the incest survivor may block out some period of her early years (probably the time during which the abuse took place). Many incest survivors "lose" years of their childhood, most frequently ages 1 through 12. In fact, it is a serious "red flag" to me when a client can't remember much of her childhood. This common occurrence, which psychotherapy has failed to attribute to any specific common theme, generally indicates severe physical or emotional abuse (such as incest).

The incest survivor may also forget what a room or house looked like where the incest took place, or trips or events during which she was abused. Laura*, for instance, molested by a close family "friend," was unable to remember his face at all. Penny does not remember what one of the apartments she lived in when she was growing up looked like.

Emotional Shutdown and "Psychic Numbing" Frequently, individuals who are forced to endure a trauma numb themselves to the experience. Psychic numbing is a numbing to external events—a closing off of perceptual or emotional reception, so that the event is not fully experienced. Emotional shutdown is an internal process where the person's awareness of—indeed, experiencing of—her own feelings is dulled. With one, the experience is not felt; with the other, feelings themselves are not felt. I know that when I ask incest survivors, "What are you feeling?" and they say, "Nothing," they aren't kidding, avoiding, or being "resistant"; they are not feeling.

Some incest survivors remember many details of their abuse but do not associate any emotional response with these events. Or some emotions may be blocked, and others may seem to be the only feelings that person is capable of; for instance, she may never get angry—instead, she may always cry. Or the opposite: anger may be the only emotion she experiences even when sadness seems the reasonable response.

Certainly this technique is effective in blocking pain (as Jessica says, "if you repress it enough, it won't hurt any more!"), but one cannot throw out one feeling without dulling the emotional richness of life. The baby gets thrown out with the bath water. As a result, some survivors experience a general flattening of their emotions. Others shut down in a crisis, becoming emotionally paralyzed when clarity is needed most. And blocking doesn't stop the pain, which lurks under the survivor's awareness.

Blocking prevents the survivor from facing and dealing with her pain; it interferes with her general life functioning; and it affects relationships because remoteness interferes with intimacy. Rediscovering her feelings, attaching names to them, and associating feelings with events are primary tasks for the recovering incest survivor. Aside from being reluctant to face the pain that she has blocked, she may be reluctant to let go of the blocking itself. "Controlling feelings" may be the only control she thinks she is capable of.

Dissociation (Depersonalization, "Splitting")

Unable to remove herself physically from the abuse, the creative child victim finds other ways to leave. Frequently this leaving takes the form of "separation from the self," or "depersonalization." Many incest survivors refer to this separation as "splitting" (which is different from "splitting off," dividing good and bad into absolute, separate realities that can never coexist). I have often heard depersonalization described as an out-of-body experience: "I left my body and floated up to the ceiling," or, more simply, "I could just feel myself slipping out of my body; therefore, it wasn't happening to me any more." At the time of the trauma, many survivors made a conscious effort to separate from what was happening to their bodies.

The adult incest survivor may lose control of this technique, however, and "split" when experiencing stress or in response to an experience that recalls the incest. Depersonalization can easily become terrifying, out of control. It could make anyone feel crazy, and often leads to misdiagnosis of borderline personality disorder or even schizophrenia. It is crucial that professionals and survivors work to determine what function depersonalization has in a woman's life.

Due to this "separation from self," and the ways in which incest is blocked from consciousness, the incest survivor (and her therapist) must always remain open to the possibility that her story is unfolding, and that more may be uncovered at any time. While 43% of Russell's respondents reported being molested only once (as did 48% of those women molested by their biological fathers), authors Janet O'Hare and Katy Taylor state that, in their experience, incest virtually never happens just once.

Partializing and Fantasy During the dissociation or splitting that may take place during the trauma of incest, several changes may occur. The child victim may develop a perceptual tunnel vision, focusing on some element of her surroundings (a light, a cartoon on TV, wallpaper) to the exclusion of the rest of the experience; sometimes she may retreat into fantasy, expanding on what she sees. For example, Polly created an invasion of bees that filled her field of vision in the bedroom, and their buzzing pushed out all other sounds. Or she may "leave" the scene for a safe, fantasy world. Later, these fantasies become substitute or "screen" memories that replace memories of the abuse. In the extreme, these become multiple personality disorder.

Creating Fantasy Identities, Friends, Worlds, or Alter Egos
Merely escaping from an unsafe place into a vacuum is not enough. Many child victims imagine alternatives to the unacceptable world they know. Laura, for instance, made up fantasy friends and family who always loved her and treated her well. Dottie found herself in a world with little people who told her never to trust, ordered her about, scolded her, and controlled her; nevertheless, these creatures "did it for her own good," and they never physically hurt her.

One is reminded of the world experienced by Deborah in *I Never Promised You A Rose Garden*. Originally described as "a young schizophrenic," Deborah hated being touched, had a fierce sense of boundaries, and constructed a world whose language she defined and characters she named. She now appears to have Post-Incest Syndrome. Since the book acknowledges an early hospital stay, she could have experienced sexual abuse.

In addition to recreating their environments, child victims often recreate *themselves,* developing alter egos who offer a positive life alternative to their own. Most commonly, this is a male persona: female survivor clients may either substitute alternative male personalities, or attach to a male fantasy companion. This is simple to understand: as a victim, and a female, she associates her vulnerable state with defenselessness; males, however, are seen as physically stronger, and not easily targeted for victimization. Victims are also aware that "women get raped, but men don't"—they see the position of social vulnerability for sexual violence that women are subject to, and they "choose" the relatively nonvictim status of men. These clients describe their actual or wished-for fantasy selves as strong, powerful: they "don't take any shit." Although it is not, of course, necessary to have a male persona to achieve power (nor is it true that boys are never raped, although rape is not as common for them), many survivors have independently developed this technique.

These are not the product of a "mental illness." They do not arise from a loss of reality such as the hallucinations experienced by someone genuinely suffering from schizophrenia, but are an active manipulation of reality. The child or adolescent is conscious and aware of what she is doing. Although in adulthood the survivor may not remain totally in control of this experience, and may not understand it, she is not necessarily, therefore, suffering from a mental disorder.

Schizophrenia and What Looks Like It For some incest survivors the trauma is too difficult to bear. These women "go crazy"—they leave reality and experience uncontrollable hallucinations and delusions. They become schizophrenic. (Severe trauma can affect brain chemistry in serious ways; therefore, other forms of extreme mental disturbance such as manic-depression probably often result from the trauma of incest.)

There are many types of schizophrenia. Current thought is that schizophrenia is a "brain disease" that has nothing to do with how a child is raised. This is true for some forms of the disease, but not for all. No matter what its origin, schizophrenia renders its sufferer unable to take care of herself, and unable to respond to "talk therapy." Mental hospitals are full of incest survivors who have never been able to escape their private hell. However, many incest survivors in mental hospitals are not schizophrenic and do not require such serious treatment as institutionalization, but have been incarcerated by family members or psychiatrists who misunderstand Post-Incest Syndrome.

Many incest survivors appear to be schizophrenic but are not. At risk for misdiagnosis, incest survivors are especially vulnerable when they experience these events: some have mild hallucinations that are topic-specific—that is, limited and related to experiences that the incest survivors have had. For instance, they may have hallucinations during sex. Some survivors frequently imagine hearing their names called, or being touched, or watched, when no one is there. This relates to the shattering of boundaries represented by the abuse, which leaves the survivor no privacy, no personal space. It is not, however, craziness, although it often feels and looks as if it is.

Multiple-Personality Disorder

Of all the cognitive creations that incest survivors resort to for protection, multiple personality is the most inventive. Research has indicated that the overwhelming majority of people who have multiple personalities were victims of particularly sadistic, relentless physical or sexual abuse in childhood, which usually involved confinement.

The lay person may be familiar with multiple-personality disorder through movies and books such as *The Three Faces of Eve, Sybil,* and *The Minds of Billie Milligan.* It is often confused with schizophrenia, because of the traditional, inaccurate lay definition of schizophrenia as "split personality." But multiple-personality disorder is actually not a psychosis. Born in the victim's early childhood, multiple-personality disorder is a form of depersonalization where, during amnesia, the personality divides into separate, fully functioning aspects of the emotional or personal life of the individual. These personalities are all fully in touch with their environment when they are "out," but they don't all know about each other and the sufferer may not know about them at all. Although the personalities are generally of different ages (children and adults), for their assigned age they are each fully functional and internally consistent.

Before I began working on the subject of incest, I (like many other professionals) didn't believe that multiple-personality disorder existed as described. I was unconvinced that the individual truly was not aware of the personalities. Research findings that one personality would have knowledge or skills or even brain wave patterns or an IQ that the others did not struck my interest but did not convince me. What convinced me was seeing the unfolding of Post-Incest Syndrome, particularly when women who had absolutely no awareness of an incest history began to remember. The inventiveness of the cognitive resources that incest survivors create in childhood—the totality of their denial, the functional purpose of splitting—demonstrate that such altered states of consciousness are possible. Someone can indeed split off parts of herself and not be aware of those parts. To see an incest survivor divided from herself persuaded me that it is indeed possible for someone to go the further step and divide into totally separate personalities.

In multiple-personality disorder, which has sometimes been described as a post-traumatic stress reaction, more than 200 personalities can be created that embody aspects of the child that she cannot face in herself: the angry one, the vulnerable one, the sexual one, the creative one. Personalities evolve over time; old ones may die and new ones may be born. They may be of different genders or nationalities (speaking languages that there is no record the individual ever learned.). They may age or stay children forever. The woman with multiple-personality disorder may not know any of this. All she may know is that the experiences repeated periods of amnesia, after which she may find in her closet clothing that she didn't buy, or may encounter people whom she does not know but who insist they know her by another name.

Frank Putnam, a physician specializing in this relatively new field, warns us that this syndrome "protects itself from detection"—women who "lose time" bluff to cover this up. The syndrome, he states, can be detected through clues such as discrepancies in personality, aggression levels (anger is an emotion that a person with MPD often cannot own and encapsulates into one or more personalities), and dress. He advises to look for changes in facial expression, speech (including pitch, loudness, rate, accent, and vocabulary), body posture, and "affect" (emotional presentation). However, he cautions that these changes may be very subtle and may in fact appear as "moodiness." He also states that migraines and self-mutilation (which is often "punishment" of one personality by another) are common.

Researcher Rosalyn Schultz from the St. Louis Medical Center has found that "multiples" are more intelligent and creative than the "average" person. This is not surprising. One reason that multiple-personality disorder is easily confused with schizophrenia is that perhaps as many as 50% of persons with auditory hallucinations may be multiples. The personalities even have different body temperatures, allergies, and insulin levels! Psychiatrist Richard Kluft, noted expert on the subject, calls it a "maladaptive persistence." Persistence indeed!

Treatment, which often requires hypnosis, involves developing an alliance with one personality and the unlocking of memory through, Kluft advises, art, music, movement, or mutual support groups. Pure psychoanalysis is not advised. He urges that professionals be very gentle and proceed slowly.

Making Memories Tolerable: Selective Memory, Minimizing, and Rationalizing

If memories or reality must be faced, perhaps they can be reduced or excused. This is called "rationalizing." If an incest survivor tells herself "he did it only because he was drinking," or "he had an awful childhood himself," then her abuse may not seem so bad.

Or her memories may be sanitized so as to be less threatening. She may think of what happened to her as "tickling." She may remember less traumatic events, or abuse at the hands of a less important person before she remembers events that would be more upsetting to face. For instance, she may remember an incident of touching but not one of penetration, or she may remember abuse at the hands of a sibling or her father's friend instead of the times her father molested her himself. She may also envision a scene of abuse but not be able to see the face of the abuser.

Many incest survivors remember abuses that occurred later in adolescence rather than ones from early childhood. She may minimize the effect of the abuse, or its intent: "It wasn't that bad." "It was only touching." A clear example of this tendency is found in Russell's book: Bonnie was abused in childhood by her brother, who would hide under her bed, from where he would touch her breast. While she admitted being "very upset" by the experience, she claimed that it had only "some effect." But she said she has "no feeling in my breasts, which *could possibly* be due to that experience" [emphasis mine].

When Memories Cripple: Depression

In simplest psychological terms, depression is a reaction to loss, real or imagined: loss of a person, loss of a treasured belief, loss of a limb. During one difficult period of my life when I experienced a depression, I learned that depression is also protective because as not merely sadness, but *apathy,* it is a state where nothing matters. One feels discouraged, disgusted, despairing; in depression one loses all hope. But because of having lost all expectations, one can no longer be disappointed. And if you cannot be disappointed—if nothing feels good—then nothing else can hurt you; you can start to heal, protected from additional damage while, psychologically speaking, you lick your wounds. Indeed, contrary to popular opinion, a metered amount of self-pity can be very nurturing.

Deep depression is a survival alternative, for the numb state it creates is like being "a little bit dead." With her emotions and mental processes flattened, her responses slowed to a virtual crawl, her energy levels reduced to virtual paralysis, the depressed incest survivor is blocking untenable reality and protecting herself from the sharpness of her pain. However, she can suffer greatly from this emotional "remedy." Relationships, work, parenting, and other responsibilities suffer as well. She can lose weeks or months, even years, and there is a strong possibility that alcohol or drug dependency can develop. But short of her actual death, or a psychic death from which she never returns, depression can be life-saving: the lesser of two evils, perhaps, but one from which, like hibernation, she can return.

The adult incest survivor often endures paralyzing depressions, or, when memory is impeded, depressions that seem to have no basis. In their refusal or inability to see incest, uninformed general practitioners or psychiatrists are likely to prescribe antidepressants for her, treating the symptom without any attention to the cause. When she cries "for no reason" (is that ever possible, or is it more rightly stated as "a reason not yet uncovered"?), she is especially at risk of looking "crazy."

A less serious depression is also common, wherein the incest survivor lives a humorless and solemn existence, free of excitement or joy. One component of this state, which is partly designed to ward off unwanted feelings or memories, is a rigid control of the thought process.

Depression is also said to be "anger turned against the self." This applies to the incest survivor as well. Frequently she is robbed of her anger, because without memory she doesn't know what she's supposed to be angry *at* and because she truly believes that if she faces her anger, she will die, in one way or another. Accustomed to blame, she turns her anger around—hating herself for what was done to her.

Depression is a reasonable and necessary response to certain events. After a loss, it is healthy to mourn. The incest survivor has much to mourn, and many reasons for despair (even if she doesn't know what they are). She has suffered many losses, including her child-hood and innocence. To mourn loss is to acknowledge the pain of the inner child, to validate herself in a way that perhaps no one else ever has. Indeed, it is possible that the more she rants and rails and protests, the more she howls and rages, the healthier she is. What can make this depression counter-productive is if her early powerlessness and aban-donment lead her to spend her future years in resignation with an atti-tude of "oh, what's the use?" Active mourning—with its stages (as described by Elisabeth Kübler-Ross) of shock/denial, bargaining, guilt, anger, sadness, and acceptance are an alternative to nonproductive de-pression.

Psychiatry today defines most serious depressions as "biochemi-cal." The chemical composition of the brain may be altered by early trauma. The real questions are these: Which comes first, changes in brain chemistry or emotional disruption? And in what order should they be addressed? Some people suffer depressions so debilitating that they are unable to respond to any kind of recovery aid, such as group support or therapy; they cannot function and require urgent medical attention. However, the continuing tendency of psychiatrists to medi-cate first and ask questions later—and the recent rediscovery of electro-convulsive (shock) therapy (ECT)—are disturbing to many cli-nicians who specialize in working with clients concerning incest. Psy-chiatry continues to prescribe mood-altering medications for natural human responses. For instance, I repeatedly hear of widows who were prescribed antidepressants for the natural, healing process of grief. In-cest survivors, whose reason for grieving is less obvious, are even more at risk for this type of abuse or neglect.

When Pain Cripples: Suicide

Not surprisingly, many incest survivors are at risk for suicide. In-deed, Judith Herman found that more than a third had attempted to kill themselves. "There are things worse than death," many incest sur-vivors have told me.

Some incest survivors develop an ongoing relationship with sui-cide. They may be actively self-destructive or passively so. They may attempt suicide occasionally or frequently. Or they may maintain a kind of romance with suicide, similar to that described by Sylvia Plath in her poetry. The relationship of these women to suicide is addictive. Suicide is a constant companion; they never let go of the attachment, which is heightened in times of crisis. When the incest survivor is at serious risk of making an attempt, support is necessary until the crisis passes.

But for some survivors, suicide is not as much about depression as about reclaiming power—taking action. It is an attempt to stop abuse when everything else has been tried. It is another example of survival spirit, albeit an extremely paradoxical one, as described dramatically in the following poem.

Child Sexual Abuse Prevention

I try to look dowdy, plain, awful,
to avoid him in my bed.
(And her telling me
I want him there.)
It doesn't work.

I eat like a hog.
Everything edible.
Balloon.
I develop acne again,
hair like a mop.
I look like hell,
and still it goes on.

Asexual.
Living in church,
reading about God all the time,
getting callouses on my knees.
It doesn't stop him.
My death stops him.

Maire MacLachlan

Life often hasn't been worth much to the woman whose early years were filled with fears, horrors, and virtually totally disregard for her needs and feelings. The betrayal of trust represents perhaps the deeper pain. What can it mean to a child to have her own parent, her beloved babysitter, her trusted rabbi disregard her pleas and hurt her anyway?

In the true egocentrism of the child, she feels as if she "let him," or "made him" and feels responsible for her abuse. She hates herself, and hates her life, and is resigned to it. *Nobody* cares, she feels. (At least when she cries—as out of control, raw and without reason as it sometimes might feel—she is giving voice to the child's pain.)

What fertile ground for despair. What sorrow in the life of a kid in fifth grade. Or first grade. How tiny a drop of this poison it takes to emotionally destroy an infant. It does not surprise me that, to these women, death feels like a release. What surprises me is how many of them resist the urge to kill themselves.

At the same time, as Marilyn Stromsness, founder of Sexual Abuse Anonymous in St. Cloud, Minnesota, continually reminds me, many incest survivors do not become seriously depressed. Perhaps they were able to free themselves from the abuse. Perhaps their inner strengths were substantial enough. Whatever the reasons, they survived their abuse to live productive, positive lives. Whether these women are merely fortunate, or their success in life is because they worked hard not to let their incest histories destroy them, they are powerful examples of the human survival spirit. Yet even those survivors who go on to develop Post-Incest Syndrome acknowledge that the aftereffects are their allies.

Hail!! Hail!!

I have already proven to the world that I possess many
qualities, tested as a child like many adults will never be.

HONOR—When my breasts were ravaged I went further and
held my heart—piece by piece I work to put it back together.
Kindness to myself was learned.

PRAISE—When I close my eyes I can see what others can't;
smiles in the sun. Insight was learned.

RESPECT—When hands slid through my legs I became stiff.
Would I be able to walk away when he was done? Strength
was learned.

GLORY—When my ears were filled with sounds of moans, I
listened for birds to sing of future times; patience was
learned.

SALUTE—When all this happened I protected myself without a formal "how-to" class. I used my own mind and body and survived. Confidence was learned.

TRIBUTE—I will not hang my head, for shame does not do me. Well I will hold it high and let them see how a spirit was not broken.

Robin R. Devino

And . . .

There are other aftereffects that are further removed from actual feeling states, and that is both the good news and the bad news for those who experience them. "Hysterical symptoms" (in fact, the original patients that made Freud aware of the prevalence of child sexual abuse all had these symptoms) are mysterious numbness, pains, or loss of functions in limbs or organs (such as eyes). These disorders are not physical in origin but psychological, and represent unremembered trauma or unacknowledged feelings. Because there is a physical distraction, the survivor is at once protected and blocked, and so her recovery is impeded. Her body remembers, but her mind does not.

* * *

At whatever point these coping mechanisms occur, they must be respected; the incest survivor is taking care of herself as best she can. Until she can consciously set limits to how deeply she experiences a threatening feeling, until she can exercise choice in what she gets in touch with, and when, and how much—her inner guide makes her "check out" at threatening moments. Sure, these mechanisms interfere with her current functioning. And they're uncomfortable. And they get in her way in therapy. But they're what she needs to do. They should be accepted. I often urge her to "be gentle with herself." Well, that's just what she's doing.

Nor do I push her if, while we're talking, she seems distracted, or spacy; or if I ask a question or make a statement and a moment later she looks at me and says, "Uh—sorry, what did you say?" I tell her, "You split off. That tells me you weren't able to hear what I was saying." I give a conscious description to this automatic, unconscious process, acknowledging the need behind it, and I give her permission for both. As she gets stronger, and healthier, and more familiar with achieving power directly by being assertive, these tactics are no longer necessary. Until then, at difficult moments—if she is still living with her parents and her father was her abuser, if she goes to the gynecologist, if she is having sex and it gets scary—her guide watches over her and calls forth whatever trick is necessary.

The Ongoing Struggle

I do not wish, in my romantic vision of the inner guide, to minimize the survivor's experience with "the crazies." They can frighten her until she understands them and accepts them as coping mechanisms. However, by avoiding stigmatizing, defect-oriented attitudes and labels, and focusing on the strength and health of the woman's will to survive, therapists and others who care about the incest survivor will help her to develop respect for what she has accomplished.

Similarly, we must not minimize the seriousness of any of these responses to incest. While helping the incest survivor to accept the *normalcy* of these responses, we must understand that they are the emotional scars of incest. They can and do cause problems that must be addressed, and they represent trauma whose seriousness cannot be overestimated. The incest survivor opts for this course despite the hefty cost, because the cost of facing the truth would be greater. Indeed, even after she has broken through her denial and acknowledged that yes, this awful thing was done to her—yes, he did that to her—she may yet continue to struggle and resist seeing that he would do such a thing.

Make up incest? On the contrary. Incest survivors would sometimes rather die (if not totally, then in pieces) than acknowledge its existence.

ONCE REMEMBERING BEGINS:
The Crazies (Part 2)

*B*efore the fact of hidden incest breaks into the survivor's consciousness, often a pattern of hints bleeds through. At each new awareness, defenses such as those discussed in Chapter 5 protect the incest survivor from aspects of her reality that she is not yet strong enough to face. The uninformed professional, or the survivor who needs to protect her denial, can easily remain blind to the meaning of the clues. However, even the slightest awareness and willingness allow an observer to see the message these aftereffects express.

THE PROCESS OF REMEMBERING

With the help of blocking, denial, etc., the incest survivor grows into adulthood relieved of the burden of her memories. Remembering takes different forms for different incest survivors.

As I described in Chapter 3, I have often heard the concern expressed by both survivors and therapists that once started, the memories will not be contained. The expectation is that they will flood in, drowning their victim—perhaps even "driving her crazy." Yet remarkably this "drowning" very rarely occurs.

Often, memories are not released until the survivor has found some support (such as a peer support group or therapy). Even then there is often no more than partial awareness, a fragmentary memory. The entire course of the incest survivor's abuse rarely becomes available in the first moment. When, early in the process, survivors voice the concern that they're going to remember more than they can handle, I often predict that, instead, they will soon be complaining that they can't remember enough.

Even though, technically, she may be "handling it," the incest survivor may be emotionally overwhelmed, so stressed that she becomes drained and exhausted. She may in fact wonder whether it's worth dealing with the memories, and contemplate quitting therapy. This is her right.

There are women for whom this awareness is too much. Perhaps her memories have been triggered by some event like the death of the perpetrator. Perhaps she was addressing incest in therapy but went too fast. It is the survivor's right to remember at her own pace.

The ability of some incest survivors to set limits on memory or surging emotion is damaged or nonexistent. They are overwhelmed by the horrors from their past and the pain they cannot contain. Some really do go "crazy." Some become catatonic in their depression. Some try to kill themselves. And some succeed. The therapist who wishes to help these women needs to help them learn to slow down. Some, however, resist slowing down, insisting on pushing themselves until they break. We must face the sad reality that some survivors cannot find their way toward hope or control. *This is a small minority of incest survivors,* at least among those who seek help.

The incest survivor's task, at least until she can protect herself, is to listen to her inner guide. If there is something that she doesn't remember, it's because she's not ready. She must learn to respect her own pace. Although she can stop, she can't turn back once she starts.

One can learn to hear the guide, but not to control her. By learning to understand when and why her guide puts the brakes on, the incest survivor learns how to take over the job herself. Until such protective pacing is well within her conscious command, her guide will, one hopes, continue to use the techniques developed in childhood.

No Absolute Stages

Remembering incest, and working on recovery, do not occur in a rigidly ordered series of stages. Splitting and shutdown can occur throughout recovery. Denial and minimizing also continue to resurface.

DENIAL, MINIMIZING, RATIONALIZING

Denial, minimizing, and rationalizing are not stages that the incest survivor conquers and then leaves behind. Throughout much of her recovery, she may grasp any opportunity to "make it not be true" again. Charlotte*, for instance, fantasized about telling family members about her abuse—and imagined their response (perhaps accurately): "NO! DADDY would *never* . . . !" Then she used this imagined resistance to bolster her own resistance: "They don't think it happened. I guess it wasn't true after all!"

Many incest survivors with whom I have worked have periodic episodes of "pulling back" from their realizations. As Laura* began to be flooded with clearer memories than she'd ever had, she found it was so hard to acknowledge what she was seeing that she held on to the view—or the wish—that she was really "making these things up." "OK," I told her, "for now, why don't you come in and tell me the things you 'made up' this week?" Doing this, it wasn't long before she was able to face reality: "It's getting harder *not* to believe what I see," she told me.

I watch so many women shake their heads in sessions, as if they were trying to shake off their awarenesses, as if they were saying, "No! This can't be!"

Kathy's denial took the form of a very short memory. She would visit her father and be surprised when—over and over—she saw he had an erection. Every time, she "forgot" all the previous times.

Betsey, a home health aid, had a male patient who exposed himself and, when her back was turned, masturbated every time she visited. But her denial of her own abuse and her lack of trust of her perceptions made her doubt what she saw. It took many visits and many therapy sessions, but she was finally able to say—"I know what I see!" Then she found the courage to complain—and complain and complain, until she found a supervisor who supported her refusal to attend to this patient any more.

Many incest survivors behave this way because they have a difficult time letting go of their perpetrators. As a woman interviewed by Sandra Butler in *Conspiracy of Silence* says, "Little kids need the idea of a family, even if they never really had one." Well, so do *big* kids—*especially* if they never really had one. It's hard to give up the fantasy of "the good father." It is hard to accept that Coach Smith, the only friend she had in the world, might not have thought she was so special after all, for then she might have to think she was not as lovable. It is harder still to let go if she has not had enough love and security to fully nourish her.

Both the incest survivor and her therapist must understand that these retreats from the truth are not failure or "regression" (moving backward), but a normal part of the cycle. They express a need not to let go of the love and self-esteem she drew from the relationship she thought was there.

SLEEP AND DREAMS

Conscious thought can be controlled; conscious awareness can be altered by defenses. But in sleep realities that are carefully masked during wakefulness can leak out. The dreams of many incest survivors are specific versions of the nightmares predicted by post-traumatic stress disorder. Horror-filled, terrifying, full of images of entrapment and violence—they represent the themes of incest. Occasionally, particular aspects of an incest survivor's actual experience may be repeated in her dreams, although often the identity of the abuser is masked. Dora, for instance, dreamed of "a big, white presence" but could never see her father's face. Her father was a doctor, and she often saw him in his white coat.

A survivor's nightmares may contain pursuit and threat—being chased, being threatened with or trapped in a violent situation. Often these dreams are bloody. Often she dreams of a man or men breaking into her home. Often, she dreams of rape or sexual abuse.

"Night terrors" are nightmares that occur at such a deep state that the dreamer may thrash, sleep restlessly, awake screaming, drenched in sweat, or paralyzed, but unable to remember any of the dream, as if too horrible to be faced. While sufferers of both night terrors and nightmares may find it impossible to shake their terror for many hours after awaking, those experiencing night terrors are particularly inconsolable.

Nightmares and fear of the dark are such common experiences of childhood that we take them for granted and dismiss their possibly serious underlying cause. However, we do not accept nightmares in the adult as readily—and do not hear of them as often, because the fear of the dark is often embarrassing to admit for most adults. Yet in the traumatized adult, nightmares are also common, especially among those who repress or fail to deal with a traumatic memory. These dreams may be a screen where portions of the abuse flash, distorted or out of proportion. For instance, a survivor may dream of a giant hand, whose size makes no sense to her as an adult but is in proportion to the child who first saw it.

In childhood the helpless state of sleep may have put the victim more at risk for the real abuses that she suffered. In her later life, the sufferer may fight or fear sleep (for instance, staying in a "twilight" state) as an attempt to avoid remembering this unwanted reality.

SENSORY FLASHES AND IMAGE FLASHBACKS

A number of my clients reported a similar, mysterious experience: when faced with a particular combination of environmental stimuli, they would get what they all called "the feeling." No amount of direct attention to the problem ever uncovered what was going on. It wasn't until we approached the experience indirectly, by working on the incest whose presence was indicated by other aftereffects, that we uncovered the real meaning of these "sensory flashes." In Terri's case, for instance, "the feeling" came when there was rain, or water running down (such as a shower), in combination with a bright light. She later remembered being molested by her aunt and grandmother, as she lay on the kitchen table, under a glaring kitchen light, while outside it was raining.

Some survivors experience image flashbacks. For Patti, it was a picture frame; for Delores, the color yellow; for Laura, a toy rocking horse or Mickey Mouse cartoons. These images, which can be of smells, colors, textures, or specific visual images, fill up their senses, blocking their ability to see any other part of the picture.

Sensory flashes and image flashbacks are manifestations of the tricks of concentration that the child victim was able to play, in combination with blocking techniques she developed later. She focused on a comparatively safe aspect of the abuse experience to avoid focusing on the abuse itself. Later, she pieces together the perimeter of a jigsaw puzzle before she assembles the center pieces that reveal the picture: the actual incest. She remembers pieces, and has "the feeling," but does not know what any of it means, at least in the beginning. One of Monica's first clues to her incest was the mysterious negative feelings toward the uncle whom she had always thought she loved intensely. She then began flashing on a particular corner of her aunt and uncle's bedroom. Then she began to see herself in the mirror that was on a closet door in that room. Like the pieces of a puzzle, these clues began to come together to reveal the incest from which she had so long shielded herself.

SKEWED REACTIONS

Emotional, as well as sensory, hints to the survivor's past occur in her adult life. She may experience unexplained strong negative feelings about a particular person, place, or event from her childhood, or an entire ethnic group or gender. For instance, an Asian woman abused by her cousin may hate all Asians, even though she is Asian herself. Or an incest survivor's hatred of men may be so absolute that she might phrase it something like this: "I hate men. They only want one thing. All of them, they're all assholes. I *know* some of 'em are OK, but I don't *want* to know any of them are OK. I just hate all of them, all right?!"

FLASHBACKS

Flashbacks are the reliving of a traumatic experience, or an aspect of a trauma, as if it were happening *now*. Along with sensory flashes, they are a virtually universal component of Post-Incest Syndrome.

For some incest survivors, flashbacks may be triggered by normal life experiences or "rites of passage" such as marriage, the birth of a baby, or a death—especially the death of the prepetrator. Flashbacks are often stimulated by a sexual encounter, such as the way a lover touches the survivor, how her partner's breath feels against her skin, or a particular sexual act. They can occur in response to hearing a certain laugh or a particular phrase.

Flashbacks often "wait" to occur in a climate of safety, such as in the therapeutic environment or support group. Once they begin, however, they do not always limit themselves to those safe spaces. Instead, they may, for example, invade the survivor's consciousness while she is driving or when she is trying to sleep. They can be very disruptive and frightening, but these "flashes" of the picture of the abuse last only a moment.

Sometimes, a woman reports that she is feeling out of control in her daily life, suffering renewed eruptions of problems that had seemed under control, or feeling urges to return to substances she had previously abused. She is often disoriented and feels a sense of urgency. For instance, Laura, a recovering alcoholic, would feel like drinking, have trouble trusting people, and be unable to focus on her problems. A long-time, active A.A. member, she began to arrive late at meetings and sit in the back of the room, hiding behind folded arms. What did this mean? It did not connect to any current problem or external event. Frequently this pattern indicates a flashback that is pushing to be vented, but which the survivor is fighting. Releasing the material of the flashback in therapy, the survivor is freed of the strain and complications of resisting it, and functions at her previous level or better.

Flashbacks can be frightening, astonishing, painful, and overwhelming for the therapist with whom they are shared as well as for the incest survivor herself. One might well feel intimidated by the intensity of the pain and drama that are unfolding, when the survivor most needs her ally to be unruffled, calm, and in charge. However, flashbacks do not represent mental illness; they are not psychotic. They are controlled experiences—events relived to release, cleanse, and heal. That they occur at all indicates that the incest survivor is strong enough to face her memories. That they occur in the therapist's company represents the trust and safety that the therapy provides for the survivor. Flashbacks are an opportunity to learn, and to be free. They are not something to be fought or medicated; they are a painful, necessary, hopeful part of recovery.

During a flashback, some incest survivors go into a "fugue" state, temporarily leaving consciousness and returning after the flashback is safely over, with no memory of the experience. (This is a relatively rare but more dysfunctional state.) Many survivors—if not most—remain aware during the entire flashback. If the survivor is in therapy when the flashback occurs, gentle, careful, fearless questioning helps the client to experience all the elements of the flashback (aspects that remain undone may require that she return to redo the scene.) Sometimes, the inner guide lets her do only part of the experience; both participants should stay attentive to indications that she needs to stop. Because she may not be able to say that she needs to do so directly, both should listen to the signs that the guide is sending.

Flashbacks are often accompanied by nausea (or, more rarely, actual vomiting), specific pains, numbness or locking in specific parts of the body, and deep chills.

Flashbacks are only technically "re-experiences." The incest survivor is like the Vietnam veteran who went through the war "on automatic," only to be walking down a street years later and, hearing a car backfire, throws himself under a bush to escape the exploding grenade. The incest survivor, too, endured life in a war zone; like the veteran, she got through it by blocking out the most traumatic parts. Therefore, when she has a flashback, *it is as if she is experiencing the trauma for the first time.* In fully experiencing it all—the event, the feelings, her sensory experience in all of its pain and horror—she can "work through it" and let the trauma go.

Because flashbacks do not always occur in a safe setting, the incest survivor must develop coping skills that she can implement when she feels unprotected. The following article by Laurieann Chutis, ACSW, a Chicago-based therapist, covers the range of partial to total flashbacks that are described earlier in this chapter, and outlines the steps that the survivor can take to "help" herself through the experience.

FLASHBACKS

What Are They?

Flashbacks are memories of past traumas. They may take the form of pictures, sounds, smells, body sensations, feelings or the lack of them (numbness). Many times there is no actual visual or auditory memory. One may have the sense of panic, being trapped, feeling powerless with no memory stimulating it. These experiences can also happen in dreams.

As a child (or adolescent) we had to insulate ourselves from the emotional and physical horrors of the trauma. In order to survive, that insulated child remained isolated, unable to express the feelings and thoughts of that time. It is as though we put that part into a time capsule until it comes out full-blown in the present.

When that part comes out, the little one is experiencing the past as if it were happening today. As the flashback occurs, it is as if we forget that we have an ADULT part available to us for reassurance, protection, and grounding. The intense feelings and body sensations occurring are so frightening because the feelings/sensations are not related to the reality of the present and many times seem to come from nowhere.

We begin to think we are crazy and are afraid of telling anyone (including our therapist) of these experiences. We feel out of control and at the mercy of our experiences.

We begin to avoid situations, and stimuli, that we think triggered it. Many times flashbacks occur during any form of sexual intimacy, or it may be a person who has similar characteristics as the perpetrator, or it may be a situation today that stirs up similar trapped feelings (confrontation, aggressive people).

If you are feeling small . . . you are experiencing a flashback.

If you are experiencing stronger feelings than are called for in the present situation . . . you are experiencing a flashback.

Flashbacks Are Normal

Vietnam vets have normalized this experience and have coined the term *post traumatic stress syndrome.*

Even the diagnostic category book for psychiatry defines post traumatic stress syndrome as the *normal experience* of all people experiencing an event that is outside the range of normal human experience.

Flashbacks feel crazy because the little one doesn't know that there is an adult survivor available to help.

What Helps

1. *Tell yourself that you are having a flashback.*

2. *Remind yourself that the worst is over.* The feelings and sensations you are experiencing are memories of the past. The actual event took place long ago when you were little and YOU SURVIVED. Now it is time to let out that terror, rage, hurt, and/or panic. Now is the time to HONOR YOUR EXPERIENCE.

3. *Get grounded.* This means stamping your feet on the ground so that the little one knows you have feet and can get away

now if you need to. (As a child, you couldn't get away . . . now you can.)

4. *Breathe.* When we get scared we stop normal breathing. As a result our body begins to panic from the lack of oxygen. Lack of oxygen in itself causes a great deal of panic feelings; pounding in the head, tightness, sweating, feeling faint, shakiness, dizziness. When we breathe deeply enough, a lot of the panic feeling can decrease. Breathing deeply means putting your hand on your diaphragm and breathing deeply enough so that your diaphragm pushes against your hand and then exhaling so that the diaphragm goes in.

5. *Reorient to the present.* Begin to use your five senses in the present. Look around and see the colors in the room, the shapes of things, the people near, etc. Listen to the sounds in the room: your breathing, traffic, birds, people, cars, etc. Feel your body and what is touching it: your clothes, your own arms and hands, the chair or floor supporting you.

6. *Speak to the little one and reassure her/him.* It is very healing to get your adult in the picture so your little one now knows that he/she is not alone, that you are not in danger now, that you can get out if you need to, that it is OK to feel the feelings of long ago without reprisal. The child needs to know that it is safe to experience the feelings/sensations and let go of the past.

7. *Get in touch with your need for boundaries.* Sometimes when we are having a flashback we lose the sense of where we leave off and the world begins; as if we do not have skin. Wrap yourself in a blanket, hold a pillow or stuffed animal, go to bed, sit in a closet . . . any way that you can feel yourself truly protected from the outside.

8. *Get support.* Depending on your situation you may need to be alone or may want someone near you. In either case it is important that your close ones know about flashbacks so they can help with the process, whether that means letting you be by yourself or being there.

9. *Take the time to recover.* Sometimes flashbacks are very powerful. Give yourself the time to make the transition from this

powerful experience. Don't expect yourself to jump into adult activities right away. Take a nap, or a warm bath, or some quiet time. Be kind and gentle with yourself. Do not beat yourself for having a flashback. Appreciate how much your little one went through as a child.

10. *Honor your experience.* Appreciate yourself for having survived that horrible time as a child. Respect your body's need to experience those feelings of long ago.

11. *Be patient.* It takes time to heal the past. It takes time to learn appropriate ways of taking care of self, of being an adult who has feelings, and developing effective ways of coping in the here and now.

12. *Find a competent therapist.* Look for a therapist who understands the processes of healing from incest. A therapist can be a guide, a support, a coach in this healing process. You do not have to do it alone . . . ever again.

13. *Join a self-help group.* Survivors are wonderful allies in this process of healing. It is a healing thing to share your process with others who understand so deeply what you are going through.

14. *Know you are not crazy . . . you are healing!*

* * *

RECALL AND RECOVERY

The cognitive techniques described in this and the preceding chapter, while they may seem like symptoms of a mental disturbance, are specifically designed to control the flow of information about the abuse into the consciousness of the incest survivor and thereby protect her. *Some* aspect of the trauma is blocked for virtually every survivor, whether it be memories of events or feelings. Whatever damage the incest itself does is compounded and complicated by these "protections." Indeed, it may be that whatever damage incest does is *exceeded* by the disruption and confusion resulting from these mental distortions.

The sooner the child victim or adult survivor successfully shares the secret of her victimization, and the sooner she gets to deal with the trauma, the less complicated, and quicker, her recovery can be. It is not the incest alone that creates Post-Incest Syndrome, but the matrix of complicated psychological, political, and social circumstances that surround it—including the aftereffects that are designed to help her survive. The adult incest survivors with whom I have had contact generally are dealing with (if not revealing) their abuse for the first time. When we attempt to do therapy, our job is made more complicated by the years of entrapment with the secret that lay behind them.

A current topic of debate among both incest survivors and professionals is whether, and how much, memories of the abuse must be uncovered for recovery to be considered "successful." Recognizing that "success" is a relative term and "recovery" is a process rather than arrival point, I would like to say this: Each completed flashback does seem to cleanse something in the incest survivor. Something inside her finds better order, is less weighted in confusion and pain, is more clear and centered. These are abstractions, I know, but there is a definite lightening of the emotional load of the survivor after a flashback is over. There is no way to know what is left, of course, for one cannot know what is not remembered. Apart from this, the survivor has many themes to address, pains to heal, new skills to learn.

Post-Incest Syndrome is a complex experience with many possible intervention points. Even before she has her first actual memory, the incest survivor can work through many incest-related complications such as trust and feelings of powerlessness. She can and should address addictions, without necessarily looking to unveil the incest. All the other aftereffects have lives of their own in the present: relationship issues, phobias, splitting, all can and should be addressed directly.

I believe that the denial of an incest history must be broken through in order for healing to begin; one cannot recover from what one does not acknowledge and "breaking the secret" helps the survivor to acknowledge that she was unfairly harmed and is not a bad person. I also believe that the more totally the previously buried traumas are uncovered and worked through, the deeper the recovery. But an enormous amount of growth and healing can accompany examining the healthy need behind each aftereffect and working toward replacing outdated, counterproductive behaviors and attitudes with healthy, assertive, freely chosen alternatives. Indeed, most details may *never* be remembered, but that does not doom the survivor. It probably simply means that she is so wounded that her guide will not let her see the trauma—and as long as she can function in treatment, or in a self-help group, or in her life, then her guide is taking care of her well enough.

With a trauma as devastating and murderous as incest, we must not impose abstract, universal standards of "health" on all who have been affected. If she is *here* today, she has survived; the goal is to reduce pain and enhance functioning, help her discover some joy and, hopefully, peace. It is not wise, and not possible, for any outsider to attempt to determine how much of any of these she should have.

SPOILED AND SOILED: Guilt, Shame, Self-Blame, and Self-Esteem

*B*y blaming herself, the incest survivor blocks her awareness of her victimization. "I was not *abused*," she tells herself, "it was *my fault*." Sadly, it is often easier for many types of victims to view their abuse in this way than to face the implications of what was done to them.

At the time of the original abuse, the perpetrator says things that feed self-blame. He tells the child victim that what he does is somehow because of her. He may say, "I'm doing this to you because *you make me want to* do it." Or: "You make men *have to* do things like this to you." He describes her as a "seductress." In other words, the message is, "I can't control myself—and it's *your fault*."

EXCUSING THE PERPETRATOR

The myth that female victims are responsible for what men do to them is applied to victimizations of adult women as well as children: "I raped her because she was *asking for it*." "What was she doing in the park so late at night?" "Why'd she have to let me get this far, so I couldn't stop?" "Why does she wear such short skirts" (low-cut blouses, blonde hair, high heels)? Or: "I beat her up because she kept pushin' at me." "She provoked me," and the more subtle but insidious, "Why does she stay and let him beat her up like that?"

As a society, we are extremely reluctant to hold men accountable for their violent acts. With regard to incest we say that "he molested his daughter because his wife wouldn't satisfy him." And if the child or woman is not seen as directly provoking the abuse, we hold them accountable for "permitting it" or "tolerating it," or we hold the mother responsible for not rescuing her child. Although women who are capable, and not themselves too abused, can be held accountable for how they fulfilled their parenting obligations, the fact that the focus is on a nonperpetrator is the issue here.

Perhaps even more dangerous are some views voiced by "experts." One is the "family systems theory" that incest is an "expression of a problem in the family system" to which everyone contributes. This theory is dangerous because the next step is to look at how a woman—or even the child—"contributes" to a father's rape of a child. Incest is not seen as the sole responsibility of the perpetrator; his behavior is merely an "expression" of a problem in the family system.

BLAMING THE VICTIM

Unfortunately, rape survivors, battered women, and children who are victims of incest are likely to feel responsible for their abuse without any outside "help." It is part of women's training to blame themselves when something goes wrong in their lives. Self-blame is a significant part of the experience of being a survivor of sexual violence, as expressed in questions such as, "What did I do to deserve this? Why didn't I stop it?" The survivor of sexual assault feels that somehow, she was "bad," or that she "wasn't enough," or—the most damaging—that she "invited it."

Women who were sexually active before a rape are especially held accountable. If she had *any* sexual relationship with an acquaintance-rapist, then she "must have wanted it." (She's not allowed, it seems, to want *some* of it and then want to stop.) And if, God forbid, her body responded in any way with arousal, even as the rest of her wanted to puke from the violation, then she must have *loved* it, the most awful guilt of all.

These attitudes damn the child incest victim with her naïveté and dependence. Of course she wants *some* of it. She wants to be noticed, and she wants to be cared about. She wants what is every child's birthright: to be adored, by *somebody*—but to be loved for what she is, not for her sexual usefulness.

It is especially hard for most child victims to know the difference between what she wants and what she doesn't want because of the insidious way an abuser sneaks the abuse up on her. He is likely to begin before she is old enough to understand what is being done to her, even before she has words to define her experience. Or he initiates the abuse slowly, with seemingly innocent stroking and caressing. By the time she is sure she has something to complain about, it is too late.

Although powerless to stop the abuser, the child believes that somehow she should have been able to stop him. There must have been some way—she just cannot think of what it is. Now, it's too late—and it's her "fault."

"Participating" in Incest

The child victim of incest often sees herself as a participant rather than a victim. The term "incestuous relationship," used casually today even by the relatively well informed, illustrates how pervasive this attitude is. Actually, in incest one person is active and one passive, one dominates and one acquiesces. The incest survivor herself often fails to make this distinction.

To some degree this attitude is a protection, similar to the self-blame of the battered woman or the spouse or child of an alcoholic. Both think that if they were just better people, bad things would not be done to them. The battered woman feels that she must be doing something wrong and that, if she could only correct it, her husband would stop beating her. She maintains this self-blame as a way of preserving the illusion that she can somehow control her husband's or lover's behavior—that she is in control of her environment. The child victim of incest also maintains this view. For both, the alternative would be even more difficult to face: *powerlessness*. It is less threatening to see oneself as somehow responsible and, therefore, guilty than to admit that one has been basically powerless and, therefore, the victim of a situation out of control.

Responding to Threats and Favors

The perpetrator's threats feed her guilt. For instance, to a child, tolerating sex abuse may seem like a lesser threat than the possibility of a beating. At her level of development, she understands how awful a beating would be, but it will be years before she understands the full damage done by the sexual violation. So even if she understands that she "chose" the lesser of two destructive experiences, she will carry guilt for "choosing" the sexual abuse. Or if she "allows" the incest for fear of losing something else she wants, such as attention, affection, or closeness, she tends to focus on the fact that she sanctioned the abuse, minimizing how little choice she had and how important nurturing is to a dependent child. She fails entirely to see the cruelty and absurdity of holding a child accountable for making such "choices." These are not choices, for the child has no freedom. Nor is her cognitive or emotional equipment sophisticated enough to evaluate what she is faced with.

Often incest comes with special favors. The siblings of a child victim of incest might endure beatings that she is spared. Or she might receive gifts that are better than those given her siblings. For this aspect of the situation, she denigrates herself and feels guilty.

"Permitting" incest often results in increasing webs of entrapment from which the child sees no escape. How can she tell her family that she doesn't want to be with that babysitter or piano teacher any more? (A young enough child will, in fact, "tell" her parents this by crying and protesting before being sent off to be with an abuser.) To ask for help, she must first break the secret and admit what she has already done. She fails to take action because, in her powerlessness, it would be meaningless—or it might result in punishment. Her options have been closed off, but in her soul she sees only her "cooperation."

Many survivors of childhood abuse draw a simple inference from their experience: "If all of these bad things happened to me, then I must be bad; if I didn't fight and scratch to the death, I must be responsible." This is truly *survivor guilt:* "If I lived, I must not have done enough." And in her guilt, she turns her anger on herself, removing it from her abuser and blaming herself.

These circumstances combine with the shame that is also intrinsic to sexual abuse. The victim's shame is exacerbated by the abuser's secretiveness—he talks to her in hushed tones; he does what he does in private, behind locked doors; he seems agitated if there is the threat of discovery; and he wants her not to tell. All this tells her there is something dirty in what they are doing, something embarrassing, something bad. Later she will associate this feeling with what she feels at the thought of being discovered while she is experimenting sexually with her own body or that of a playmate; sex can become dirty in all its forms.

THE AFTEREFFECTS: OUTGROWTHS OF
GUILT AND SHAME

One feels *guilt* over something one did that violates one's moral code, is likely to be met with social disapproval, or hurt another. *Shame* is a deeper sense of worthlessness, a sense of inner, innate badness, not in relation to one's actions, but one's very self. The child victim of incest feels shame as well as guilt. We feel guilt over what we have done, but shamed by what we *are*. Guilt says, "I did something wrong." Shame says, "*I* am bad for this." Incest survivors are so good at shame that they blame themselves for otherwise positive characteristics; they say, for instance, "I was too pretty."

Many incest survivors feel ashamed to be "victims of incest," which sometimes becomes their primary way of defining themselves in adulthood. As guilt is an alternative to powerlessness, shame is also an alternative to a more threatening reality. If I am not bad (that is, if I have nothing to be ashamed of because I am a *victim*), then someone I relied on has hurt me. He has not been safe for me, and I cannot count on him. Shame, therefore, is the alternative to being alone, to facing that I really do not have this person—I have been abandoned.

Because Post-Incest Syndrome is "life out of balance"—because a problem is expressed by going to one extreme or another—a self-hating, guilt-ridden, shamed person needs to be either invisible, perfect, or perfectly bad. These are alternatives to having a balanced sense of self.

Low Self-Esteem

The child victim of incest feels *soiled* and *spoiled*. She feels contaminated by the dirty act of incest that she "permitted" or even "asked for." Because the event(s) occurred in childhood, while her self-esteem and her identity were still developing, and often before she was even verbal, these feelings weave their way into the very fabric of her being. Unlike a rape survivor who might feel guilty or dirtied because of an event in her adult life, the incest survivor grows up with sexual abuse as part of her development, and it becomes part of her view of herself. She grows up feeling as if something inside is putrid, disgusting. Feeling dirty is endemic to the post-incest experience, often complicated by the fact that the incest survivor doesn't know what soiled her. Feeling dirty becomes a part of her character rather than the response to an event that happened to her. Simultaneously she feels both bad and responsible. Whatever self-esteem she is able to muster is based not on her own belief in her self-worth but on what she can do for others.

If it is her fault—if *she* is bad—she has no reason to criticize a beloved adult (or brother, or cousin). No reason not to trust, no anger to feel at them. So nothing interferes with her relationship with her needed family member or other childhood caretaker.

For Teresa* this experience was so fundamental that it interfered with her ability to function in therapy. She was unable to get past the shame enough even to talk with me about the abuse or related feelings. Unfortunately, at the time there was no support group to send her to. So taking charge (for the first time!), she started one! "I felt like you were judging me, even though you weren't; it was just so hard to talk to someone who was on the 'outside,' " she said. "I felt like the only place where it wouldn't be 'us' versus 'them' was where it had happened to all of us, so nobody could point the finger and judge me."

One of the primary benefits of a self-help group is the feeling of belonging. It remedies what Laura calls "terminal uniqueness." Teresa, fortunately, had the strength and initiative to "turn lemons into lemonade." Many other incest survivors respond to these attitudes by growing contained, retreating into themselves, for any attention reveals their worthlessness.

Lack of Assertiveness

Self-blame, guilt, and shame of this magnitude are difficult to bear. While these attitudes may, in childhood, seem to be preferable to their alternatives, they can virtually cripple the adult survivor's daily functioning.

Particularly affected is *assertiveness*. Already a difficult skill for women to develop because of their indoctrination to be compliant, "ladylike," and "nice girls," assertiveness is virtually impossible for many untreated incest survivors. They feel that they do not deserve even the smallest gesture of good will.

One manifestation of this pattern is the dynamic of "high appreciation." Often the incest survivor can't understand when other people go out of their way for her, doing something for her with nothing in return. For example, a co-worker says, "I'm going to get coffee. Would you like some?" The survivor, with unspoken discomfort, says yes (because she hasn't the courage to say no). The co-worker brings her coffee today, and again a couple of times. The survivor knits her a sweater to thank her. (I told this example to Barbara, thinking I had made up a clever fiction to prove a point, and she exclaimed, "I *did* that!")

How much more difficult it is, then, for an incest survivor to ask for something. Many incest survivors never expect kind treatment, and when their experience is unsatisfactory they think they deserve it. Because of this expectation, they often go into situations defensively. If they don't ask for anything, then no one can respond by pointing their "badness" out to them.

Invisible

In adulthood, the incest survivor expects bad treatment because she feels she deserves it. Being invisible means her "innate badness" won't be noticed. Feeling marked, she feels her being announces and reveals her innate worthlessness. To avoid attention is to stay out of harm's way.

The desire to be invisible starts with the abuse: if she's invisible, maybe her abuser won't molest her. Sexual abuse often occurs where other abuses thrive (such as alcoholic families or families where there is child- or wife-beating). If he doesn't notice her, she might be spared other forms of emotional or physical abuse. Even when the abuse comes from outside the immediate family, in many cases the child victim is more vulnerable to the emotional enticements of the abuser because she is running from a similarly abusive family. The fact that these abuses are in the past has no meaning for many incest survivors, who feel the danger very much in the present. To ensure invisibility, she may dress in quiet colors, not raise her hand in class, withhold her opinions.

Unfortunately, for some, invisibility means slinking apologetically through life. This pathetic posture—carrying herself "like a victim"—sets her up for continuing victimization. She often expects—even invites—disrespectful treatment. (Then she may get angry over the way she is treated, but that is a distraction from deeper, more threatening anger.) Or she acts so helpless, passive, and apologetic for herself that others find her difficult to deal with. They may become impatient or hostile toward her, or verbally abusive. Or they may avoid her. Expecting abuse or rejection, she may become antagonistic and provocative. She unwittingly sabotages her own welfare.

On one occasion, Polly was twisting herself inside out over a problem with her boss. She took a work assignment for a particular day, "forgetting" that she had a previous commitment—in effect "setting herself up" to have a problem. Then she felt unable to call her boss to request a change, because she felt like a bad person for having done the thing to begin with, and therefore *unentitled* to ask for an adjustment. Guilt, shame, and self-blame can pull the survivor into the quicksand of powerlessness, paralyzing her, drowning her in a cycle of self-destructive acts. This stance makes her no longer invisible; in some cases, it makes her a target.

One effect of this aftereffect of invisibility is seen in relationships. Many incest survivors (as well as adult children of alcoholics) expect to be invisible in the eyes of others; they do not expect relationships to last. Thus they do not expect others to think about them when they're gone and are surprised when someone does.

Perfect

An incest survivor might instead try to be perfect. This overachieving stance, an overcompensation for her negative view of herself, is commonly found among children of alcoholics, whose ego may drive them to cover their lack of self-esteem with the pursuit of extreme power and influence. Struggling to achieve an impossible goal (because she is human, she is necessarily "imperfect"), the incest survivor appears infallible from the outside, but never feels good enough on the inside. She must be in total control of everything all the time, get perfect grades, be above reproach, never bump into things or look silly, always have the right answers, always be whatever everybody else wants her to be (which breaks down the minute two people want different things of her), be the perfect lover, the perfect daughter, the perfect mother—the woman who "has it all," dresses for success, rapidly climbs the executive ladder—and never feels tired or annoyed!

Of course she cannot possibly reach these impossible goals, and she never feels even adequate, let alone perfect. In fact, things always feel out of control. And she is always under pressure. She is especially prone to alcoholism, eating disorders, and other addictions; perfectionism is also an aspect of obsessive-compulsive personalities. What anger she must feel at herself for never being good enough! But of course she can't admit to this anger, because it would mean admitting to being imperfect. To achieve and impress other people may feel good for a time, but she is always performing, and she is hollow inside. (Incest survivors are not the only women who feel this drive. In my own therapy I heard my favorite quip regarding perfectionism. My therapist Leslie Diamond once listened to my self-criticism and said, "Do you have to be perfect to be adequate?")

Mandy expressed one way in which the incest survivor twists herself up: "It's not enough for me to be perfect. I need to be both perfect and invisible. That's because I must be perfect—but I don't want anyone to notice!"

Another example of the extremes to which this need can be manifested is that even when an incest survivor does something for someone else, she torments herself and apologizes for not doing it well enough, no matter how well she does it.

Perfectly Bad

An alternative is to be "perfectly bad." Rebellious, "out of control" teenagers are perfectly bad. They are also angry. When people— especially teenagers and women—are angry, we as a society feel threatened. So we try to medicate away their anger, or discipline their anger, or (literally) lock up their anger. Adolescent girls, and adult women, don't need to do violence or break laws to be incarcerated in mental institutions; being angry is often enough grounds. We want to stop their anger. We train females that it's not ladylike, not "socially appropriate," and if that doesn't work, if somehow their anger breaks through, we try to get rid of it—sometimes by getting rid of them.

But we don't ever say, "What's wrong?"

"If this is what you think I am," the perfectly bad survivor is saying, "then this is how I'll act. Life sucks anyway."

The incest victim as rebellious adolescent is a paradox of a fighter who has given up. She feels she might as well be bad—there's nothing left. Life has trapped her. She has been treated as if she were bad so many times—by the abuse, by those close to her who did not see her pain, by systems that abandoned her and a society that blamed her. So she wonders, "What's the use of trying?" Her attitude toward life becomes, "Fuck you back, world!"

A quitter would have gone passive, but she is hardly passive. Impossible to reach, awful to deal with, maybe. But in her anger there is fight. There is spirit. There is life.

I do not condone abusive behavior, if that is what she does. Nor do I think that a child benefits from being out of control. But, while we work on the behavior of the angry person, we must acknowledge her pain and desperation—and we ought to appreciate her spunk.

The "perfectly bad" survivor exhibits one form of the grandiosity found among alcoholics and other addicted persons, as put forth in one of my favorite descriptions of an alcoholic: a person with an inflated ego and no self-esteem. However, many incest survivors do not have inflated egos to compensate for their diminished self-esteem. The form their "grandiosity" takes is a negative one: whenever something bad happens around them, whenever someone in a relationship with them is in a bad mood, they're convinced that they caused it! Although they feel they are so powerful that they can influence the rhythms of everything around them, these incest survivors often feel silly or unentitled when they consider acting as if they were worth something. Their situation fits a term I heard years ago: "delusions of adequacy!" (One way some people, not only incest survivors, compensate for feeling most people are better than they is to choose some others whom they see as rather pathetic and whom they can feel superior to; again, in a life-out-of balance, others are either above them or below them; no one is ever equal. This sets them up for the problems described in Chapter 15.)

REBUILDING

The adult modes of being perfect, bad, or perfectly bad result from the derailment of the child's developing self-image. For self-blame to be altered, survivors need to understand that the abuse had *nothing to do with them*—the abuser chose her because he could have this power over her—not because she was an "irresistible seductress!" She must let go of the distorted, self-exploiting sense of power she thought she had, and realize that she could be said to have been invisible.

But it may be easier for her to feel that she was bad than to believe that she had no importance. This is worse than being invisible; it is being nothing. Not being. Feeling empty, hollow. Having nothing to offer a relationship but sex, and no right to ask for anything. Being unable to be alone; for when she is, she is with no one. She lives with an unspoken terror, the existential fear of nonbeing. This fear can man-

ifest itself as the feeling that "negative attention is better than no attention." She feels used; she internalizes this, believing that she can expect
to be, and deserves to be, treated this way in later relationships. This
belief affects all her relationships, especially intimate ones, and later
situations of victimization.

The incest survivor's self-blame, shame, guilt, and destroyed self-
esteem become a double bind. She doesn't feel she deserves to be
treated well, so she tolerates abusive or neglectful treatment that further reduces her self-esteem. And she often doesn't feel good enough
about herself to pursue the help she needs to feel good about herself.

The survivor feels trapped by life, by the wills of everyone around
her, by the emptiness and pain of relationships that she feels are all she
deserves, by a society that has disregarded her cries and continues to
do so, by the abandonment of others that has led to an abandonment
of the *self*. She isn't there for herself because she has no role models of
healthy caregiving. Because she believes that she deserves the abuse and
neglect that have defined her life, this is the way she treats herself in
adulthood. This is one reason that an incest survivor cannot look you
in the eye.

Rebuilding self-esteem is complicated, and difficult to help someone else do. You cannot *give* self-esteem to someone. Even loving her
won't do it, because without self-esteem she cannot accept love. It
frightens her. It makes her feel even more unworthy. It bounces off her.
Only she can do the painful healing work that rebuilds self-esteem;
only she can replace the behaviors that sabotage her self-esteem. Although this process involves other people, it starts with her.

She struggles with this even while she is in recovery. She slowly
travels from seeing herself as a bad one to seeing herself as a weak,
pitiful victim. To define herself as not being to blame is a major victory; to call herself a *survivor*, another. To finally define herself not
through her past, but her potential, not through what was done *to* her
but through what she is making of herself—these are the ultimate re-
claimings of her self-esteem, of her *self*.

FEAR, ANXIETY, TERROR, AND PHOBIAS

Fear and its less directed cousin, anxiety, are constant for the incest survivor. From the moment the abuse begins, or perhaps from the moment the child victim realizes that it could happen again, they are her normal state—a state that easily leads to an adulthood full of anxiety.

In a sense, every aftereffect in Post-Incest Syndrome is related to fear, and serves to protect the fearful victim. That she often is not able to develop and rely on direct and assertive methods of taking care of herself is partly due to old fears—fears related to the threats and possible losses faced by the child that are still with her in adulthood. She views the world through the eyes of the child; she does not believe she will survive the threats that would have crippled the child. Her life is drenched with fear and dammed with restricted options.

THE CHILD VICTIM'S WORLD: CONSTANT FEAR

The child victim of incest lives within the paradoxical circumstances of chaotic unpredictability and inevitable abuse. Apprehension fills her days: When will danger come again? What awful thing will happen next? Will I die?

Repression Breeds Anxiety

Some child victims protect themselves by repressing the abuse even as it occurs. One woman who first remembered in her 40s that her

121

childhood had been riddled with almost constant abuse said that to her, "every time was the first time." Blocking awareness of events does not block the impact of those events. It only makes life more confusing and unmanageable because the child knows that something is wrong but does not know what. She develops "free-floating anxieties," anxieties that are not attached to something real.

Active Awareness

If consciously apprehensive, the child constantly steels herself for the inevitable. Times of day, persons, places, and situations (especially being alone with her abuser, who is also her father, brother, school teacher) fill her with dread. "When everyone else was asleep and I heard his footsteps coming down the hall . . . or when we went swimming . . . or when we went on ski trips. . . ." Barbara's voice breaks, like an eight-year-old frightened child's. "I knew what that meant . . . I knew that he would be—" she gropes for a word. No word can be as strong as the memory. She does not finish. She simply cries.

In addition to this foreboding about the abuse itself, the circumstances surrounding the abuse breed many fears in the child. Nothing is safe. Will he do what he has said he might do? Will he do it if she is not "good" enough? Will he carry out his threats just because he wants to?

Other Fears

Conditions, such as alcoholism or violence, that are separate from the abuse might make her fearful. The perpetrator might be the only ally of a lonely, insecure child (whether he is within or outside the nuclear family), providing what little security she feels, sanctuary from an existence full of fear. The threat of losing him, of losing the role he plays in her life, is terrifying. If he is alcoholic or physically violent (to her, her siblings, or to her mother), the rest of her existence will be frightening. Because paternal incest represents a skewing of power in a family, an extreme imbalance of power, the child—like someone in a dictatorship—may live in constant intimidation.

If her abuser is outside the family, a parallel fear occurs. For a nonfamily member to maintain the power necessary for the commission of incest often indicates some weakness in the victim's primary kinships. She may see her family as unsafe or unavailable. For these children, the family cannot be a site of deliverance. (A lucky few have strong enough bonds with a family member to whom they can go for help in halting extrafamilial incest. Being able to do so—and doing so—seems to reduce considerably the incest aftereffects she will suffer.)

However, her perceptions may be denied by those around her, the perpetrator, family, neighbors, counselors, the criminal justice system. Life is crazy, after all. She is trapped. The abuser imprisons her by his demand for silence, society abandons her into the arms of her abuser, and she is trapped with the poison of the abuse.

THE AFTEREFFECTS: FEAR'S LONG SHADOW

The child victim carries into adulthood a sense that life is fragile and that she scarcely dares *breathe* lest it shatter. She does not speak loudly, walk loudly, make big movements; her whole existence is a whisper. She holds her shoulders rigid and her arms tightly at her sides, as she tiptoes through her life of glass. She does not argue, cry out, or complain. And she is always, always scared.

Not remembering makes a fearful existence even more fearful. "Who *am* I," the incest survivor wonders. "What happened to me?" And even more frightening for these women may be the question, "If I can't remember everything that was done to me, what could I have done to someone else?"

She is afraid because horrible things have been done to her and because there was no protection. She is afraid because she has been stripped of her memory and of the right to tell what was done to her. Later, as she learns to take better care of herself she says, "I shouldn't be doing this, telling people I won't give them anything they want from me, saying no to them. I can't put my needs first, ever." She expects something awful to happen. She doesn't know exactly what, so she can't even prepare. But she's scared. Again. Still.

Specific Fears

Various fears are associated with the incest experience as with sexual abuse. When rape survivors are interviewed, they generally report being afraid for their lives—even if no additional physical violence or use of weapons accompanied the rape. As victims of absolute access, whether overt or covert, many incest survivors likewise carry a sense of mortal fear into their adult lives.

Fears accompany other themes of the incest trauma. The incest survivor is often afraid that if "they" know her secret, they will not care, afraid that no one will want her if they know. If she is religious, she may be afraid that God will punish her.

Twilight: A Frightening Time Twilight is often a time of great discomfort and apprehension to the incest survivor. Julie, who knew that she had been molested but had never explored or discussed the abuse, hated twilight. She didn't know why. "It just gives me the creeps."

For incest survivors who spent the night in the same place as their perpetrators, twilight is when danger began. It was when he would come into her room—when she was sleeping, or when she was pretending to sleep, hoping that would discourage him, or block out the experience. (Sleep, in fact, is a common "escape" for the child victim, and later, for the survivor; many can fall asleep at will, whether by conscious choice or not, at a moment when safety or escape is needed.) Twilight foreshadows darkness, and danger slinks in darkness.

Sleep and Night For the incest survivor whose trauma often occurred under cover of darkness, night was a time of monsters in her bed. Sleep is the most defenseless state. In sleep, she is unable to perceive or sense danger; she cannot take action to protect herself; she cannot hide or, if she is so inclined, fight back. It is dark and scary in the best of times, scarier still when incest lives with her. "I thought there were arms that would reach over the side of the bed at me, grasping, grabbing. I was terrified of that." Connie found that this childhood fear returned when she was detoxifying off alcohol. Insomnia is a natural consequence.

Sleep time is also when others in a household are unavailable, and so the perpetrator in a home where she lives or visits has easier access to her. Access and privacy are integral aspects of this kind of secretive contact, and nighttime ensures both. At night, in bed, asleep, the child victim is at her most physically vulnerable.

In adulthood, the survivor is vulnerable to the fears and memories through dreams that she cannot control. Concomitantly, she is likely to be *afraid of sleeping alone in the dark*. However, if she was molested in daylight, night is likely to be her safe time. If she was molested by, or in the presence of, several people, she might feel safer alone.

Lilly* told me she had no fear of sleeping alone in the dark . . . until she realized that, between roommates, husbands, and sister, she *had never done so.* This need not to be alone at night is one component of the survivor's tendency never to be without a relationship, but it may then be necessary for her to trace back to a time when she was uninvolved before she can assess the presence of this aftereffect.

This aftereffect may be buried in other ways. Cynthia slept with the television on, but didn't realize that the TV light in the room served as a nightlight and the voices offered company. Many incest survivors keep lights on around the house at night. This relatively specific and obvious aftereffect is easy to disguise and ignore. If an incest survivor is afraid of being alone in the dark, she may not know it.

The vulnerability of sleep time also contributes to the incest survivor's *tendency to sleep clothed.* She needs to protect her body. She is afraid to be alone . . . and not comfortable when she has company either!

Closeness Having been betrayed by someone she needed and trusted, the incest survivor often spends adulthood afraid of people and, especially, of closeness. (This fear will be explained in more detail in the chapters on relationships.) As her nights replay the trauma of incest, her days replay the betrayal.

Anxiety

Years later, the incest survivor cannot associate actual circumstances with her fear. She cannot say, "The world is unsafe *when.* . . ." So she generalizes it. She does not see how much of this fear is about being a defenseless child. Besides, she is not a child anymore, although she still sees herself as that child in many ways. In her guts, she cannot distinguish past from present, realistic from unrealistic. She feels yesterday's fear as if it were today's, and is as overpowered by it as if she *were* a helpless six-year-old. She has no awareness of her adult powers, which are undeveloped but do exist. She can't count on strength that isn't there yet; she can't use skills that she doesn't know she has. And—full circle—the thought of risking anger or assertiveness often fills her with terror.

Because she cannot associate an event with her reaction, her fears generalize into the vagueness of anxiety. Anxiety is an un-fixed fear, a state of apprehension rather than a specific response to a specific thing. For the incest survivor, the world is a dangerous place, period. It is not dangerous at this or that time, or for this or that reason; it is simply unsafe.

In our early days on earth, we humans, when faced with physical danger, experienced a rush of energizing adrenaline as we prepared to stay and fight or escape. Now, when our dangers rarely come from giant fanged animals, the threat may be no longer physical, but our bodies react as if it were: we still prepare for "fight or flight." Over time, this state of anxiety produces a state of stress. Our bodies go through several stress-related physiological changes, resulting often in certain physical diseases (known to occur frequently in incest survivors).

The "fight or flight" response is designed to protect its bearer from the (real or imagined) dangers of a hostile environment. What more hostile environment is there than that which holds a child captive to sexual abuse? Her psyche and body are altered by this stress. As she grows, constant anxiety that arises from her incestuous experience alters her development. Finally, she lives with not only the fear of certain things, but anxiety as a daily condition.

Severe anxiety can become a way of life for the incest survivor. As Laura said, "I've had to be so alert my whole life. As a kid, I could never just relax and let the grownups around me do their job. I had to be always on my guard. And I don't think I've relaxed since!" To live in this constant state of stress is destructive physically, interfering with the immune system, hiking blood pressure, straining heart function; once again, she pays a price for her "protection." But she hasn't quit on herself. She hasn't "lain down" in the path of whatever comes. She's watching out for the kid, as best she can, ready to defend her, one way or another.

Terror, Acting Little, and Acting Big

Many incest survivors live constantly with terror, a state of extreme fear. This distortion of fear occurs when the fear might be held in, when there is not the freedom and safety necessary for honest self-disclosure, and when the situation causing the pain cannot be prevented.

Both feelings and distortions of feelings arise from life experiences and need to be expressed and dealt with. "Dealing with" in this context can best be described by the three tasks expressed in the "Serenity Prayer" used widely in Twelve-Step recovery groups such as Alcoholics Anonymous: "the serenity to accept the things I cannot change, courage to change the things I can, and wisdom to know the difference." However, in an abusive environment, I suspect that mere expression is not sufficient; *change* of the environment is necessary, though not always possible.

Terror is often commensurate with the degree of the real or perceived threat, in combination with the degree of control that one has over the situation. One may be afraid of being punched; one feels terror over a life-threatening danger. For example, adults who are securely trained in the martial arts have little to fear from another individual, but they may experience terror over the threat of nuclear war. The child, having neither physical strength nor the power to change her environment, has much to fear.

Many incest survivors come into adulthood feeling and acting like frightened children. They manifest behavior that first occurs in childhood: hiding (cowering in corners, in stairwells, closets, under the bed, under porches) and hanging on (for security). Terri describes a poignant example of this. When she was a child, she remembers hanging onto a telephone pole in front of her house. For hours she would stand with her arms wrapped around this wooden pole, a skinny, dark-haired kid with eyes like the children painted by Keane, wide and sad. For hours she would stand there, in front of the neighbors, next to the street, and no one ever asked why.

The child victim hides so that she won't be seen and targeted for abuse; the adult just hides—from the world, in which she feels equally at risk. In fact, another aftereffect is a "disappearing act": incest survivors sometimes "drop out of sight," not returning phone calls, not going to meetings or socializing, making themselves totally unavailable. This hiding is not the same as being alone or learning to feel comfortable in one's own company; it is extreme in its totality. Avoiding others and isolating oneself, while growth inhibiting, can be effective methods of protection.

At the other extreme, some survivors overcompensate for their fear by acting loud and "big"—sometimes even being big. These women protect "the kid inside" by putting forth to the world the most intimidating face they can.

Panic and Phobias

As terror and anxiety are distortions or exaggerations of fear, another fear reaction, panic and phobias, is common among incest survivors.

Panic is an adrenaline overload, with heart palpitations, light-headedness, rapid pulse, and similar symptoms. It can feel like a heart attack, an inability to breathe, a sense of imminent doom or craziness. It is "flight or fight" gone haywire, without an obvious stimulus of danger.

When a woman has this genuinely terrifying experience, she may take it a step further. "What if I feel this when I'm somewhere that I can't get help?" And so she can become "agoraphobic" (literally, having the fear of open spaces, but loosely applied, it becomes a fear of leaving the safety of the house). This disorder affects women much more often than men because women are relatively powerless and their acculturation ties them closely to home, whereas a man's training focuses on "making his way in the world."

A phobia is an overwhelming, irrational fear of something. Common phobias for incest survivors are fears of driving (especially tunnels and bridges), fear of elevators, fear of enclosed spaces, and fear of open space. For example, some of my clients feel protected by being in a therapy setting where all the doors are closed; others need to have one door open. Once when my exit door was momentarily jammed, the client who was present panicked; her trauma manifested as a phobia of confinement. This client would go far out of her way while driving around the block so as not to make four successive right turns—drawing with her car a closed square.

Underlying these phobias are themes of entrapment, suffocation, fear of hurting oneself ("I'm afraid I'll drive off the bridge and kill myself"), which may actually represent wishing to kill the perpetrator, and fear of going out of control ("I'm afraid something will happen and I won't be able to do anything about it"). In these themes we can see the clear connection between phobias and Post-Incest Syndrome, for these are the primary concerns of one who has been traumatized by the child sexual abuse within the confines of a dependency.

Post-Incest Syndrome contains a number of syndromes with which we professionals have occupied ourselves as ends in themselves. The addictions, self-injury behavior, multiple personality disorder, phobias and panic attacks—all are independent and full-fledged problems, and we are correct in attacking them as primary problems, with the goal of arresting hurtful behaviors. But we fail to consider whether these signal a deeper problem, incest. Many clinicians deny the common existence of the incest experience. Many simply lack knowledge about the far-reaching consequences of incest.

These self-contained problems, especially when seen in clusters, can be like spokes with incest at the hub. We must learn to associate the possibility of an incest history with certain other presenting problems. Panic and phobias are an example of problems with which we fail to do this.

Among professionals there is no fixed answer as to what causes the phobias and panic disorder. There is also disagreement about the remedy, although most professionals and self-help groups focus on behavioral treatment and/or "psychoactive" drugs, usually antidepressants or tranquilizers. Many clinicians and persons in recovery find this tendency to remedy psychological problems with tranquilizers and other psychotropic medications dangerous, especially when prescribed (as they often are) to active or recovering alcoholics. Programs that combine behavioral desensitization with "walking through" support are extremely successful, although not everyone has found her solution this way.

For many, the elusiveness of a proper diagnosis complicates the problem. A panic disorder can feel like a heart attack or other physical crisis, and many sufferers waste enormous amounts of time and money going from doctor to doctor, emergency room to emergency room, until finally someone is wise enough to suggest to them that their real problem is a panic disorder. (This is very different from being told, "It's all in your head, honey, why don't you learn to relax," which is the way many male doctors treat their female patients when they don't know, and don't care, what's wrong.)

It is beneficial—even necessary—to approach the crippling symptoms of phobias first. But once this is done, once the panic has been relieved and the sufferer can function in the world again, we must stay aware of the possibility of an underlying incest history and explore issues and feelings that the phobias might cover. This task is further complicated by the possible hidden nature of repressed incest for some women. Other signs of the Post-Incest Syndrome may need to be considered for the woman's therapeutic needs to be fully understood.

FROM FEAR TO ANGER TO HOPE

Fear often accompanies every moment of the incest survivors life and, later, every step of her recovery. She knows her fear—its is an old, familiar companion. She does not as readily see her courage. Others see her courage long before she has the self-esteem to see it.

At some point, fear and anger become enmeshed. She becomes afraid to feel anger. Then she gets angry at her fear. To move from fear toward anger is one of her first steps toward healing.

ANGER AND RAGE

Anger is a healthy, natural, useful reaction to abuse. It is healthy for a child or adult, if abused, to feel, "Hey! What's the matter here? How dare someone treat me that way?" A healthy, strong individual feels indignation at mistreatment. The infant or child naturally feels anger in a life where basic nurturing needs are not met. She experiences this anger on a "gut level," without being able to describe or analyze it. At that level, its primal nature could more properly be called rage.

ROBBED OF ANGER

The adult incest survivor has *so much* to be angry at. She has been hurt. Her needs and feelings have been disregarded. She has been forced to take care of those whose job and moral responsibility was to take care of her. She had no childhood. She never got the chance to develop into a healthy adult. And now she must maneuver through the world handicapped by emotional deficits and a history of trauma and pain that is often buried beneath her consciousness. Yet she is often robbed of her anger by fears, family rules, and social injunctions.

Anger Stifled by Fear

Fear and anger are often joined at the time of the original incest. An abused child feels intimidated and has learned two lessons about anger: it means danger for her and it is an "out of control" emotion for the abuser.

Expressing any anger can result in further abuse, leading her to conclude, "If I get angry, I'll get hurt." Or it can lead to a caretaker's emotional withdrawal, thus giving her the view, "If I get angry, I'll lose someone or something that's important to me." The more emotionally impoverished her environment, the less she feels she can afford to lose and, therefore, the more threatening her anger becomes.

The normal anger she feels over being made to do something hurtful jeopardizes the environment she is struggling to preserve. So, perhaps without being aware of the anger, she converts anger into fear. Now the fear that results from the incest experience combines with the fear that underlies the anger at being abused.

During her perilous early life, this fear could be an ally: it prevents her from doing what might put her in further danger of abuse. In later years, however, the actual threat long behind her, she still cannot experience her anger. As Barbara said, "It's like I have all these friends: fear, anger, love, hope, courage, the ability to ask for help. Only I kept feeding fear and paying attention to fear—and fear grew so much bigger than all the others. I never even see my anger, because the fear blocks it."

If fear is too big, anger is too small.

No Good Role Models

Even in healthy families, anger is difficult to accept and deal with in direct, nonabusive ways. As children, we often are victimized by our parents' inability to deal with their anger—an inability passed down from their parents. Emotional bungling often passes from generation to generation.

Many of us, when we expressed anger as children, felt that our parents neither heard nor accepted it. Sometimes they ignored our anger, or punished our anger (instead of the behavior, if it was not OK). Sometimes they got angry back. Sometimes they told us "Don't be angry." Sometimes they wanted us to look at a situation as they did, not understanding or tolerating our own view. In these cases, our parents' discomfort with their anger leads them to react this way to the child. But the child cannot see this: she thinks the problem must be about *her*. And so she learns that anger is "bad" and that by having or expressing it, she is bad. She also learns that anger leads to the loss of much-needed and wanted approval from others, especially parents.

In families where addictions (such as alcoholism) or violence exist (these are families also likely to contain incestuous abuse) as well as families where incest is the only such behavior, anger is prohibited for a reason: to tell someone that you're angry or that you have been hurt is to threaten the denial that shelters him from facing how out of control he is. Everyone in such families works hard to preserve this illusion. Also, in families where the father batters the mother or the children, or drinks heavily, the mother might be afraid that the child's anger will provoke him to further violence or drinking. (Where the mother is the abuser, the father is generally uninvolved with family responsibilities and, therefore, unavailable to turn to.)

And so a trap exists: although all these situations—emotional and physical abuse, addiction, incest—can be expected to anger all family members, they often cannot acknowledge this anger or cannot express it in a healthy way. The abused child cannot help but be angry at her abuse, and she cannot afford to complain.

Social Injunctions against Anger

As adolescence begins, the pattern of repressed anger may shift for some daughters. No longer the defenseless, overpowered children, some may rally their developing sense of self into "acting out" behavior. However, girls are not as likely to do this as boys, and adult women are even less likely to do so, because they are neither expected nor permitted to be angry.

Anger and aggression are power, and our definition of women—ladies—does not include power. An angry woman is "a bitch" or "castrating" or "domineering." Anger is "unfeminine"; it is not appropriate for females who derive their value from being "nice," "good girls," "ladies," especially when they depend on the approval of others. This restriction effectively prohibits girls from growing into adults. They are kept children: powerless, small, submissive, sweet.

THE AFTEREFFECTS: DISTORTIONS OF ANGER

Anger is like raw garbage—banana peels, chicken bones, old brown dead lettuce. If you don't deal with it, you add it to the pile, and over the years it loses its form and turns into sludge, until you no longer can say, "I'm angry because this or that happened." You're left with brown yucky stuff, without anything in it that you can name.

After a lifetime of this, the incest survivor probably doesn't know what she's angry about. In fact, she may not know she's angry (even if everyone else does). She has long disassociated her anger from the events that caused it, and has not learned the skills necessary to address anger.

Inability to Recognize, Own, or Express Anger

While growing up, many incest survivors spent all their energies *dissociating* from their anger, stuffing it down, distracting themselves from it.

The incest survivor who disowns her anger is not aware of experiencing this emotion when it would make sense to express it. She never acts angry because she never *is* angry. She can endure disrespect, abuse, any unpleasant experience, and, if you ask her what she feels, she *never* says "angry." Or she minimizes her anger, shrugging it off as if it were "no big deal." Sometimes her stance is akin to the Alfred E. Neuman slogan: "What, *me* angry?" She may seem angry to an observer, but she does not acknowledge the fact. To be angry is to be a bad person.

During psychotherapy, many incest survivors must do some work before they can identify that they are dissatisfied over something that happened. The old injunction "Don't make waves" still operates for them. They seem to go along with everything. They are quintessential doormats. They allow everyone to make demands without a complaint. Assertiveness is not even a consideration. They are either the most agreeable women you've ever met, or the most passive. These incest survivors may look like adult women, but they are really terrified children.

When questioned, when they can look at the *possibility* that they *might* not have liked what was going on, these women might benefit from being helped to identify their fear. Perhaps then they can face their anger—anger at the power they've given away, anger at the abuses they've suffered and at no one's being there for them, and anger that their anger was taken from them.

Constant Anger

At the other end of the continuum is the incest survivor who is angry all the time. Her mouth is turned down in a perpetual scowl; she may snap or growl at anyone for anything. She may react especially strongly to current violations of her boundaries (perceived or actual), victimizations, or injustice. Although these events warrant anger, it is disproportionate—it is not, after all, solely over the *current* abuse. We may call her "bitchy" or hostile. But she is no more aware of what is going on for her than the anger-phobic incest survivor. Her anger leaks out all over the place, indiscriminate and undirected. In her fury at everything, she blinds herself to what she is reacting to.

Another example of distorted anger is the incest survivor who is not constantly hostile, but who does not express her anger directly. (Originally, it was often wise, whether conscious or not, to avoid expressing her anger directly, for her abuser was much bigger than she.) One example of this is the woman (generally given the psychiatric label "borderline") who sees the world in absolutes: you are either perfect in her eyes or absolutely evil. She cannot accept that there are good and bad sides to everyone, that everyone in our lives makes us happy and unhappy, is sometimes what we want them to be and sometimes not. (The psychiatric term applied to this is "splitting off." In this context, this term does not mean "dissociating"; it means separating the bad from a person in whom it cannot be accepted.) She either idolizes and idealizes you, or turns on you in a rage, using whatever criticisms that she feels would be most damaging. She might attempt to harm you in her rage, either directly, by hurting you emotionally or physically, or by turning others against you. She wants what she wants when she wants it; she likes you when you please her, but your rating drops dramatically when you fail to meet her needs.

Displaced Anger

Some incest survivors who cannot face the original objects of their anger pick a fight with someone else over the same theme. Frequently they are angry at a person upon whom they are currently dependent. They unjustly criticize this person for being selfish or abusive.

A client may get angry at a therapist for "feeding her ego needs" when the therapist attempts to explore the client's feelings about her therapy or the therapist. (Although there are valid reasons for challenging some therapists, lawyers, and others, this example refers to incest survivors with a distorted emphasis on the imperfections of the other.) Some survivors come to sessions religiously, every week, in rain or snow, to tell the therapist how awful she is. One colleague who was overly generous with his time and services was attacked by his client for being self-serving. The theme of these criticisms is that the helper is *taking something away* from the incest survivor, or that, in meeting his or her own needs in a healthy or professional way, the helper is doing something wrong or abusive to the survivor.

This incest survivor knows she is mad at a caretaker for taking; she just has focused her anger on another who is easier to reject. Or her anger may result from her need for this current person. Needing someone is dangerous for the power it robs her of—it puts her in jeopardy of being a slave to the needed person. In this light, some of her anger might be at herself for needing someone, and some might be at the needed person for putting her at risk. She might actually be angry at being cared about. In these examples, displaced anger is a survival tactic. It is safer to face this incarnation of her anger than the situation from which it sprang.

The therapist or other caregiver faces a difficult set of requirements: to allow for the fact that the client has been seriously damaged and cannot help what she feels or how she behaves while, for the sake of both sides, refusing to tolerate abuse. I have heard of situations where a professional was genuinely harmed by a client's acts. It is not acceptable for a victim to victimize others, whether by molesting a new generation of children or by unjustly attacking or slandering a helper.

In most cases, firm and patient "working through"—helping the survivor understand the true source of her anger—helps her and avoids this destructive behavior. Sometimes, however, this cannot occur, and the helper must protect herself or himself. This might include challenging the way the client speaks to her, calling in a third party to mediate the relationship, or even terminating the therapy. If the problem can't be worked out in the therapy, it is more damaging to both the therapist and the client to remain in this destructive relationship and continue feeling and acting this way than to discontinue therapy.

Although the themes of incest in this aftereffect are easy to identify, the self-defeating nature of this behavior often makes the survivor unwilling to look at *herself* when she's stuck in this threatened, blaming mode. In her childhood, an adult who should have taken care of her used her in a selfish way instead. Now, when she is dependent on someone (such as a therapist or lawyer), she confuses being helped and being used, misdirecting this accusation on someone who is safer to attack than was the abusing caretaker. She finally knows she's angry over being taken advantage of, but she's angry at the wrong caretaker. The caretaker might feel as if her client has turned on her, but she must be aware of the trap inherent in reacting to this behavior, even though the caretaker feels abused or angry.

Disproportionate Anger

Distorted anger at all men or at all members of the ethnic group of the abuser, and the idealization of the perpetrator even when all around him are critical of him, are examples of how anger is skewed for the survivor. Disproportionate anger can be directed at a non-abuser as well, and can later result in exaggerated resentment—not at the gender of the abuser, but at the gender of the parent who is seen as not "protecting."

Idealization of Men in General Nonfeminist heterosexual women who are protecting their primary emotional bond to men are particularly likely to idealize all men. This woman can't find her own identity without a man or men in her life; she idealizes men and denigrates women. She is unable to be angry at men or critical of what they do, even if their treatment of her is demeaning or abusive.

In families where incest or alcoholism exist, which results in an environment of scarcity, fear, competition, and coercion, there is little chance of bridging the gaps of gender, age, and individual differences because everyone's interests are divided. The conventional (already unforgivable) societal gender roles are exaggerated to bizarre proportions. A girl in these families sees her mother constantly worried about not pleasing her daddy enough with her womanness. He probably doesn't believe in "letting a woman feel like she's got him by the balls" and so is unwilling to be pleased with her anyway.

The child who grows up in this type of family can view reality in one of two ways. She may say, "My life is a miserable, unfair, exploited, wasted, hopeless mess because I am powerless and my parents are insane and so is the whole horrible world." Or she may say, "Daddy is wonderful, his every wish is important, and femaleness has to be adhered to exactly as he wants it. I must be positive, Daddy likes that and I need Daddy." The latter view is safer.

Anger at the Mother   In my experience, children with incest histories and children from other families where the father was abusive are much less angry at the father for his actions than at the mother for not rescuing them. Over and over I see in my clients the tendency to idealize the father, despite the fact that he was alcoholic or abusive, while holding the mother responsible for everything that went wrong in the family. The mother is held accountable for the abuser's behavior, and the abusive father is relieved of this blame. Even when denial is broken and pain is unlocked in therapy, the survivor often discards the inner child's pain again and again as she attempts to re-connect with her father, only to be repeatedly reminded—often much to her surprise—of how he has hurt her.

This pattern results from a wider social tendency not to hold men accountable for what they do and to blame women instead. Our first question about a battered woman is, "Why did she stay?" not "How could he do such a thing"; we demand to know how rape survivors were dressed; we focus immediately on where the mother of an incested child was. This attitude takes the focus off the actual perpetrator of the violence. It feeds the daughter's natural reluctance to see her needed father (or other bonded abuser) as bad, her ambivalence and reluctance to let go of him. However, she does not struggle with similar ambivalence toward her mother, of whom she is so relentlessly unforgiving. Mothers seem never to be allowed any failings. They are held responsible for the behaviors of fathers, whose failings are excused, minimized, or forgotten.

This is an extension of "mother-blaming" (described in Chapter 11). Some therapists allow the incest survivor to maintain this stance unchallenged or promote it themselves.

Therapists who are incest survivors, who have not worked through this skewing of their anger, are especially likely to allow their survivor clients to get stuck at the same place that they themselves are blinded. I once had a conference with a psychologist who was both an incest survivor and a founder of a local chapter of a support group for parents who have abused their children. Her attitude, expressed to me with great certainty, gave me chills: "Oh, yes," she told me, "I've worked on my incest and I have come to terms with it. I've forgiven my father. And I was able to realize that my real anger should have been at my mother! I mean, there was more reason to blame her—after all, women are stronger people, so she should have taken responsibility and stopped it!"

The research findings of Herman, Russell, and Finkelhor (see Chapter 2) reinforce the tendency of survivors to skew their anger toward their mothers. Nearly 50% more survivors reported being hostile toward their mothers than were angry at their abusers.

In addition to social and political attitudes, there are a number of reasons that the survivor of paternal incest may be more easily angry at her mother than her perpetrator.

1. The survivor generally (as do most of us) charges her mother with more responsibility for maintaining family welfare; she has higher expectations of her mother. She barely expects her father to have control over himself; in many cases, she makes excuses for his behavior, excuses that often strikingly resemble the excuses that perpetrators use to justify their behavior. For example, when asked why the incest occurred, Russell's respondents gave reasons like the excuses used by the abuser: "That's the way he taught me about sex," "It was an unsure time of his life," "It was OK because it was all in the family," and, most often, "Mother wasn't good enough."

2. The perpetrator often gave her more safe or positive attention than anyone else, but the survivor often sees her mother as cold, controlling, critical, or unavailable. The mother is, therefore, easier to give up than the perpetrator. She can simply be seen as bad, while the abuser elicits ambivalence, a far more complicated emotion to deal with. As Dottie told me, "I can't face what he did because then I'll have to get angry at him, and then I'll have to take an action, like letting go of him. I'm not ready to let go of Daddy!"

3. It is safer to face anger at her mother because if the incest survivor faces her anger at the abuser, the abuse itself must be faced.

Rage vs. Anger

Anger that is not given its proper expression and resolution becomes distorted, in this case, into rage. Anger may be described as red and warm; it can be spoken, it can be yelled. Rage, however, is white-hot and freezing cold; it may come out in a screech, but never in words; more often, it is paralyzing, tightening all the muscles and causing the jaws to jam, limbs to stiffen, fists to clench.

Whether it is the survivor's initial aftereffect or what she comes to after opening the door on her anger, rage serves a protective purpose. In rage, she's spinning, flailing her arms; she is fast and big. No one can get close. No one can touch her. No one can penetrate her wall so no one can hurt her.

I remember once walking in New York City late at night with an incest survivor friend. Beth was short, quiet, soft spoken, and passive. She has been abused a lot. As we walked down the short street we had chosen to cut from one avenue in the theater district to another, I realized we were surrounded by groups of men sitting on stoops and standing on the corner. Many were drinking, and all were staring at us. I was suddenly more frightened than I had ever been. I felt in danger for my life. We walked faster and, much to my surprise and relief, we got out unharmed. I said to her, "I have never been so scared in my whole life. I was sure we were going to be attacked, maybe raped." Quietly she replied, "I wanted them to try something. I was ready to fucking kill them." She had stored her anger for so long, had endured so much abuse, that she welcomed the opportunity to fight back.

When rage leaks, ever so briefly, into the survivor's consciousness, she becomes afraid of the rage she feels or thinks she might feel. When survivors are asked what it would be like to tell someone that they're angry, they often say things like, "The anger is so strong I can't talk about it" or "I just couldn't." They say they are afraid that if they felt their anger, they'd "break things" or "kill someone" or "lose control."

"Losing control" of their anger is, as with other issues of control, a defining theme for many incest survivors, who think that their anger is unmanageable because they have never learned to manage or express it. They are also aware of how much it has grown over time. An incest survivor may not understand that if she lets a little out she will survive, because she's never let any out. She also carries forward the old lesson that the cost of anger is punishment or abandonment—even if *she* doesn't lose control, her *life* will go out of control. When I ask survivors what will happen if they say no or if they get angry, and instruct them to tell me their absolute gut reaction, without censorship, they often say "I'll die."

Holding in anger because you are afraid that it means "loss of control" can be self-fulfilling. This is often the dynamic of batterers who were the children of batterers: they hold in their anger and hold it in and hold it in, until it leaks out destructively or explodes abusively, and then they think, "See—I told you anger meant being out of control."

Rage is the emotional consequence of entrapment, abuse, and a lifetime of protests that couldn't be made, of anger that could not be let out. When you hear the actual stories of incest survivors (the stories of your clients if you are a therapist, or your loved ones or those in current books on the subject), it is easy to share rage, to feel it for them and with them. The therapist can afford to feel anger; the victimized woman, at least as yet, may not be ready.

LEARNING TO DEAL WITH ANGER

The incest survivor's task in recovery is to learn to acknowledge her anger and to express it in a productive way.

Experiencing Anger

As the incest survivor gets stronger, as her therapist or support group validates her other feelings, she usually begins to experience her anger or rage. This experience may frighten her. She needs to learn ways to deal with her anger and to learn that she *gains* control by dealing with it properly.

She may not, however, do this well in the beginning. The pendulum may push her into feeling angry at everything, all the time. This phase may be extremely difficult for those around her who are uncomfortable with anger and who have never seen her angry. However, it is not more unhealthy than her old anger-denying ways. Actually, it is a big step *toward* being healthy because the consequences of anger that is not vented or dealt with are far-reaching. They can include "acting out" (lashing out at or abusing others, destroying property), "acting in" (abusing the self), depression, eating disorders, chemical dependency, ulcers, sleep disturbances, anxiety, physical problems such as the jaw joint disease called temporo-mandibular joint syndrome (TMJ), and suicide—many of the aftereffects discussed in this book!

Women who disown their assertiveness and anger are negative, manipulative, dishonest ("What's wrong?" "NOTHING." "Are you angry?" "NO!"), or whiney. In labelling women these ways, we are "blaming the victims," criticizing them for what they must resort to because they've been robbed.

Anger is healthy, although a critical, attacking, demanding person is not dealing with anger properly, and a person who lashes out in rage is not. But in anger is power, and with power can come change, energy, and strength.

The first step toward a healthy attitude about anger is for the incest survivor to recognize when she is angry. She needs to be able to say, "I'm mad," to *feel* anger and attach a label to it.

Facing Anger at the Past

The next step is to face her anger at the past. This task will be influenced by the social attitude described by Alice Miller, with which therapists often collude to defend parents against their children's anger. Children are encouraged to forgive, understand, and excuse their parents' behavior; essentially, then, they are urged to abandon themselves for the sake of their parents. Also, being angry jeopardizes her need to be accepted or loved, or her need to win the abuser back. She may be scared or guilty over this anger, but to face the well-deserved anger she feels at her incest (and at any other abuse) is necessary. This anger may take a long, long time to clean out of her system. After it is done, however, the anger she feels at current experiences will become cleaner, no longer clouded by anger at the past.

Connecting Current Anger to Its Cause

Her old angers purged, her next task is to connect her current anger to its cause: "I'm angry over the way that man whistled at me in the grocery store," or "I'm angry that I'm being paid too little in my job." Then comes venting, or expressing the feeling in an angry way. This may be a hurdle that requires creative intervention, and it might take much time for the survivor to feel entitled to complain about unwarranted treatment. The survivor's issues of entitlement are a part of this process. Not only does she need to develop the ability to feel justified in complaining; but she needs also to develop the judgment to know when another person is disregarding her needs. Incest survivors, like adult children of alcoholics, often become involved with abusive partners. It is a significant task for both of these groups to find how angry they are, and to refuse to take the blame for everything that goes wrong in their lives.

She needs to be able to see genuine abuse, when it occurs, and abuses come in many forms. Of course, one type of abuse is the violence of her past; no one should tolerate verbal and physical abuses. But there are other instances—when a friend is never on time for appointments, where others always talk about their problems but are never interested in hers—that are also abusive. She must face her anger here to end the abuse, or, if necessary, end the relationship.

Learning from One's Anger

This "housecleaning" done, the survivor must join the mainstream of people learning how to deal properly with their anger. Like the rest of us, she must look at what makes *her* angry about each experience. In other words, she must look beneath the top layer of the anger to what it says about her. Not, "I am angry that my partner always ignores me," but "this is what being ignored brings up in me."

When we express anger, we often point the finger. We say things like, "You make me angry," or "I'm so angry at my mother! She's so controlling!" Our anger is often blaming. *We* are angry because of the *other* person, and we are angry because the other person is *bad* or *wrong*.

Actually, we are usually angry because something didn't happen— or someone didn't behave—as we wanted. Abusive and oppressive acts must be labeled wrong, but usually we are angry because of our expectations, not because the other person was intending to hurt us. Even if we react to something that by legal or moral standards is a crime, for our own growth we must understand specifically how it affects us. What makes us angry—the particular aspect of it that triggers us in a particular way—*comes from inside us*. Someone else in the same situation could react to a different aspect.

This task helps us understand ourselves, and helps us express our feelings in a way that the other person can understand, whether that person is a therapist, friend with whom we are discussing an experience, or the object of our anger.

It is easier, but less productive, to project that anger onto the person who has wronged us: "I'm angry at you because *you* . . ." rather than, "I'm angry that you did that because *it made me feel.* . . ." Only when we avoid projecting our anger can we investigate our reactions, the meaning the event holds for us, and the themes with which it connects in our lives. We could all benefit from this approach. For the incest survivor, it offers the opportunity to help see the impact, specifically, the abuse had on her life. Even if the end goal is to say, "I was wronged, and here's what it did to me," this way of exploring anger helps us to know ourselves better.

Yet exploring our own reactions is difficult for those whose feelings have always been "turned around" by others who were unwilling to face reality or take responsibility for their actions. If an incest survivor has been told that something is wrong with her for having her feelings ("You're too sensitive," "You're only thinking of yourself," "You're crazy" and the like), if *she* feels like the bad guy, then her protective inclination is to make someone else the bad guy. If she has been blamed, believing that *someone* must be blamed (and having colluded with that message, by blaming *herself*), in her anger she wants to blame the other person. But, again, with the exception of abuses such as incest and battering, life is rarely broken down into villains and victims. Emotional health is being able to deal with the gray areas, even in relation to feeling wronged.

AVOIDING PAIN:
Addictions and Compulsions

The incest survivor has so much to struggle against that it is a surprise when she does *not* retreat into the relief and illusion of control that addictions and compulsions provide. Like all other after-effects, addictions serve a survival purpose.

Only recently have addictions professionals recognized the association between addictions and incest. Research confirms it. For instance, an enormously high percentage of women with eating disorders have reported incest histories. As one addictions specialist told me, "At this point, I'm surprised when I *don't* find sexual abuse in the past of a woman I work with." Many incest survivors also develop alcohol and drug problems. When I worked in a therapeutic community for substance abusers in upstate New York in the mid-70s, we didn't even consider the possibility of childhood sexual abuse. Looking back, I believe that most of the women clients were indeed incest survivors. (I have no doubt that a large number of the male clients were as well.)

Lasting addictions recovery is often elusive unless survivors face the truth about sexual trauma and its resulting feelings. Even after becoming sober, a woman might relapse repeatedly, or bounce from one addiction to another until she identifies the "core" of her problem.

WHAT IS ADDICTION?

An addiction is a progressive, debilitating illness. It is characterized by the obsessive concern with the substance and its effects, a compulsive need to pursue the addictive behavior, an inability to choose when or how much to do, and a distortion of the thought process. For example, the social gambler bets a few dollars more than she can afford; the compulsive gambler gambles away the rent money and then tries to borrow more because she is sure that *this* time she will win enough to remedy the problem. Like all addicts, she sees her problem as one of bad luck rather than of gambling. She cannot control the consequences of getting high, and gets high regardless of the consequences. The addict is bewildered by the mess her life has become; her significant others feel frustrated and powerless.

Addictions ruin lives—the addict's, her loved ones', her children's. No addict who recovers feels that her years of "using" were worthwhile and productive—they were lonely, out of control, and full of dangers.

Addiction, or chemical dependency, does not depend on how much of the substance is ingested or how often a "high" is sought. A woman may switch addictions from one drug to another; she may switch from a more visible substance (alcohol) to a less obvious one (food) or a virtually invisible one (addiction to a relationship). It may not be obvious to her, or to an outsider, but she is still addicted. In fact, she may still be very sick even if she has stopped using any "substance" at all: there is a difference between being "dry" and being "sober."

"Denial"

Persons with addictive disorders are generally the *last* to know that they have them. We in society tend to be impatient with them, believing that they "*must* know" there's a problem; in reality, although they may know there is a problem, they do not know that the problem is their use of a substance. They see the substance as the *solution* rather than the cause. And so, "I don't get along with my boss because he's so picky" is reality for an alcoholic, rather than the more accurate, "My boss yells at me because I'm always late for work and I'm groggy for most of the morning due to a hangover."

Someone who is not addicted looks at a drinking episode and thinks, "Oh, gee, I can't get up in the morning after I drink so late at night. I'd better get a grip on this partying." But an alcoholic is flooded by anxiety, shame, guilt and resentment, and *drinks to drown out these feelings*—instead of facing them or experiencing them at all.

Inevitably in this cycle, problems will come, and she will feel powerless and out of control; in response, she will drink even more; this will cause more problems and pain, over which she will again drink—and on and on. This is the merry-go-round of the addictions.

The chemically dependent person doesn't feel she can survive without her drug. This attitude, as she experiences it, is one of nonnegotiable need. She does not know there is another way; instead of learning coping skills, she has been drowning in her high. Feeling that the choices available to others are not available to her, she may become convinced she is "different" and that there is "something wrong with her." And so she cannot, as we would like her to, "just stop drinking so much"—not alone, not without help in breaking through her denial and finding another way to live.

Denial Among Family Members

Many times, when partners or children of alcoholics seek treatment with me, buried among their litany of complaints—around #5 or so—is "and, oh yeah, (s)he drinks too much." That is, if they recognize the problem at all. *The alcoholic is not the only one who experiences denial.*

The addict's family members are frequently blind to the real problem. This denial is also often found in families where paternal incest exists. The reasons are strikingly similar.

To some degree, denial results when people simply are not aware of how commonplace the addictions (or incest) are and how possible they are for *any* of us. Like incest, addictions may be the last thing that a parent or spouse may suspect to be disrupting her family.

Even if they suspect or have proof of addiction in a partner, many women resist facing the unwanted reality. If they faced it, they might also have to face the limits of a loved one or question a relationship (which may include letting go of fantasies or expectations). A woman's social training may have focused on the self-esteem, security, and "accomplishment" of "getting a husband". This upbringing may leave her ill-prepared for a life on her own. To lose her husband is to lose her job, her retirement plan, her health insurance, her identity, and often her self-worth. If her childhood home was traumatic (damaged, for example, by addiction, incest, or overt violence) she may especially need to maintain the reality or illusion of a stable family life. These women desperately cling to a "white picket fence illusion" no matter what their senses—or their children—tell them.

The children maintain a balancing act between what they feel (pain and confusion, the source of which they may not understand), what they know (Daddy beats us up; Daddy is always drunk; Daddy molests me); and what they need to hang on to (this is the only family I've got). Thus a "conspiracy of silence" frequently divides siblings into isolated, competitive, insecure cells. They share a secret; they also share the same feelings and pain. Sadly, this pain is held inside like some shameful reality.

Addictions Must Be Treated First

Until abstinence from the chosen substance is achieved, nothing else can change. "If only I could get over this depression, then I wouldn't have to drink so much" is actually the opposite of the truth. An alcoholic can either work through feelings or drink—not both. Therefore, therapy while drinking actively is a waste of time, unless the goal of the therapy is for the client to get to the point where she can stop drinking.

The stress of facing deeply painful feelings causes the addict to need *more* of the chosen substance, because there is more to anesthetize. The addictive "disease" has so many complications, affecting the addicted person on all levels—physical, emotional, mental, and spiritual—that dealing with deeper issues is impossible. Those who suffer from these diseases and have experienced early abuses must deal with the addictions first.

Addictions Cannot be "Controlled"

It is useless to urge the addict to stop after two or three, or not to drink so much. She cannot. After all, an alcoholic, by definition, cannot realistically predict how much or when she will drink or what the consequences will be. Facing this is crucial for the substance abuser, her significant other, and health professionals.

Helping the Addict, Not the Addiction

The rules for helping people with addictions are the reverse of what they are in other helping situations. Generally one should nurture clients or friends in pain or healing from pain—be warm, supportive, and nonconfronting, to help them make their own choices and find their own ways to lighten their load. Doing this when the pain is caused by an addictive behavior, however, "enables" the addiction. For instance, if my client comes to a session complaining because of rejection that resulted from her drug abusing behavior, it would only prolong the problem to give sympathy. Concern for her struggle *must* be combined with helping her to see what she has done that led to the rejection, or else she will continue to get high and complain about the consequences and never change. The ultimate consequence of these progressive diseases is death or institutionalization.

There is a risk in confronting the behavior of chemically dependent people, who generally protect their addictions, for this challenges their relationship with their needed substance. At the same time we all must face that we are powerless over the addict's behavior and that only she can decide to change.

THE COURSE OF ADDICTION

All addictions, whether chemical, behavioral, or emotionally based, follow roughly the same course.

In the Beginning

When an addiction starts, the user derives from the substance a feeling of excitement, euphoria, control, and power, all of which are absent in her "real" life. Under the influence of the substance, the user feels no pain, anger, or fear. Many feel real, or "like themselves," only when they use their substance.

Yet there is often a personality change during the high. For instance, a normally shy person becomes publicly seductive, or a person who is unable to express anger becomes irritable or explosive. Thus the individual violates her sober value system, with resulting guilt, shame, and confusion.

As Time Goes On

Along with feeling weak, inadequate, and guilty, in a life that is increasingly unmanageable, the addict feels compelled to have and use the "drug" at any cost.

The responses of those around the addict change. Tensions, conflicts, and distrust result from the negative behavior of addiction and the inability to work out problems.

The addict cannot receive the "information" provided by the internal or external environment about the consequences of her behavior. Unable to evaluate and modify her behavior and improve her situation, she feels stuck and confused. Her inability to admit to herself what is really wrong causes her to convert her complaints to resentment, self-pity, and self-justification: *she* has no problem, everyone *else* does. Instead of resolving the tension within her, she medicates it away by getting high, and continues on the merry-go-round. She builds a tolerance to her substance or behavior of choice. More and more is necessary to satisfy the need for the euphoria of the original high. With some substances such as alcohol, this increased tolerance is chemical: the organs, from the liver to the brain, *alter* their functioning because blood that is supposed to deliver needed nutrients is partly ethyl alcohol, a liquid whose chemical structure is like that of ether.

Alcoholism is more clearly understood in this framework than gambling, for instance. Some current theories suggest that brain chemistry is altered by any addictive behavior, whether or not chemicals are involved. There still remains the chicken-egg question of what leads to what.

Eventually, the level of euphoria diminishes. Real-life consequences of the addiction make life more and more complicated. The addict must develop a repertoire of manipulations, lies, and coverups to protect her disease.

Finally . . .

The euphoria is lost, although it remains a memory—and a goal. The addict pursues the addictive behavior to pull herself out of feeling "sick" into feeling OK. The horrors of withdrawal lurk behind every delay in the next fix. There is no longer any high; she needs to get high just to feel normal.

Whatever *other* feelings she may be needing to mask are long buried, lost to awareness and resolution. Now she has new problems: the craziness of her addiction and the deterioration of her body, mind, and relationships that have occurred.

USE VERSUS ABUSE VERSUS ADDICTION

Not all use of a substance is overuse, and not all overuse is addiction. These categories are difficult to distinguish from each other, and opinions vary on what they represent. For instance, many people who condemn "drug" use approve the high achieved with alcohol and overlook the addictive nature of nicotine.

Social use of a chemical or activity for enjoyment, with no negative consequences, might not fit into the value system of some people, but is not abuse. Many people, when "down in the dumps," go shopping. Gambling can be an exciting activity, a special event. Alcohol use can harmlessly end a hard day or lubricate a social function. Many college students and professionals smoke a joint occasionally and suffer no ill effects. And how many can resist the smell of Swiss chocolate?

Substance use becomes a concern when it is done to mask feelings instead of deal with them, face life, and grow; or when it interferes with interpersonal relations, personal finances, school or job functioning; or when it jeopardizes health or safety. After some period of drug abuse, many people can see the damage they are doing and discontinue or modify their use of the drug. This renewal may entail counseling, but not necessarily an ongoing recovery program or inpatient treatment.

Addiction, however, cannot be controlled or merely stopped. It requires continuing involvement in a recovery support system, and often some form of professional treatment as well. To some degree, once a substance is used not for fun but for self-medication, whether the problem is abuse or addiction is moot. The substance use must be changed or eliminated (the latter in the case of addiction) if such issues as incest are to be addressed. Although one can certainly understand—even endorse—an incest survivor's need to medicate her feelings, she makes a choice not to work on feelings when she chooses to numb them, and therefore recovery is inhibited.

EATING DISORDERS

What makes eating disorders occur so much more frequently among women than men? Women have reduced involvement in, or access to, such world experiences as gambling, but they have primary responsibility for providing food for those around them. The kitchen is their domain. A person with no outside source of gratification and control can still manipulate her food intake. Most men can achieve mastery in the real world, but many women can exercise total control only over their own bodies. Additionally rigid social expectations define women through their appearance. Body size relates to power, sexuality, attention, self-worth, social status and the aftereffects of incest.

Which of the manifestations of a disturbed relationship with food might a survivor develop? Each eating disorder takes care of a different need.

Anorexia Nervosa

Anorexia is the "starvation" disease. Sufferers lose much of their body weight in a short time. Anorexics have extremely distorted body images, feeling themselves to be fat even when they are in danger of dying from starvation. Some anorexics do starve to death. Some die of heart attacks when they begin to regain weight.

Anorexia is difficult for an outsider to understand or analyze. Those who suffer from it often say that it is a monstrous entrapment but, at the same time, as one theorist has said, "intensely negative self-esteem is akin to a powerful moral commitment that keeps their souls together." Any analysis of external or political aspects are not alive for the sufferer, who feels only a force she cannot resist.

To some degree anorexia correlates to the social attitude that women "can never be too rich or too thin." Women in society are expected not to "take up space"—not to be too loud, too tall, too commanding. Men can sit expansively, with their arms and legs spread, but women are expected to exhibit "ladylike" posture: legs wrapped around each other, hands huddled in the lap. These expectations reflect the powerlessness of "ladies." They are left with nothing to control but their bodies, no way to express power except through self-deprivation, and no one to take anger out on but themselves.

Anorexia results in the loss of secondary sex characteristics such as breasts, pubic hair, and menses. According to current psychoanalytic and psychiatric theory, anorexic women can't deal with their femininity or their sexuality. This analysis fails to recognize that the incest survivor's experience of sexuality is distorted. Sex is not something that she owns whose purpose is to gratify her; it is not *sex*, but violation, abuse, and subjugation. The average woman experiences difficulty when construction workers catcall at her. This is not discomfort with her femininity, but with the sense of violation she feels; it is the *social* consequences of being a woman. For many survivors, however, even respectful sexual interest is such an extreme violation that it leads to virtual emotional paralysis. Knowing no other way, the incest survivor protects herself through the building of walls that substitute for the power she cannot exercise. In the case of the anorexic, perhaps that wall is the facade of the child: on some level, looking childlike may seem the key to dissuading others from being sexual with her. (Ironically, however, the body she seeks is the very body which was the recipient of the original abuse: that of the child.) And, like sufferers of all other addictions, they are counterproductive: she actually perpetuates her state of defenselessness while achieving the illusion of power through the manipulations of others.

While the *behavior* is consciously addressed by the anorexic, her compulsion is neither conscious nor a choice, and she is not aware of the process as it unfolds.

Anorexia is a pure expression of anger turned inward; anorexics often hate themselves, but cannot express anger at all. In light of what we know about the self-hate, powerlessness, and body issues of Post-Incest Syndrome (such as alienation from the body), the prevalence of anorexia among incest survivors is easy to understand. It is the ultimate achievement of the delusion of power derived from deprivation at the sacrifice, often, of life itself.

Bulimia

Bulimia is a disorder whose sufferers, to the average outsider, do not appear to have any problem. They do not waste away; rather, they appear to be the perfect image of womanhood. Often they are very attractive, successful women. Yet underneath this facade that so pleases others is a woman whose life is no less out-of-control and who is in no less danger than the anorexic. The bulimic is trapped in a cycle of binges and purges: she eats uncontrollably, and then eliminates the food through self-induced vomiting or the excessive use of laxatives before most of it can be digested.

Bulimia can result in medical problems ranging from an electrolyte imbalance that creates disturbances of heartbeat, to a ruptured esophagus from vomiting. Malnutrition can occur, as it does with anorexia. With malnutrition comes dulled mental, sensory, and emotional functioning.

Vomiting after eating is not a painless form of weight control, as some women think it is when they first hear of it. Bulimia can be so extreme that women induce vomiting 50 to 70 times a day. One woman had so disabled her gag reflex that she had to put large tubes down her throat to make herself vomit. The incest-related symbolisms in this disease are obvious.

The bingeing of bulimia can occur in a frenzy that resembles the desperation of any other drug use and can include "blackouts" just like those the alcoholic may experience. In a blackout, events and surrounding feelings are blocked from awareness and not remembered. Both the bulimic binge and anorexic starvation numb the individual's feelings, distracting her from whatever she is trying not to face, while resulting in substitute complications such as guilt, feelings of powerlessness, and interpersonal problems.

After the "high" of the binge comes the violent elimination of the food, vomited like a poison. This experience symbolizes the experience of the incest survivor, whose guts are filled with poison, self-hate, and deep rage—all of which she feels the drive to purge herself of.

Bingeing and purging give the illusion of control over emotions and anxieties. Simultaneously, however, they create the feeling that life is out of control (which it is) and deep feelings of guilt and shame over the addiction. These are a substitute for the original guilt and shame that accompanies incest.

Although anorexia might help some incest survivors to feel "invisible," bulimia, by helping her to stay beautifully thin, helps the bulimic in her quest for perfection. Both take care of the incest survivor's need to be "perfectly bad"; guilt and feelings of worthlessness are part of any addiction. Addictions produce a substitute focus for these feelings while distracting from their original source, the incest.

Compulsive Overeating, Overeating, And Fat

Not all weight problems are due to objectively measured overeating, and not all people with enthusiastic appetites are compulsive overeaters. Obesity specialists are now realizing that repeated dieting can become compulsive and can contribute to a weight problem. The body adjusts to these cycles of deprivation with a "starvation mentality": it lowers its metabolism to adjust to lowered food intake and so future food intake within a normal range results in weight gain. Thus, although an overweight individual might be eating more than her body needs, she may not be eating more than normal-weight individuals.

Food can serve as a substitute for friendship or nurturing, as a comfort or a reward, as an activity when one is bored, or as a replacement for love or attention that were lacking in childhood. It can numb feelings or cause a high.

Yet there are other overweight persons whose problem, as Molly says of hers, is caused by a combination of "too much enjoyment of too many of the wrong foods, and too little interest in physical activity." To eat junk food, or to be part of a culture that uses a lot of deep frying (as in soul food) does not define an eating disorder. What is necessary for that definition to apply is a combination of distorted attitudes and feelings.

Not every compulsive overeater is too fat. Similarly, not every woman who *thinks* that she is overweight actually is. A number of surveys have shown women's body image to be so distorted that normal-weight and *underweight* women frequently describe themselves as undesirably heavy. A 1984 *Glamour* study, for example, found that 82% of all women saw themselves as too heavy, including almost half of the women within normal weight ranges. Many women have been so brainwashed by society's demand that they be diminutive that their view of themselves is seriously inaccurate.

Compulsive Overeating To become a problem that parallels substance abuse or addiction, overeating may involve bingeing or steady overeating to achieve a high or an altered emotional state. Compulsive overeaters, (many of whom are also alcoholics) often react to sugar in extreme ways. Some get a high, some get dopey, some become irritable, but all experience mood changes. There is an anesthetizing of anxiety, anger, or pain, and a similar distortion of attitude to those associated with other addictions.

Compulsive overeaters may hide or hoard food; they eat without enjoyment, for the effect; they will turn to food when any unmanageable feeling or situation arises. Joanie, for instance, would often find herself sitting in front of the refrigerator at 3 o'clock in the morning without any awareness of how she got there, shoving food into her mouth as fast as she could, yet tasting none of it. She felt powerless to stop the process and hated herself for it.

Not all women who eat too much are as psychologically impaired as a woman who is a compulsive overeater, even if that eating is done in response to feelings. It is the way food is used, the way feelings are mismanaged, and the alteration of attitudes that distinguishes this problem from a weight problem.

Recovery

When an eating disorder exists, treatment is necessary—not weight-loss treatment, but psychological treatment that addresses the emotional addiction. Not all persons with weight or food-habit problems are suited for, or require, such programs as Overeaters Anonymous (OA). Counseling, or other types of support groups, can be very beneficial for them. But those with an eating disorder will need to do more intensive work.

Other Views

Another approach to women who manifest eating disorders focuses on women's social realities. One such view is found in Susie Orbach's two volume, *Fat Is a Feminist Issue*. From this perspective both the overuse of food and the attitude of deprivation that comes from dieting are an outgrowth of the lack of nurturing that women (who are always taking care of others) receive, and an outgrowth of women's lack of entitlement to put their own needs first or to take power or express anger. When a woman's assigned manner of expression and communication is through food, this is the predictable form her problem will take. The problem is seen not as the responsibility of the individual alone, but as a response to a situation that women as a group share. Much of the solution focuses on women developing healthy "selfishness" and empowerment.

For some women, rebellion against a tyranny of thinness is a way of taking power. Size is power. Although being "big and fat" does often prevent these women from achieving the (sexual) approval of men, such approval is not their goal. Being a woman of size often give these women a sense of strength.

WOMEN INCEST SURVIVORS AND ADDICTIONS

Women have been largely overlooked in research on addictions. In the field of alcoholism, for instance, studies have looked at men's experience and then the results have been applied to everyone.

Women experience addictions differently than do men; their "substance of choice" and the course of their addictions are correlated to their social/political life experience, as well as their physical differences.

Generally, women are more quickly addicted, more likely to develop an addiction in response to a crisis, more at risk for physical deterioration and more likely to be multiply, or "cross"-addicted. Because of their different body structure, they metabolize chemicals and detoxify at a different rate.

While both male and female incest survivors are at risk for alcoholism, women generally are much more likely to become prescription pill abusers, and are also more likely to combine this with alcohol abuse. As stated, disorders related to food and body size, such as eating disorders, are much more commonly found among women, who can also suffer from exercise addiction for similar reasons. Self injury behavior, an addictive pattern that is explored in detail in Chapter 11, is found most commonly among women incest survivors as well.

Sex and relationship addictions (codependence) are also frequently found among incest survivors of both genders. Women are prepared throughout life to take care of others, and to measure their worth through their relationships. Thus they are very vulnerable (due, not to personal weakness, but to the expectation of society) to relationship addiction, or "codependence;" they are more likely to become involved with partners who are addicted.

Both women and men who were molested as children may maintain an addiction to the escape that suicide promises, as well as to control, power, and danger. Where addictions to spending and gambling exist among survivors, women are more likely to experience the former. "Workaholism" which associates with the need to "produce" and the need to be perfect, can occur as well.

In addition to being shrouded with more denial, women's addictions are often hidden. There is more discomfort surrounding women's addictions. We can laugh at drunk Uncle Arthur, but we are not comfortable when we see a drunk woman. That is because when women are high on chemicals they violate all the rules of ladylike behavior by which we judge their value; they also (like all addicts) become selfish, instead of being the caretakers of others that society expects. Also, their problem is not as often spotted in drunk driving arrests or job performance; women addicts are frequently more isolated in the home. These invisible addicts deteriorate faster and further without the intervention or crisis that can lead to recovery.

Treatment programs, facilities, and recovery groups are generally designed to meet the needs of men, and women are far less likely to seek help from these services. Some do address women's issues, both psychological and concrete (such as women's need for childcare). Alcoholics Anonymous has women's meetings, and there is a separate program called Women for Sobriety, which grew out of the dissatisfaction that some women felt in AA. For the most part, however, no such alternatives exist for the other addictions.

When women develop an addictive disease, they are much more likely than men to have to "go it alone." "Among alcoholics, the rule of thumb is that nine out of ten wives or girlfriends will stay with an alcoholic man," says Patricia Hughes, Director of the Alcohol Awareness Project of Mt. Holyoke College. On the other hand, "nine out of ten men will leave an alcoholic woman."

Why Addictions Are So Common Among Incest Survivors

The high rate of addictions among incest survivors occurs for two reasons.

First, for incest survivors, chemical use/abuse/addiction serves a survival purpose. It numbs pain, and creates a sense of aliveness or excitement for one who may feel "dead" inside. Also, each disorder may provide a secondary and specific protection: for instance, fat provides a sense of protection from exposing raw nerves to an unsafe world. Emily, a nurse, observed that only when she lost weight did she feel the need to hide behind the body cover of her lab coat; without it, she felt too exposed. Although primary in one sense, addictions can be seen as secondary, as well, in that they are an outgrowth of the incest trauma. While they are diseases that must be arrested, they have also helped the survivor.

The other reason for this frequency is that incest occurs frequently in alcoholic families, and ACOA's are several times more likely to become addicted or to become involved with an addict.

Addictions Recovery and Incest Recovery

In early sobriety or abstinence, it is advisable to focus on strengthening the addict rather than on the incest. I know of one hospital on Long Island whose 30-day eating disorders unit insisted on addressing the incest of a bulimic whose bulimia had not even been arrested. She felt very threatened and left the program prematurely. Generally the weakened physical and mental systems of the addict need to stabilize before incest can be addressed without hurting or overwhelming her. Although an incest history should be identified, if present, addicted survivors in outpatient therapy and/or support groups should wait until their one-year anniversary (at *least!*) before exploring incest.

Many survivors do not have the luxury of waiting, however. Their incest is causing them intense distress and disruption *right now*. These women need help to vent their pain, rage, and guilt, reducing these feelings to levels at which they can be endured until the time to again unleash them for active exploration.

Addictions are complicated and destructive. Their sufferers are not OK simply because they have stopped the addictive behavior. Recovery from addictions involves re-adjustment of attitudes and behaviors, healing of damage, and development of skills and strengths that addictive behaviors had precluded. It is often said that chemically dependent persons stop developing emotionally at the point they started "using"; an alcoholic who started drinking alcoholically at, say, 13, has emotional development arrested in the beginning of adolescence. Certainly, anyone who gets high instead of facing problems learns only to get high, not to work through one developmental task in preparation for the next. For the incest survivor, crippled so early, it is crucial that cognitive and emotional functioning be as clear and strong as possible before addressing Post-Incest Syndrome. However, true recovery will not be possible unless the underlying issue of incest is ultimately addressed.

OBSESSIVE-COMPULSIVE BEHAVIOR

According to the Obsessive-Compulsive Disorder Foundation, Obsessive-compulsive disorder (OCD), "is characterized by recurrent, unwanted thoughts (obsessions) and/or repeated ritualistic behaviors which the person feels driven to perform (compulsions). People with OCD know their obsessions and compulsions are irrational or excessive, yet find that they have little or no control over them." Unlike the addictions, which they resemble, OCD offers no high, no euphoria. All the sufferer can hope for is the temporary relief of some perpetual inner struggle. (Another way in which OCD is distinguished from the addictions is in the absence of denial.)

Many of us experience obsessive-compulsive patterns. We may need to check electrical appliances repeatedly before we feel comfortable that they are turned off; we may follow rigid and specific bedtime rituals. But for many sufferers, OCD is a tortuous entrapment that ruins lives and relationships.

Michael Liebowitz, Director of the Anxiety Disorders Clinic at the New York Psychiatric Institute, categorizes obsessive-compulsive behaviors into the following patterns: hoarding (which can be understood literally—these people cannot throw anything away); arranging (such as lining things up, or spacing things perfectly); horrific thoughts (the sense that one must avoid or maintain a certain ritual in order to prevent loss of control of an impulse to do violence); magical thinking (behaviors or thought patterns designed to maintain safety or achieve success, such as the childhood game of not stepping on a crack). Checking and counting are other ways to achieve relief and control. A fantasy underlies many of these patterns: that following them allows a person to control her destiny. They are, for incest survivors, an attempt to control *something*, to have a sense of control in a life that feels out of control. Where obsessive thoughts exist compulsive behaviors make them more manageable.

The themes of incest are clearly shown in obsessive-compulsive disorder. For instance, many of the manifestations of this disorder relate to issues of control, boundaries, and territoriality (such as the inability to sit in a room with a door open, or with a door closed). The compulsive repetition of certain behaviors may control the thought process, inhibit unwanted memories, or emotions such as guilt, anxiety, or anger. What Judith L. Rapoport, in her best seller on OCD, *The Boy Who Couldn't Stop Washing* calls "an obsessive fear of contamination," is especially pertinent for incest survivors who feel "soiled and spoiled." (At the other extreme may be the incest survivor whose sense of being dirtied is manifest in a literal way: she may neglect personal hygiene and appear unkempt, her hair oily and uncombed. Her entire presence screams, "STAY AWAY!") Compulsive hand-washing is a manifestation of the obsession with cleanliness—a desperate need to remove some stain from the soul.

According to current theory, there is a connection between obsessive-compulsive disorder and brain chemistry. Current wisdom regarding treatment suggests behavioral or pharmaceutical treatment. As with the addictions, the person with obsessive-compulsive disorder cannot stop through will power. Additionally, symptomatic relief is necessary before deeper issues can be explored. Long-term insight-oriented psychotherapy has proved relatively ineffectual.

There are many theories about what problems, if any, lurk behind this disorder. Many professionals who work with Post-Incest Syndrome, and some literature about the consequences of incestuous abuse, see the high rate of occurrence among survivors. With such themes as control and powerlessness, such emotions as anxiety, shame, and anger, and the functions of distraction and mastery, it is easy to understand this high incidence of obsessive-compulsive disorders as well as the related concerns of chemical dependency/addiction among the adult survivors of childhood sexual abuse. Yet nowhere in the brochure of the OCD foundation, or the recent comprehensive article contained in *Psychology Today*, which offered Dr. Liebowitz' analysis, is any mention made of incest.

PROFESSIONALS NEED TO UNDERSTAND
SPECIAL POPULATIONS

Alcoholism conferences today increasingly incorporate the subject of child sexual abuse into their agendas. The field of Adult Children of Alcoholics, with its down-to-earth attitude toward real-life consequences of childhood abuse and trauma, was ahead of many other groups in its willingness to address incest. Yet even when workers in addictions agencies recognize the prevalence of incest among the people they treat, they are often no better prepared to deal with it than many other professionals. Adequate training is scarce and many administrators are reluctant to take the side of victims and survivors (children and women) against their abusers (usually men).

The chemically dependent incest survivor is further at risk because therapists outside the field of addictions cannot recognize such disorders as alcoholism when their clients evidence them. I frequently hear of therapists, most of whom define themselves as psychoanalysts, who continue to see alcoholic clients year after year without identifying the presence of the disease or requiring its therapeutic attention.

I know of two women who were in such "therapy" for twenty years; one was alcoholic, the other had an eating disorder. Still another was in therapy for many years until she independently decided to get sober through Alcoholics Anonymous, which her therapist had never required. At that point she began to make rapid progress with many previously unsolved problems, including incest, depression, and career issues. By the time many of these clients get to a professional who understands and can diagnose a problem of chemical dependency, they have often been to several therapists, leaving behind wasted dollars and wasted lives.

Another problem occurs when therapists fail to accept addictions as disorders existing in and of themselves, rather than outgrowths of a preconceived framework. In one recent book on the secret thoughts of a psychoanalyst, for instance, the author expresses dismay that his alcoholic patient was not able to see that he did not really want to suck on a bottle, he really wanted to suck on his mother's breast!

The failure to properly diagnose or treat certain conditions is not exclusive to the addictions. Many other secondary syndromes associated with incest also remain undiagnosed and therefore untreated, because of lack of awareness on the part of medical or therapy professionals. For instance, persons with multiple-personality disorder often see a number of therapists before proper diagnosis is made; those suffering from panic disorders frequently bounce from physician to physician in pursuit of a medical diagnosis for their problem without any medical doctor offering them either the correct diagnosis or a referral to a psychotherapist. Women are particularly vulnerable to misdiagnosis. There is statistical evidence that when they complain, their (usually male) physicians take those complaints—whether physiologically or psychologically based—less seriously than those of male patients. When she is sent home with the injunction to "relax," a woman's problems (dismissed as the hypochondriasis of a hysterical female) remain untreated.

Thus the blindness of the system impedes the recovery of the incest survivor at two levels: many problems remain unidentified and untreated; their function as indicators of possible incest cannot be recognized. When combined with the inability or unwillingness of many therapists to see the incest itself, this omission transforms Post-Incest Syndrome into an iatrogenic condition, an illness that is caused by medical personnel or by medicine.

Another problem in the assessment of Post-Incest Syndrome is a consequence of the tendency of psychiatrists to see feelings as "symptoms" to be treated with medication, rather than as expressions of a problem that deserves attention. A psychiatrist may diagnose accurately the presence of depression in a patient but fail to consider the real-life factors that contributed to it. If such an obvious experience as grief can be so easily misunderstood, then incest, so buried from survivors and professionals alike, is even more at risk of invisibility. Similarly, untrained professionals tend to see schizophrenia in the flashbacks or unexplained emotional explosions of Post-Incest Syndrome.

The solution to the shortsightedness within the profession of psychotherapy demands that we acknowledge the *specialness* of our clients. It does our clients an enormous disservice to continue to squeeze certain populations into presumed truths. But the dilemma of these theorists is clear: if the dynamic of a particular problem challenges their presumed underpinnings of human functioning, these professionals must abandon either the theory or the client. Those of us who are therapists must be willing to adopt the variety of treatment skills necessary for these specials populations. *We* must accommodate our *clients'* needs, rather than demand that they accommodate our training or belief system. The needs of the incest survivor particularly demand that we do this, for to fail is to rape the victim again.

This hidden trauma *insists* on being heard. Through the challenge presented by incest survivors and women's groups, we have finally begun to repudiate such psychoanalytic presumptions as the "oedipal fantasy." Using trauma theory as a framework, we can separate from psychiatric assumptions about internal defects or conflicts and see feelings as the human reactions they really are. Through a broader understanding of gender roles we can transform theories of mother blaming and the view that sexual violence is the act of "a few sick individuals" into a true understanding of the power abuses inherent in society. With any disorder or life experience we must learn about the experience from those who endure it and must see it in its cultural context. By telling society and people in therapy our various untruths, we have failed them both. It is time to listen to the truths they can teach us through their experience.

VICTIMIZATION AND SELF-DESTRUCTIVENESS

*I*ncest is a crime of dominance. Implied and actual threats combine with the relationship bond to entrap the child. The closer the relationship between victim and abuser, the less likely her escape. She may be unable to explain to her nonabusing caretakers why she doesn't want to be around a certain person anymore. Or she may be too scared to try to separate.

She may also tolerate the abuse to protect others in her family (such as sisters or her mother) from being hurt. She often reaches for help, not for herself, but for others; she has given up on getting help for herself. Often she takes action to protect other children in the family or community.

The most common reason that child victims reported incest to authorities, according to O'Hare and Taylor's experience at NYWAR, was "an attempt to rescue younger siblings." According to newspaper reports, this altruism motivated Cheryl Pierson to kill her father. She had long since stopped trying to save herself, but when she saw her father begin the "tickling games" with her little sister, she took action.

MOTHER BLAMING

Much has been made of the responsibility of the mother in families with paternal incest. But often these wives of abusers are themselves victimized by their husbands.

Wives as Victims

Several researchers have found a clear correlation between wife battering and child abuse, including incest. Donna Truesdell, John McNeil, and Jeanne Deschner, whose findings appeared in *Social Work*, found that about 75% of the wives of men who sexually abused their children reported at least one incident of physical attack; the same percentage reported psychological abuse. A quarter of the women reported abuse that was life-threatening. Because the same threats, shame, and resulting secrecy shrouds violence against wives as surrounds incest, both are under-reported. These women fear for their lives and suffer little deaths every day. Through battering and verbal abuse, the husband controls and isolates his wife, diminishes her self-esteem, degrades her, and undermines her authority.

Many more subtle forms of dominance and control can render a woman powerless as well. In his article "Grown Men Fearful Before Incest Offenders," from *Aegis* magazine, Rich Snowden describes the attitudes of abusing men and sheds light on what many women and children experience in households with paternal incest. In 1982, when Snowden volunteered to lead an incest offender's group, he expected "crazed psychopaths." To his amazement, the perpetrators reminded him of men he knew growing up: ordinary guys who, like him, were "taught that privilege is our birthright, so we take, we do not give," and who "get affection, or express it, mainly through sex." These men had received the social training that all men receive: "women and children belong to men . . . to use for their benefit . . . and . . . pleasure . . . and . . . anger."

Like many of us, he had heard therapists say there was nothing criminal about these men—that they were "nice," really, but had simply "made a mistake." But when he started to push them a little, their appealing manner fell away, replaced by tension and anger. He says, "I could only think about a child facing one of these men alone . . . the fear she must feel . . . knowing that her father is her master and she must either obey or risk the rage that lay under the surface."

He thought then of how mothers are expected to stop these men who "turned out line after line about the 'dangerous desires of little girls' . . . these 'demon nymphettes.'" When one man shouted to Snowden to stop telling him what to do—"Nobody is going to make me do anything I don't wanna!"—he realized that no woman was going to stop an abuser. These are not men who ask for—or are interested in—the opinions of others. Some of them rule their homes with violence, but some merely use the power of their presence and the certainty of their socially guaranteed dominance.

In most families where paternal incest exists, the caste system of the nuclear family is rigidly enforced. Herman's research revealed that the father's "role as breadwinner was honored with almost ritual solemnity." Incest perpetrators, like batterers, "exercise minute control over the lives of their wives and daughters, often virtually confining them to the house, [enlisting] the boys in the family . . . as deputies in this policing role." Both mothers and daughters were prevented from developing outside contacts: like battering husbands, "the fathers consolidated their power in these families, isolating their wives and children from the outside world." Half of Herman's respondents reported that their fathers were habitually violent and that they themselves had seen their mothers beaten (and other children as well). As Russell says, wives "are isolated in one-to-one relationships with the person who has power over them."

Herman continues:

> These men were described as the unquestioned heads of their households. Their authority within the family was absolute, often asserted by force. They were also the arbiters of the family's social life . . . and were often feared within their families, yet *they impressed outsiders as sympathetic, even admirable men* [italics mine].

In fact, she notes, "the daughters themselves were often impressed, for their fathers did have many strengths." Herman sees these incest-perpetrating fathers as "the perfect patriarchs."

Myth: Mothers Cause Abuse

Despite the obvious physical and psychological effects of this unbalanced family structure, society holds mothers at least equally (if not mostly) responsible for the abuse. Mothers are blamed either for causing perpetrators to do what they do or for failing to stop them. Psychotherapy—even in its more "progressive" form, family systems theory— blames mothers for causing the abuse. In one view, mothers have been described as "the cornerstone of the pathological family system." Mother's sexual "unavailability" is generally seen as driving him to his daughter; or she's seen as too demanding (she can't, it seems, get it right no matter what she does). On one hand, she's expected to meet her husband's sexual needs, and not her own; on the other, as Butler says, if she is "too" aggressive, she fails as well, by "having caused her husband to feel emasculated." But this presumption clearly ignores reality. As Nicholas Groth, who is well known for his work with men who molest, says in *Men Who Rape:*

> The men were having sexual relations with their daughters and sons in addition to, rather than instead of, their wives. Those offenders who confined their activities to children did so by choice. There was no one for whom no other opportunity for sexual gratification existed.

One woman in Russell's book says she "used to beg him to go to bed with me," yet the whole time he was molesting her daughter. Other opportunities for sexual satisfaction may exist, *but incest is not about "sexual satisfaction."*

Such abusers often feel they have the right to take what they want, even from adults. Russell tells us about Ann, a mother of an incest victim, who endured nine years of violent abuse from her husband before rejecting him sexually. In response to her long-overdue assertion of her own needs, he raped her. Shortly after, he began molesting his daughter. To blame the woman for "failing to satisfy her husband," Herman points out, assumes that "without question a wife is required to service her husband on demand"; failing to do this justifies his seeking satisfaction from a person who can never deny him, fail to satisfy him, or have her own needs: his daughter.

Women in Russell's book state that of all the horrors they endured—near-fatal beatings, rapes, and their own victimization through incest—their daughter's abuse upset them the most. Even though incest was only one of the abuses perpetrated by Daphne's husband, who would pin the children's hands on the table with a fork until they bled, she felt that "the kids love and respect him dearly."

After their divorce he refused to pay child support. Subsequently he remarried and became a minister.

Blaming the mothers not only victimizes women who are already often victimized; it also gives the perpetrator more opportunity to shift the blame from himself. Daughters become confused and their fragile bond with their mothers is further weakened. In *Father-Daughter Incest,* an incest survivor named Janet says, "He would just talk in very personal terms about how deprived he was. But then my mother says that she always did have sex with him, so I don't know who was telling the truth."

We place unrealistic expectations on a woman in such a family. To take the steps we expect of her, she must have power—power that she is prohibited from having, both by the family structure and the culture.

Yes, some of these women are not what their husbands want them to be. True, some refuse sex. But by focusing on this refusal, we not only impose the unreasonable expectation that a woman is responsible for her husband's behavior; incest almost becomes the woman's crime if she denies her husband (sex or anything else). No matter what she wants, or how she feels, she's *obligated.* Aren't these the same messages mirrored by incest? When her mother is blamed for her abuse, the incest survivor is further encouraged to see all women—herself, her mother, too—as extensions of the needs and demands of men. All are objects, all are powerless, and all are victims.

Many mothers of incest victims are unavailable because they are sick, some chronically. But still they are blamed. In *A Deadly Silence: The Ordeal of Cheryl Pierson,* Dena Kleiman cites a description of women such as Cheryl Pierson's mother as "quite likely to be . . . needful women, insecure in her worth or femininity . . . absorbed in her own infantile needs." Infantile needs? Needful? Pierson's mother was dying of kidney disease. And she was a battered wife.

And anyway, is it the mother who has "infantile needs"? Judith Herman says:

> Implicit in these descriptions is a set of normative assumptions regarding the father's prerogatives and the mother's obligations within the family. The father, like the children, is presumed to be entitled to the mother's love, nurturance, and care. In fact, his dependent needs actually supersede those of his children, for if the

mother fails to provide the accustomed attentions, it is taken for granted that ... he is entitled to use his daughter as a substitute.

The father is never expected to take on the mother's caretaking role. The father's wish, indeed, even his right, to continue to receive female nurturance, whatever the circumstances, is accepted without question!

No matter what illness, disability, or burden their wives were facing, "[n]one of the fathers adapted ... by assuming a maternal role in the family. Rather, they reacted to their wives' illnesses as if they themselves were being deprived of mothering." At the same time, many daughters were "assigned a special duty to 'keep Daddy happy.' "

> *But no degree of maternal absence or neglect constitutes an excuse for paternal incest,* unless one accepts the idea that fathers are entitled to female services in their families, no matter what the circumstances.... It is this attitude of entitlement ... that finally characterizes the incestuous father and his apologists [emphasis mine].

High Expectations of Mothers

If mothers aren't responsible for causing the abuse, then they are responsible for letting it go on. Survivors of paternal abuse are often angrier at their mothers for not stopping it than at their fathers for actually doing it. Mother is, first, presumed to have known. "She *must* have known," many incest survivors tell me. In some cases mothers do know: mothers walk in on, or are told about, an incident. But often the answer to "How did she know?" is "I don't know. But she must have." Survivors blame their mothers because the trauma is all-consuming; the victim feels marked—she expects that the incest shows. They blame their mothers because of the unrealistic expectations we have of mothers to know everything that happens around them.

Mothers do not know everything that happens in a family. They cannot see through walls or telepathically know what happens in another building (especially true when the abuser is outside the home). And their ability to know is further reduced by the particularly secretive nature of this kind of abuse. Also, "the offender and the victim used every possible means to keep the abuse a secret," as O'Hare says.

Even of those who know, some are strong enough to rescue their daughters, and some are not. Some women who are married to the perpetrator are so totally dominated by their husbands that they can't save themselves. In either case, what is the message when we continue to focus on where the mother was? Russell challenges us to wonder, "What does it say about male behavior and sexuality if young girls are unsafe in their own homes with their own relatives without an adult female to protect them?"

Many of these mothers are also incest survivors. Some are so crippled by their own histories that they cannot see what is before them; to acknowledge the child's incest would be to acknowledge their own. This applies not only to paternal incest, but that committed by siblings, cousins, uncles, and non-family members as well.

Some partners of abusers *do* see, but feel that they have no practical options. Like battered women and wives of alcoholics, many of these women are more than economically dependent on their husbands. A society that limits a wife's economic base forces her into the powerlessness that can result in victimization. "Where can I go, with no job skills and five little kids?" they ask. For many, economic dependence goes hand in hand with emotional dependence: her marriage provides not only her income, her health insurance, and the roof over her head, but also a structure that gives her a sense of security not available from inside. Dominated, these overburdened and weakened women are often incapable of, or believe they are incapable of, independent functioning. They wonder, as Penelope Russianoff's book asks, "Why do I think I am nothing without a man?"

Herman describes this scenario:

Economically dependent, socially isolated, in poor health and encumbered by the care of many small children, these mothers were in no position to challenge their husbands' domination. . . . No matter how badly they were treated, most simply saw no option other than submission. . . . They conveyed to their daughters the belief that a woman is defenseless against a man, that marriage must be preserved at all costs, and that a wife's duty is to serve and endure.

This type of mother might seem responsible for giving her children a role model of self-hate and weakness. But she is not responsible: if we hold her responsible, we blame the victim for her victimization. And we do blame her, even though one study (done shortly after the airing of the television show "Something About Amelia") found that almost 60% of mothers take the side of their abused daughters against molesting fathers. Russell, acknowledging that some mothers do abuse or abandon their children, says that "Some mothers are also victims of the incest between their husbands and their daughters . . . placed in [the] profoundly humiliating position . . . of having to deal with their own feelings of pain and rage . . . while at the same time having to try to understand and accept their daughters' rage at them for what their husbands did."

Some see and take action. Sometimes the system hears them and helps protect the child. Often, society refuses to believe a mother's complaint against the minister, principal, or family doctor. In cases of paternal incest, the system often blames the *mother* and removes the child from her custody. By thus invalidating her, the system tells the mother that her word is never as believable as a man's, and no more believable than a child's; the system says that she doesn't matter any more than the child. Thus another message about the worth of women is given to the victimized daughter.

For us to ask *first*, "What did the mother do?" is to suggest that she is more responsible than the one who committed the abuse. Although only a few women have the inner power, the economic capacity, the ability within the family structure and the legal system to do what we expect of them, all women are expected to be more powerful than those who are actually in control. When men abuse power and women are powerless, it is the *woman* society criticizes. Thus the abuser's blame is validated by the system's blame. This distortion continues even among some incest specialists. A flyer from the Incest Recovery Association of Texas, a well-respected advocacy organization, says that incest occurs because the family "is not . . . emotionally healthy. The bond between the parents may not be strong. . . ." Henry Giaretto, founder of Parents United, requires in his "humanistic" treatment program that mothers confess and apologize for their failure to protect their daughters. An approach that suggests equal blame for both parents fails to acknowledge the basic power issues of incest.

The *perpetrator,* and only the perpetrator, is responsible for the acts he commits. However, we excuse or minimize his responsibility in many ways, such as when we analyze the offender as having been hurt by *his* mother. Alice Miller says that "men who were not respected by their mothers will take revenge on women and little girls." Yet the literature is clear that the person these perpetrators were abused by is their *father*. A *Life* article by Cheryl McCall states that few abusers had "passable" relationships with their fathers. When fathers fail sons, women are hurt or blamed.

Not all mothers who fail to protect their children are completely debilitated. Some mothers have the resources and knowledge necessary but choose to ally themselves with the perpetrator and abandon the child. They fail to validate and nurture the child. They fail to reach out for the support (such as women's support networks) they need to help them be strong. They choose their husbands over their children. Yet in doing this, are they doing anything different from the society that denies the cries of the child and says of the man she accuses, "He's a nice man! He would never do that"? Society defers to men. Women do it because we have trained them to do it.

Evan Stark, Rutgers professor and co-director of the domestic violence training program in New Haven, published these observations in an article called "The Invisible Men in Child Abuse Cases" in *Newsday:* "Women who fail to control their batterers are labeled 'bad mothers' and held legally responsible for the child even when a male is the assailant." Stating that Yale-New Haven research shows that mothers are battered in 45% of general child abuse cases and that battered mothers of abused children are more likely to have their children removed from their custody, he asserts: "Emphasis must be shifted from child saving to the protection and empowerment of women, from being the mother's adversary to being her advocate."

I agree that a child deserves to be rescued from a rapist, even if he is her father—especially if he is her father. And I look forward to the day when the rules, the roles, the laws, and the institutions of our society help women have the power, the resources, the independence to take on the role that we demand of them. And let us remember that despite all this, most of the women in Russell's study "were able to protect and care for their children *far better than they took care of themselves*" [emphasis mine].

Mothers are not responsible for this problem. They are additional victims of a structure gone haywire. Russell says it this way:

> Incestuous abuse can no longer be viewed as a problem that involves a few sick or disturbed sex offenders. Particularly when considered along with wife rape, wife-beating, and nonsexual child

abuse, it reveals an intensely troubled contemporary family. And the fact that the vast majority of this abuse is being perpetrated by males suggest that a full understanding of this problem requires seeing it within the context of severe gender and generational inequality.

Incest, after all, is the expression of a deeper social problem.

A SOCIAL DISEASE

The victimization of women and children grows out of a larger social scheme.

In 1987, the National Institute of Health (NIH) declared that the number one health problem of women is battering. According to FBI statistics, battering is the most frequently occurring violent crime in this country. One study found that half of all women are hit at least once by a partner; a government study says that one-quarter of all women who marry are struck at least once. Over half of all murders of women are committed by "former or present partners," according to Dr. Lenore Walker, author of *The Battered Woman*. Data reported by many rape-crisis centers projects that one-third of all women will be raped. (This incredible figure includes "date rape," which accounts for half of all rapes, and rape by a spouse, which many states still do not recognize as illegal.) In England, according to law, a man may beat his wife with a stick no thicker than his thumb. This is the origin of the common expression "rule of thumb." Because English common law is considered a precedent for U.S. law, courts have upheld the "rule of thumb" in many states.

Frequently, when I lecture, I am asked why women deal with incest more easily than men do. Although I am not sure either group has an edge, women seem better able to accept the reality of having been sexually victimized. The reason is a sad statement of the relative status of women and men in society: women expect to have to deal with sexual violation; men, who are socialized to take what they want sexually, do not. Virtually all women I know constantly carry their awareness of this potential. When they decide whether to go out at night alone, they always consider that they might be raped. The specter of rape confines, restricts, and intimidates them, hindering their full involvement in the world. Sexual violence is a fact of life. In March 1988, *Ladies' Home Journal* surveyed its mainstream circulation on the "most negative aspect of being a woman today." "An overwhelming number of women—no matter what age, income bracket, or education—cited vulnerability to physical attack, such as rape, mugging, or domestic violence."

The family is a microcosm of a powerful social imbalance. In families, as in society, men are taught to be aggressive and self-satisfying and women are taught to give what they don't want to give (or it will be taken from them). The power structure—in the family, as in society—distributes power in a skewed way, concentrating it in one gender while depriving the other.

Incest is only one aspect of the violence and violation that women and children too often experience at the hands of men. The messages the incest victim receives and the experiences of women around her reinforce this problem. Sadly, her childhood abuse may make her even more likely to be victimized or even victimize herself through self-abusive or self-destructive behavior in later life.

FROM THE VICTIM'S PERSPECTIVE

On a fundamental level, the child cannot—ought not—to understand any of this. If she is hurt, she has a right to complain. She has a right to expect good and healthy parenting. She has a right to be angry when neglected or abandoned. Her job is not to understand the struggles of either of her parents or to make excuses for them. Her job is to acknowledge her feelings. Ultimately, however, the adult survivor needs to understand these considerations. To blame her mother for what was, in effect, her mother's victimization, is to damn all women, herself included.

Where should we draw the line? These questions are not easy to answer. Perhaps they are not ours to answer at all, but the incest survivor's herself. But in our zealousness to save children, and assign responsibility, let us not further victimize.

THE AFTEREFFECTS: VICTIM IDENTITY

The incest survivor learns early that she is a victim. The circumstances of the abuse often lead her to give up on herself. She accepts that she will be hurt and can do nothing about it. She believes neither in her ability nor her right to escape or fight back. She has no faith that anyone will rescue her. She feels worthless as a person and as a woman (especially because she equates being female with being abusable). She often resigns herself to the inevitability of her abuse.

In families where the father or another primary relative commits incest, everyone is in it together, separately. Sandy, a 19-year-old survivor, says that in her family it's "every man for himself." No one gives to anyone else, because no one has anything to give. Each deprived and drained family member struggles so hard to survive that he or she has become, of necessity, self-absorbed, despite the deep caring that may exist for others in the family.

The child victim may have learned the role of protector, by being a deflector: she feels that by accepting abuse she can keep others from harm. Or, if the incest protects her from abuse directed at others, she may experience survivor guilt.

A child who has a problematic relationship with her parents or who is personally troubled is vulnerable to sexual abuse by persons outside her family. Her often obvious neediness sends signals to a perpetrator that she might want attention enough to pay a price for it, and be less likely to report it (because she has no one she trusts enough to tell, or possibly because she is quicker to blame herself). Researchers have found that daughters raised apart from their mothers, or in the home with a stepfather, are particularly at risk for sexual abuse by men outside the family. For instance, Russell says that "men appear to be selecting previously victimized females for further pornography-related victimization."

Economic dependency, already shown to make a child victim's mother powerless, is a higher risk for the incest survivor too. Incest interferes with her success in school, and the aftereffects often make job success difficult to achieve. This difficulty puts her at risk for dominance by her partner.

For these reasons, in addition to social and gender-based circumstances, incest survivors often are prepared to be victims—to accept victimization as their due, to feel unable to escape it, or to fail to see the victimization. The incest survivor often knows things feel bad but does not know how bad they are or how much better they can be. And her choices are confined by her narrow field of expectations and her broad field of tolerance.

A Pattern of Victimization

Victimization is familiar to the incest survivor. She feels that she deserves to be abused and does not understand that there is an alternative. Like the daughter of an alcoholic (which, in many cases, she is as well), she often becomes involved with partners who have drug, alcohol, or other addictive problems. She is also likely to have relationships with people who do not take her needs into consideration or who are verbally or physically abusive.

The adult incest survivor is more likely than a woman who was not molested in childhood to find herself continually violated. She is more likely, I have found, to be the target of lesser forms of sexual abuse, such as exhibitionism. There is research (which Russell calls "extraordinarily strong") supporting the suggestion that such a woman is more likely to be a victim of later acts of sexual or spousal abuse. Among incest survivors, 68% later became victims of rape or attempted rape (compared with the norm in Russell's sample—itself a frighteningly high 38%); 82% experienced "some kind of sexual assault" (compared with another disturbing figure—48% of nonabused women). Two-and-a-half times as many survivors experience marital rape; twice as many experience "unwanted advances" by an authority figure; twice as many were asked to pose for pornography (four times as many if the perpetrator were their father). Russell warns that these figures might be exaggerated, because the incest survivor's reaction may be different and, therefore, more likely to report. However, my professional experience and the literature indicate a pattern of victimization by both strangers and others.

The stories in Russell's book reinforce this pattern of victimization. The truth of women's lives speaks more strongly in their own words than in research data. Woman after woman tells multiple abuse horror stories. Sarah, for instance, endured incest at the hands of her foster father, a "friend rape" in her mid-teens, rape at knifepoint by her mother's lover a year later, and acquaintance rape during the same year. Like many multiple incest survivors, she reinforces that the relationship determines the degree of trauma: the abuse by her foster father, by far the least violent (no force was used) was by far the worst.

Perhaps more important than the increased incidence of later abuse, Russell says, that these incest survivors, as a group, were not angry over the rapes. Many acted as if they deserved it, as if it were punishment. One woman married her rapist one week after the rape. She had not known him before the rape.

Feeling as if she deserves abuse sets her up for sado-masochistic sexual activity. Some argue that participation in S&M is a matter of personal choice and that the person who plays the masochist is really in control, for she dictates when to stop. But women who have examined their incest and its consequences take the view that S&M continues their abuse. Claudia, an incest survivor who was involved in sado-masochism before she began her recovery, says that she has never known a woman who was into S&M and had not been molested as a child.

To be relentlessly victimized in childhood results in resignation. The incest victim knows no other way to be. She feels she has no alternative but to give in, do what the other person wants. Each additional experience reinforces that she is worthless and powerless. She does not feel entitled to any other treatment, and she is too afraid—and too emotionally exhausted—to complain.

As a child, she *was* a victim. For survival, she often turned that victimization against herself and learned to hate herself instead of her abuser. Now she carries herself like a victim, apologizing for her very presence.

This aftereffect can be misinterpreted both by those who blame women for their abuse and by those who hold the imbalance of power in society responsible for everything women do.

To what degree is "choice" applicable to this situation? For one to have choice, one must believe one has alternatives, be clear-thinking enough to evaluate them, be free enough of fear to implement them. And one must have the power, safety, and economic freedom to exercise one's options.

The Jews, gays, gypsies, and dissidents victimized by the Holocaust did not have choices. They did not understand the horror that was creeping up on them until, one by one, their freedoms had been annihilated, and then it was too late for most to fight back. But we still ask "Why did the Jews let the Nazis do that to them?" as if the victims gave their permission to be victimized.

The continuing victimization of Post-Incest Syndrome does not represent choice but a compulsive, blind continuation of an entrapment that molded the child victim's life before she had *any* understanding of what was happening. A victim mentality results when victimization starts quietly and surrounds the victim. The victim is stripped of economic resources and freedom of movement. Sometimes others become competitive with or suspicious of the victim. She may ally herself with the abuser out of dependence, fear, or awe of his status. By the time the victim realizes what's happening to her, she has lost the power to fight or flee, and is trapped.

I do not wish to imply that, when women are battered or raped, they are to blame. Nothing the victim can do, no clothes she wears, no place she goes can justify an abuser's behavior. Women get raped no matter how careful they are. We are responsible for how we carry ourselves and who we choose for our relationships, but society offers little support for a woman to leave a battering partner or child molester; many women have the strength and courage to do so, only to be met by the brick wall that is the legal system. Also, many incest survivors, once victimized, find themselves in a continuing cycle of victimization and are unable to stop their children's, because they are so damaged.

Criminals say they can sense a target to victimize. They can tell by the person's carriage, body language, facial expression. They can sense the fear, the helplessness, the passivity. A woman named Ann in Russell's sample said, "I think a man can smell insecurities." A person who experiences herself as easily victimized gives off an aura to those who are looking for conquest. A woman who is an adult incest survivor, a woman who believes she is worthless and helpless, is likely to be chosen for further abuse.

Some might contend that being abused excuses abusing others later, childhood traumas result in one's not being responsible for one's later actions.

We must, therefore, distinguish self-victimization from mistreatment of others. Helplessness can lead to the passive acceptance of mistreatment from others, but having the inability to defend or protect oneself or one's child is absolutely different from actively perpetrating hurtful acts on others. Some survivors of childhood abuse do neglect their children. Others do commit verbal, physical, or sexual abuse, although sexual abuse is the least common, and a woman is less likely to become violent than her heterosexual male partner. While overt acts of violence are less common for women, they are no more excusable. But women who have been victimized often continue to be victimized, and thus are unable to rescue (or properly parent) their children.

Paralysis is the opposite of action. Even if someone feels she or he cannot help hurting someone else, she or he is responsible to do whatever is necessary to prevent doing so, such as seeking treatment and, in the meantime, avoiding the situation. For instance, one who feels he is a compulsive child molester must never let himself be alone with a child. Likewise, a batterer must leave the room before exploding into violence, as should a physical or verbal abuser of children.

Runaways

When runaways are driven out of their homes by abuse, they are driven into instant adulthood. According to Father Bruce Ritter, founder of Covenant House, many, if not most of them, then face death. He says that if he can't save a kid fast, he knows he's lost the kid. These kids, he says, don't last long in the streets. Sadly, however, he sees it as his goal to reunite these children with their families; even though he sees therapy as a requirement for abusive parents, this goal is often tantamount to returning the victim to her rapist. These kids run away to save their lives. According to one study, many say that there is less abuse in the streets than what they found at home.

Mary Ellen Mark, who, with husband Martin Bell, made the movie *Streetwise,* photographs runaway kids. All of the images are haunting, but one has stayed with me: a little girl, maybe 11, with a tough "Don't fuck with me" expression on her face. But such a child's face. In one hand, a cigarette rests naturally between her short fingers. The other arm clutches a doll. These are *kids.* When Trudee Able-Paterson, the director of Streetwork Project in New York, asked a runaway who had been a prostitute since age 12 what she wanted for her eighteenth birthday, the girl said a coloring book and crayons.

In a poignant, frightening article in *Psychology Today* called "Coming of Age in the Streets," Patricia Hersch tells us what we may not want to know: "Block after block," she says, "I see female prostitutes, some as young as 12 years old, dressed in G-strings and not much else."

In America, one-third of the kids who run away are lured into selling their bodies within two days of leaving home. Over 5,000 kids a year are buried in unmarked graves. (These two bits of information are provided by Pete Axthelm, from his *Newsday* article "Somebody Else's Kids." But they are not somebody else's kids. They're our kids.)

James Kennedy, M.D., treats Covenant House residents. He also tests them for HIV antibodies, evidence of exposure to the virus that causes AIDS. He estimates that half of the regulars have been exposed to the virus.

Runaway kids run away from abuse in the home and attach to pimps—or are abducted by pimps—because pimps offer them something familiar: the illusion of nurturing and protection, the use of their bodies, the marketing of their souls. The girls swear that these pimps, who give them abuse, entrapment, and violation along with care and attention, are their boyfriends. They assert that finally someone cares for them. They won't let reality interfere with their illusion, because they need to believe it too much.

As vulnerable as any runaway kid is, Russell points out that little girls are even more vulnerable than boys, because they are more preyed upon by pimps and perpetrators. Their inability to say no or fight contrasts with the training that boys get in street smarts, scrapping, and self-sufficiency.

As Dr. Kennedy says, in runaways the "fire of life" dies. Bitter, abused, shaking from the cold, selling their bodies at 10 or 12, many are murdered. Many commit suicide. From the horror of incest they go to being destroyed by the streets. Incest especially kills the kids who are strong enough or foolish enough or smart enough to try to escape.

The Sex Industry

The sex industry—prostitution, pornography, and the like—relies on the involvement of incest survivors. According to some estimates, 92% of teenage prostitutes were sexually molested in childhood, most by someone known and trusted (from *The Death of Innocence*, by Sam Janus). In a study published in *Social Work*, Mimi Silber and Ayala Pines found that of the street prostitutes studied (many of whom were children), 60% of the adult prostitutes had been sexually abused by "an average of 2 males each," some having been molested by up to 11 different males; 90% knew their abusers. But most prostitutes were not adults: 60% were 16 or under, many were younger than 13, and almost 80% had become prostitutes before age 18.

A recent study by pornography researcher Edward Donnerstein compared the effects of erotica (sexual content without violence) and pornography (sexual activity that was violent and abusive). When male college students (prescreened to weed out abnormally hostile individuals), were exposed to erotica and pornography, their erotic response was significantly higher to pornography.

Not all aspects of the sex industry are directly violent, although marketing a woman's body as a commodity can never be nonabusive. One must question alleged "free agents" who claim to willingly become involved in activities that they deny are exploitive. The dividing line between pornography and erotica is debatable, and some believe that there is no difference between the two.

With the exception of erotica, which is a mere corner of the vast pornography industry, an industry that operates in the open and through secret networks of child pornographers and pedophiles, is not a victimless industry. It is based on a view of women and children that endorses and supports their victimization. Women who are involved in the industry, from prostitutes to strippers to actresses to the women who pose for what are called "split beaver" shots in the magazines, are truly at risk. Some women are battered, murdered, robbed, and raped as part of their work; other women are sexually abused as a consequence of the impact of pornography on men. (In some states, a prostitute who is raped has no protection under the law, for it cannot be rape, in the eyes of the laws of those states, if the victim is a prostitute.)

The connection between incest and later activity in these areas is enormous. Raped and exploited in childhood, these survivors later take the reins of their own exploitation, deceiving themselves into believing that they now have control over their lives. Sometimes they merely become "promiscuous," the label we use to describe women who are more sexual than we want them to be. In one sense, the difference between promiscuity and prostitution is only a matter of degree: as Sandra Butler says, many incest survivors feel that as long as they are obligated to have sex with men, "they might as well get paid for it."

Despite the judgment society places on women who exhibit this behavior, it is only wrong because the woman who pursues it is hurting herself. Like those who criticize pornography from some self-appointed stance as society's moral guardians, those who judge promiscuous women have no real concern for the woman herself; she is a new kind of object, not a sexual object, but an object for carrying out someone else's moral agenda. In this way, the moralists are like those who exploit women in the sex industry: they use women for their own purposes. They are like the incest perpetrator as well.

Like teenage runaways (for many of whom prostitution is inevitable), women in the sex industry are often imprisoned by "the life," unable to leave for practical and emotional reasons. Their self-esteem has been decimated (partly a response to the message that no straight person will ever respect them as human beings, a message that both pimps and society reinforce). They are unfamiliar with society's values, rules, and roles. They have acquired drug habits. Some women feel addicted to the control, power, danger, and money of prostitution.

The movie *Stripper* clearly illustrates this major consequence of incest. Perhaps as a straight audience, we cannot identify with the naked woman who pretends to whip herself as trails of stage blood drip down her skin, or the woman who rubs her nude body up and down a metal pole. We know the attitude society takes toward strippers: they are loose, immoral, "bad." But we are introduced to the caring and responsive mother preparing a birthday party for her daughter; we see women who work hard as dancers and athletes and are quite talented. In many ways, they are ordinary women. Yet they feel that their only choice is to perform naked on a sexual stage. Perhaps their lifestyles would make more sense to us if we understood the pain and abuse of their pasts. Survival has always meant performing and tolerating exploitation. So they, too, are "survivors." But the price they've paid is the hardness that comes from every day enduring danger, degradation, and hopelessness.

The wasted lives, the wasted strengths, the wasted hopes and dreams of these women, is a death formalized by their involvement in the sex industry. Some call this self-destructiveness. But is that term really accurate?

Self-Destructiveness and Choices

Not all women who appear to be self-destructive actually are. A woman who is trapped in an abusive situation lacks the freedom to be held responsible for intentionally, willfully, harming herself.

Similarly, the addictions (and other aftereffects that can harm the incest survivor) are not necessarily self-destructive. They are an attempt to avoid pain; whatever damage might accompany these aftereffects is merely a side effect, like the side effect that might accompany the use of a prescription drug. The person isn't really self-destructive, because she is not taking the pills for their negative effect.

Many survivors pursue behaviors that damage their minds, bodies, spirits, relationships. Can't any of this be called "self-destructive?" Labels such as these address not only the consequences of acts, but their intentions as well.

Certainly these women may damage their lives. But generally they do not hurt themselves purposefully. At first they may not know they have choices; they may not have the power to make choices. Often they do not feel that they deserve better. *But the incest victim did not cause these problems.* She was crippled by the misconduct of another. So she is not responsible for having the problem in the first place. She is responsible only for what she does about it today.

So let us use this term not to blame, judge, or criticize, but to describe. Starting today, the incest survivor owns her life. But taking ownership may require time, help, and compassion. Yes, she must work toward seeing the ways in which she hurts herself, and learn to do things differently (or some things, not at all). But let's remember how things got to this point.

Self-Injury

Although much of the victimization described so far in this chapter is done to incest survivors by others, at the end of this continuum of victimization, self-destructiveness, and self-abuse is self-injury, or "cutting." Recognized for less than a decade as an aftereffect of incest, the behavior has come much more into our understanding due to the efforts of Karen Conterio, a Chicago-based consultant for self-injury.

I had been addressing this behavior as an aftereffect of incest without encountering any understanding of it from anyone in the profession other than incest specialists, when in 1985 I saw Karen Conterio on "The Donahue Show," and we began corresponding. My clinical experience, she said, validated her own theories about common themes I'd seen in "cutters." She shared with me her substantial knowledge on this behavioral disorder, and I shared with her the relationship of self-injury to incest, of which she had been unaware. Since then, Ms. Conterio has been a valuable resource. What follows, whether in my words or a section she co-authored, is from her work.

Self-injuring behavior is an addictive pattern. Like the addictions, it is designed to relieve unmanageable stresses or emotions, temporarily dulling them but resulting in feelings of guilt and powerlessness. Like the addictions, it is progressive. It also results in highly manipulative behavior: women (most sufferers are female) who injure themselves generally are unable to identify or deal with their feelings, resorting to the "payoffs" (such as caretaking) derived from self-injury for the attention that they cannot admit they need. This is another primary disorder that must be arrested before the trauma and pain that underlie it can be addressed in therapy.

Therapists must take a firm stand for abstinence from self-injuring behavior just as they would for an alcoholic's sobriety. Self-injuring individuals can manipulate the systems they turn to for help. Psychiatric hospitals, for instance, often perpetuate the abuse by treating these patients like helpless people, paying a lot of attention to their self-induced wounds and little to their incest.

The incest survivor is a candidate for self-injury. She cannot allow herself to experience her emotional pain, but she has developed a huge tolerance for physical abuse. ("I just split off" is the matter-of-fact way many incest survivors explain what they do when faced with physical pain.) Anger, need, disappointment, fear, self-blame, rejection all tap into deep reservoirs of pain, and all may feel unmanageable to the survivor who injures herself. Cutting distracts her, relieves the tension, and provides a kind of hypnotic state or high.

The woman who injures herself may or may not feel pain from the act. For some women whose connection with the sensations of their bodies is nearly severed, to feel the pain of the self-injury is a signal that their mind-body split is being repaired.

Along with Armando Favazzo, a psychiatrist interested in her work, Conterio sent a survey on self-injury to 1250 people; 250 responded. The results were published in the spring 1988 *Community Mental Health Journal* under the title "The Plight of Chronic Self-Mutilators." Some of Conterio's thoughts follow.

SELF-INJURY

by Karen Conterio, C.G.F., and MaryJo Bever, R.N.

Self-injuring behavior has been referred to as cutting, self-abuse, self-mutilation, self-injury, para-suicide, and deliberate self-harm. We have chosen self-injury as the most accurate and acceptable term.

The most common specific behaviors are cutting, burning, breaking bones, pinching skin, ingesting, injecting and inserting foreign material, interfering with the healing process of wounds, punching, slapping, picking skin, and pulling hair.

We believe that the self-injurer is unable to accept or express uncomfortable or overwhelming feelings due to underlying emotional conflicts usually resulting from early traumatic childhood experiences. Frequently the trauma is incest.

Hatred of Body

In our study 49% of self-injurers stated that they had been sexually abused and 45% stated that they had been physically abused. (Some respondents experienced both types of abuse; hence, the overlap.)

The child makes sense of the violations against her body by incorporating a negative body image: "My body is bad or I am bad; that's why this is happening to me." Later in life, the self-injurer continues to exhibit "hateful behavior" toward her own body. This becomes a negative self-validation: "I am bad because I do bad; I deserve for bad things to happen to me." Self-injury may be a direct expression of self-blame. One woman who continually injured one of her hands was eventually able to share that she was attempting to destroy the hand that had been forced to touch a neighbor's penis. Women who self-injure frequently state "I hate my breasts. I hate my periods. I'd be better off without a vagina." Some self-injurers inject urine or feces into their bodies; this behavior demonstrates how desperate the need of the self-injurer is to make sense of her earlier experiences.

Physical Pain More Manageable Than Emotional Pain

Through self-injuring behavior, deeply rooted emotional pain is converted to manageable physical pain. Persons who are in emotional pain and who lack a capacity to express it in emotional terms express their pain physically, at the same time manipulating attention by injuring themselves. Physical pain is tangible, while emotional pain is abstract. Physical wounds can be attended to with immediate results; what is obvious can be treated. For the most part, women who self-injure can accept attention to physical wounds without having to face their emotional wounds.

Self-Hatred

Self-injurers feel deep self-hatred. They often make such degrading statements as, "I deserve to be dead," "I'm stupid," "I'm ugly,"

"I'm such a jerk, why would anyone want to be with me? I wish I'd never been born." Thus they assert the only identity that feels real to them and that makes them feel real: a negative one. "See, I was bad. That's why those bad things happened to me."

Blood

Blood-letting is a core feature of the ritual of self-injury. Blood is the universal component of life. Here are some typical statements from self-injurers: "Seeing my own blood makes me feel alive when I feel so dead inside." "I know that if all else fails and leaves me feeling emotionless and empty, the pain and blood will always be there for me." Blood is also commonly associated with worth and nurturing by self-injurers, and the absolute predictability of their being able to produce it feels reassuring. Additionally, blood shocks people and gets their attention; although that attention is negative, attention is attention. Self-injuring women state that menstruation is an occurrence out of their control; cutting is experienced as a way to control the bleeding from their bodies.

A strong component in the life experience of these women is feeling out of control as a child [an especially common outcome of incest]. They continue to strive for control, although it is achieved through hurtful methods, such as blood-letting.

Feeling Numb

One of the primary goals of self-injuring is to numb feelings. Injuring is usually preceded by a period of agitation; even though injurers report feeling dead, they are actually experiencing an intense emotional state, or they are feeling anxious in anticipation of such a state. What they describe as "dead" is probably an intense feeling of sadness, fear, hopelessness, or grief about conscious or unconscious painful memories. They have never learned ways of self-soothing, so they paradoxically resort to self-injury, because it has helped them in the past.

During sexual abuse the victim copes with the trauma by detaching herself from the act through finding a safe place in her mind to which to escape. The injuring acts in much the same way, by allowing the person to escape, once again, from feelings that are too intense. Seemingly, she escapes from one pain into another, but what is actually sought is the state of numbness. The world feels safer when she is numb; she is less vulnerable, and feels infinitely more in control.

All-or-Nothing Outlook

Physically, when self-injurers feel all their emotions, they become overwhelmed; this feeling of being overwhelmed leads them to injure, thus producing the nothing feeling. Psychologically, their outlook on the world is split into two parts, good and bad. This attitude colors how they view almost everything in their lives. Preserving the good in a parent, for example, prevents them from seeing the bad in that parent, even if the parent's behavior was destructive toward them. Therefore, when bad feelings toward a parent emerge, they often injure themselves. This is done to preserve the all-important good feelings associated with dependence and nurturing, or to distract them from feelings about a needed person that they cannot acknowledge.

Guilt

Numerous self-injurers are also incest survivors who frequently blame themselves for the incest. Guilt is often a catalyst for self-injuring. Through time, many self-injurers benefit from the reduction of feelings of guilt that comes from positive validation from therapeutic groups or individual work with a therapist. The therapeutic process is complex because as the secret of incest is brought out, frequently the survivor becomes more vulnerable. Survivors often begin to have memories and flashbacks and self-injuring incidents usually increase, controlling the terror, guilt, and confusion surrounding the violation.

Anger

Self-injurers are often angry people who cannot admit to, or do not know how to express, their anger. Their self-hate and hatred of their bodies make their bodies the perfect object for the focus of their anger. They may "take the anger out on themselves," or they may cut to cut off the anger that they do not think they can have and live. In a typical scenario, a self-injurer experiences some type of emotional crisis, a therapist or significant other tries helping by providing verbal nurturing, understanding, and a lot of attention, only to have the person injure herself anyway. The helper usually feels frustrated, powerless, and angry. The client now feels numb.

In these situations the self-injurer desires for the other person to take all of the pain away in some magical way; obviously the other person cannot. That failure stimulates intense rage in the self-injurer, which is intolerable for her to feel toward a person she depends on and needs to see as good. In her mind, then, the only safe place to direct the rage is toward herself. There is a desperate need to keep her external world under control. This need originates in the early traumatic experiences where the person felt destructively controlled; later, the adult expresses needs through negative, demanding, manipulative behaviors, thus eliciting angry feeling in others. The counterproductive nature of this method of fulfillment is striking: the person wants a drink of water; she asks for milk. You give her milk. She becomes enraged because you should have known she really wanted a drink of water!

The essence of childhood safety is trust and security. When this trust is violated, as in incest, the child is forced to create her own safety net. Paradoxically, the cutter's safety net is self-destruction [in its effect], self-abusive, and ineffective.

* * *

Overcoming Self-Injury Self-injury strongly reflects the guilt, shame, and entrapment of incest as well as other emotional themes. "Take that," the injurer's acts say to the source of her anger, which is herself. It is herself because she hates herself; it is also directed to herself because she has been cut off from other outlets.

The self-injurer often hurts herself while in a depersonalized or split state. She must trace the steps that lead to the act, as must an alcoholic who "just ended up in" a bar with a drink in her hand.

In a way, self-injuring is the ultimate denial of her hateful body, which she views as the cause of her sexual abuse. To strike out against her own body is a way of saying, "My body is not me!" If the self-injurer has so totally numbed herself that she feels no pain, she can almost claim that her offending body does not exist. When it results in bleeding, cutting can also be seen as purging the poisons of her contaminated body.

The particulars of the injuring behavior can be a window for significant aspects of the original trauma. Michelle, for instance, spent many months exploring in therapy a pattern that she could not change: her self-injury would always occur when she was in the bathroom. Thinking that this was because of the temptation that the bathroom mirror offered, we developed escape plans such as writing a note on the mirror saying "STOP!", covering the mirror, and making a phone call instead of sitting in front of the mirror.

One day, on a hunch I said, "Michelle, what happened to you in the bathroom?" Her face flushed and formed into the expression that always represented her reluctant facing of the truth. Shortly thereafter began a rapid unblocking of memories of abuses she suffered at the hands of both parents (but mostly her mother) in the bathroom.

Conterio stresses the importance of having recovery groups specifically designed to address self-injury, rather than attempting to address the syndrome through generalized models or those used for addictions (the 12-step groups). "S.A.F.E." (Self Abuse Finally Ends) is a short-term (6-week) contract-based group. Members are discouraged from identifying themselves through a "disease" (she does apply the disease model to this behavior) and are prohibited from talking about the specific methods of injury that they used. Competition to see who is the best or "baddest" is thus avoided. The focus of the group is the view that self-injuring behavior is a choice; the skills necessary for its alternative, expression of feelings, are taught.

Indeed the alternative to any such coping mechanism gone awry is, at the core, the same: deal with the feelings. If we do not tell people what we feel, we cannot expect anybody to know how we feel. Sometimes we do things that keep us from knowing what we feel and then we get stuck in our confusion. We avoid sharing our feelings honestly and wonder why communication goes sour. To identify, share, and examine our lives and choices through our feelings, especially the parts of our lives that are not working, is to reclaim our power and our peace. All our addictions have, as an alternative, facing and finding safety with our feelings.

THE UN-VICTIM

This is Jessica's dream:

I was parked in a remote area. Desolate. A guy came over to the car. He said he wanted drugs but I just had a feeling he wanted sex, you know? He said, "You're right, I want sex." And then I knew he wanted to rape me. I said, "You know what I like?"—in a very seductive voice. He said, "No, what?" "I like to sit on a hot ————." (I said it in the dream, but I can't say it to you.)

He broke into a grin. And I opened my jacket, and pulled out my lighter, and held it under his penis till it glowed!!

Revenge isn't necessary to end victimization, but dreams can be wonderful arenas for reworking attitudes. Jessica obviously no longer saw herself as a victim, which was reflected in the contents of the dream.

Victimization is about power, boundaries, trust, and security. For the incest survivor, it is about sex, self-esteem, and choices as well. If she believes she deserves nothing better, she will manifest an attitude that makes her vulnerable to continuing victimization. To end this pattern, the survivor must dare to be assertive, and risk saying NO.

12

AT WAR WITH THE BODY

We are a confused society—trapped between repressive attitudes about our body parts and their functions, and the 42nd Street mentality that equates sexual freedom with *Playboy* and Frederick's of Hollywood.

LESSONS IN AN IDEAL WORLD

In a healthy society children learn to respect their bodies, to find the beauty of their uniqueness, to discover the names of all their body parts with equal delight. They know when to be proud and when to be private. They respect the variety within their own gender, and differences from the other, without competition or criticism. Children whose early lives are free of abuse learn that they own their bodies: they can decide who can touch them and how. When they must rely on others to take care of their needs, they learn that there is safety in being taken care of. They learn that touch feels warm and reassuring, and that when something goes wrong with their body, it can and should be helped or corrected. They learn that their bodies deserve respect, positive regard, and proper attention. They learn what is appropriate touch, what is inappropriate touch, and what is truly giving or taking—and how to decide.

They also learn that their bodies can be the source of great joy, or the site of a challenge for personal best, and that one is not worth less or more because of how that body looks or performs. It is a thrill to win a race, but the runner is no more worthy than someone who is in a wheelchair. They learn that their body, mind, and emotions are interconnected. They learn that their bodies are for *themselves,* not for the use, satisfaction, or appraisal of anyone else.

WHAT INCEST TEACHES

The child who experiences incest learns that her body is not hers. She learns that touch is not affection, but violation. Touch does not bond or reassure—it hurts and confuses her. She learns also that there is no separateness between her body and that of her abuser, and that her small size and her weaknesses put her at risk. *Her body puts her in jeopardy.* If the perpetrator focuses solely on his own satisfaction, she is likely to learn that her body is designed for the pleasure of others at the expense of her own comfort; if he focuses on touching her to stimulate her, she may learn to feel betrayed by her own arousal. If she fought back at the time of the abuse, she may experience less guilt in later life; the abuser's response, however, may be violence, the price paid for emotional "security."

Her body is the battlefield on which the incest is played out. It stores her pain and her memories. It also stores her self-blame.

THE AFTEREFFECTS: THE BODY AND ITS FUNCTIONS

In the incest survivor's eyes, her body gets her into trouble, "attracts" the unwanted attentions of the perpetrator. Self-hate, shame, ugliness and alienation are common attitudes of incest survivors toward their bodies. In reaction, she generally feels disconnected from her body. During the initial abuse, and during later life when these attitudes prevail, seeing her body as the site and source of her violation, she may separate from her own physical self to separate from her pain, discomfort, and embarrassment. To endure her negative attitude toward her body, she may believe that the self and the body are not the same. She doesn't live there by choice. She's being incarcerated.

Throughout her life, all aspects of her physical self are affected: appearance, health, physical presence and experiences, physical responses, and body functions, as well as sexuality, which will be discussed in the next chapter.

Touch

Touch can be frightening, angering, or painful to an incest survivor. She frequently misinterprets it. She has no basis on which to judge the other person's intentions; therefore, she cannot know how to react. In her experience, touch often foreshadows a demand. It is, therefore, threatening.

Claudia's skin crawled when she felt someone's breath on her, or when someone's face was too close to hers. (As described earlier, the incest survivor may feel that her boundaries are extended. For Claudia to feel as if something had crossed her physical boundary, it did not need to touch her skin.) The incest survivor may hate being tickled. She may react particularly negatively to adult play that includes "forced touch" such as tickling or that impedes her movement.

Clothing

Many incest survivors are either extremely modest or immodest. Some overprotect their bodies, totally unable to dress in a way that suggests sexuality. Others seem almost compulsively provocative in exposing themselves with low necklines and tight-fitting clothes.

Many incest survivors avoid nakedness at all costs. They feel a terror associated with nakedness: to be naked is to be unprotected.

To be minimally dressed is to be exposed, available. Little girls are put on display, their miniskirts hardly covering their frilly underpants, while little boys, at worst, wear pants that reveal their knees. Adult women continue to be burdened with the expectation that they wear skirts or dresses (which makes the sexual area more accessible than pants do).

Nakedness. Exposure. Defenselessness. Clothing provides actual or symbolic protection: it covers and blocks access. One area that incest survivors often seek to protect is the neck, an area of vulnerability that is generally erogenous and is covered in some cultures. These incest survivors commonly wear turtlenecks, scarves, and the like.

The incest survivor wears clothes when others freely discard them or wears more of them. For instance, she may don shorts (or more) for the beach.

A surprising number of incest survivors feel a compulsive need to bathe in their underpants, or shower in their clothes. In addition to being inconvenient and messy, this behavior is an understandable source of embarrassment. Because of it, they avoid many social situations such as the local health club and swimming.

She may insist on sleeping in clothes, or at least reserve the choice to wear clothes to bed with a partner when she needs to feel safe. When she chooses not to do so, she is telling her partner that tonight she feels trusting, but that does not necessarily mean that she feels sexual as well.

Poor Body Image

Many women devalue their bodies whether or not they are survivors of sexual trauma. For the incest survivor, poor body image is complicated and destructive. Many incest survivors associate being a woman with being a victim, and so hate the womanness of their bodies, especially the parts connected with sexuality or attracting sexual attention.

To dissociate from the body or to protect the self from unwanted sexual attention (which is experienced as violation), the incest survivor downplays sexuality in behavior and dress. She may eschew makeup and styled hair, and may be seen as plain or perhaps, in the extreme, poorly groomed. She willingly faces potential rejection or social ridicule in order to be left alone. (Some women—who may or may not be incest survivors—dress this way as a political statement, challenging the social demand that women comply with certain manners of dress.)

Although sexual harassment and rape are not predicated upon the sexual appeal of the victim, she distances herself from unwanted personal attentions. Outsiders, including her therapist, might think that she is not taking good care of herself; in fact, she is taking care of herself in the best way she knows how, by saying, "Look, I'm not available for your sexual interest. Leave me alone." Unfortunately, by dressing this way she is not addressing the core issue—the presence of Post-Incest Syndrome and its behavioral and attitudinal indications of victimization.

Manipulating Body Size

To protect themselves from sexually-oriented responses, some survivors manipulate their body size. A survivor might choose to be large

and unapproachably powerful, or invisible and childlike in her thinness, or perfect through bulimia. (These addictive disorders are discussed in Chapter 10.) By controlling the only thing over which she
feels she has power, her body, she continues her victimization.

Sexual "Acting Out"

Whereas some incest survivors attempt to downplay or eliminate
any semblance of adult sexuality, others become what they have been
treated as being: persons reduced to their sexual purpose. They learned
to see themselves this way, they are used to experiencing the world this
way, and they continue to act this way.

It may feel like a choice. It is not. Whether she expresses anger by
proclaiming, "OK, suckers, this is what you think I am like, this is
what I will be" (which is anger turned inward, as she is the one who is
hurt) or she has stopped caring, these forms of sexual acting-out are
representative of Post-Incest Syndrome. Already detached from her
body, already accustomed to paying with her body for love, attention,
and a place in the world, already used to living her life through her
body, she may use this body as a commodity.

Feeling Unclean

Sex is a physically dirty experience for the child. It involves sweat
and semen, and it's messy, and it smells. For some, the smell never
seems to leave. It elicits negative reactions when experienced in later
life.

More significant is the sense of uncleanliness that occurs primarily
on the psychic level. The shame and guilt of the incest, the overriding
feeling of being bad, manifests physically as feeling dirty. Eventually,
the incest survivor may not associate these feelings with anything concrete; her sense of self is stained. As described in the section on
obsessive-compulsive disorder (Chapter 10), this feeling manifests itself
as either extreme of personal hygiene.

Swallowing and Gagging Sensitivity

Many survivors have an overactive gag reflex. They choke easily
on food; they find it difficult or impossible to take pills or brush their

teeth. The origin of this aftereffect is obvious: forced oral sex in childhood. To fully appreciate the impact of this experience, consider the size of the average adult male's erect penis and the size of a child's mouth. Survivors commonly associate a feeling of suffocation with various aftereffects, especially this one. Related is the experience of being nauseated over having to endure deeply repulsive acts. Nausea is another consequence, along with choking, of this gag reaction. (The child may have been choked or threatened with choking or smothering as well.)

Sensitivity to Water on the Face

Some incest survivors report being unable to breathe or catch their breath when water unexpectedly hits their faces. Some are almost paralyzed with terror. As a result, some survivors forgo showers for baths; some never learn to swim; several say they have avoided washing their faces for years.

This aftereffect might relate to the fact that water is associated with bathing and swimming, two activities where the child is naked or minimally dressed and where an adult is permitted some physical access to the child—access that may be pushed beyond permissible limits. However, the origin of this aftereffect is elusive. All I have been able to suggest is the possible scenario where oral sex was followed by rushed washing of the victim's face, often as she sputtered and struggled to breathe. Oral sex itself could also be a cause—but oral sex has not always occurred.

Avoidance of Public Bathrooms

Many survivors cannot use public bathrooms; others resist using bathrooms in other people's homes. Their discomfort may have many roots.

Using the bathroom is a private act. Generally, one is to some degree undressed. Further, the elimination of body wastes is often considered the most private act of all: many people avoid talking about it, consider it to be dirty, find it to be more private than the sexual act or other forms of simple nakedness. When in real life do we discuss these functions? With doctors? With whom else? Even when we do, what terms do we use? "Going to the bathroom," as it is euphemistically called, has no place in polite society. We have such a variety of terms for the acts of sex, but we can't integrate these acts or the words that describe them; we may walk around naked with someone present, have sex with other people, but we "go to the bathroom" in isolation.

For the incest survivor, to whom privacy is a primary need and protection, this already concealed act often requires absolute seclusion or a place that is totally within her control: her own space, her own home.

Incest experiences may involve bathrooms as a general association with a violation of privacy, or as a site of actual violation because of the privacy and protection that they afford the violator. Using the bathroom which already has associations with embarrassment, is, for the survivor, fraught with risk and the danger of invasion. When she uses public facilities, in addition to whatever reminder of trauma it may arouse, there is the feeling of exposure associated with disrobing in a public place.

At the other extreme, the incest survivor may have become so accustomed to having no privacy that she never needs or expects any. Or she may think she doesn't, and act like she doesn't when other people are around, but be secretive and furtive when she is by herself (when it's safe to "act out" the need).

Resistance to Defecation

As one incest survivor put it, "I hold it in for days, even if it hurts. Taking control in that way makes the pain feel *good*. I hold it in just for the sake of not letting it out."

Is this evidence of the psychoanalytic assumption that there is an anal stage which, if not resolved, creates an anal-retentive personality in adult life? That approach dilutes real-life traumas into universal theories that contain many unproved presumptions, when in fact something real and specific is going on. This reaction to defecation has little to do with a developmental stage and the symbolic meaning of toilet training and resistance. More relevant is the fact that the child's anal orifice is an available and much-used opening for the fingers and penis of the perpetrator. Consequently, the survivor associates physical and emotional pain with the release of feces: "After I'm done, I feel empty, as if something that had once filled me—something that had hurt—were now gone." It may be that this organically necessary act is a constant physical and emotional replay of an actual incest experience.

Alienation from Body; Failure to Heed Signals of or to Take Care of Body; Hatred of Physical Self

One way to separate from the violation of incest is not to be with one's body: my body is not my *self,* is not me. This may manifest itself in a variety of ways. Some incest survivors may not pay attention to the pains or other signals of an illness, may let a cough or skin growth go on unattended for months; they may not groom themselves, or may avoid or be indifferent to mirrors. Often they feel no wholeness with their physical selves, no continuity between the experiences of their physical feelings and their bodies.

Physically the incest survivor may be awkward, out of step with herself. She may be angry at her body or inconvenienced by it, or it may simply not occur to her to pay attention to its internal workings or external presence.

Physical Symptoms

The incest survivor is prone to stress-related diseases: migraines, headaches, joint pains, gastrointestinal problems. One aspect of this problem is being investigated by Barbara B. Young, a researcher from Silver Spring, Md., who is investigating her hypothesis that cluster migraines, a particularly relentless form of migraine headaches are characteristic of the post-incest experience. She sees them as "an existential as well as a medical expression of rage, [whose] periodicity serves to 'drain off' excess rage and relieve the guilt caused by murderous feelings resulting from the abuse."

Considerable attention has been paid to the relationship between stress and disease. The mind, the feelings, and the body interact. Strain in one area affects the others. Pain, disease (dis-ease), or dysfunction in one can weaken the others. There is a physical explanation for this, concerning the effect of stress on immune system function and brain chemistry. The untreated incest survivor, with traumatic memories and pain trapped inside a body from which she has long been alienated, is a prime candidate for stress-related illnesses such as these for two reasons: first, she continues to endure systemic stresses (on the physical, emotional, and intellectual self) of unhealed wounds, and, second, she may continue to act in the self-abusive and neglectful manner of post-incest syndrome.

She is also swallowing a lot of pain. Holding pain inside and not expressing it or dealing with it can result in illnesses of the body, addictions, and emotional or mental disturbances. Her body is expressing what she cannot: this *hurts*.

At the same time, her existence is defined by a number of destructive emotional states: fear, guilt, hopelessness, internalized anger, powerlessness. There is the absence of such healing states as self-esteem, and the ability to trust and bond with others. These conditions not only take a deep emotional toll, but can also, as states of stress, create toxins that reduce the effectiveness of the body's autoimmune system and lead to physical deterioration. All these circumstances convene in the body of the survivor, putting her at increased risk for stress-related illness.

Whether we describe these medical problems as stemming from internalized anger, stress-related illness, or through other schools of thought—whether we see them from a holistic, psychological, or feminist point of view—the important factor is their prevalence among incest survivors, and their relationship to the meaning of the incest experience.

Researchers at Southern Methodist and Ohio State University have discovered some interesting information regarding these stress-related illnesses. They found that trauma experienced in childhood had more to do with health problems in adults than did more recent traumas. They found a significant correlation between the nonexpression of feelings and medical problems: respondents who said they never discussed their problems had more major and minor illnesses. Not surprisingly, the facts of a situation were not important to share, but the feelings.

Additional research has revealed that child abuse and rape contribute to heart attack and stroke. Christina Crawford, whose (nonsexual) abuse at the hands of her mother, actress Joan Crawford, was revealed in *Mommie Dearest,* suffered a stroke at the relatively young age of 42; from age 14 on she had migraines. She attributes both to having been beaten as a child.

The good news is that talking about these feelings actually boosts immune function, actually correcting the reduced functioning that trauma produces. As reported by Jamie Talen in a 1987 *Newsday* article, while initially people felt worse both physically and emotionally (probably from the stress of facing the pain), over time they proved to be happier and healthier than those who had not talked about their problems. Talking helps. As the Hungarian proverb says, when you share joy, you double it; when you share your pain, you halve it.

Crying helps too. Scientists have found that tears from sadness contain toxins—the toxins manufactured by the body in stress. Crying really does cleanse not only the soul, but the body as well!

Gynecological Problems

The mind-body connection of stress-related illnesses, in conjunction with the nature of incest as being experienced through sexual and localized body functions, yields a particular grouping of aftereffects that is, once again, highly symbolic and specific: incest survivors frequently experience physical problems that are concentrated in the female or reproductive organs. Some survivors are so alienated from their bodies that they are unable to do breast self-examinations or submit to necessary tests, thus compounding the problem.

The experience of incest produces medical problems that would not otherwise exist in children: urinary tract and vaginal infections, syphilis, gonorrhea. To these problems are added others in Post-Incest Syndrome: ovarian cysts, fibro-cystic disease of the breast, uterine fibroid tumors, painful periods (dysmenorrhea), endometriosis, and the cessation of menses (amenorrhea). There might be a correlation between an incest history and postpartum depression or psychosis; for many incest survivors, childbirth triggers incest issues. These medical problems offer a variety of directions for research.

There is also a high occurrence of premenstrual syndrome (PMS), which is experienced as an emotional syndrome although it is thought to have a physiological base. It is difficult at this time to ascertain whether PMS occurs disproportionately among incest survivors. In my clinical experience, women who suffer from this disorder feel victimized and act nonassertively; then, being unable to take charge of their lives or express the resentments that accumulate, they experience depressed or explosive mood swings when their hormones go out of whack. This passive/victim life view is similar to that of the survivor who has not had treatment. I recognize that PMS is largely a physiological malfunction, but I suggest that various forces may be interacting.

Psychoanalysts have long explained gynecological problems as representing women's rejection of, or reaction to, their femininity or their feminine role. Incest survivors do not reject womanhood per se; they reject powerlessness and sexual victimization—which, in many ways, happen to overlap with the traditional definition of femininity, but are not about womanhood in itself or the survivors' attitude toward (victimization-free) womanhood. These women are reacting with disease at the sites of their abuse. For many incest survivors these areas, and their female status, equate with the abuse; sexuality and victimization become synonymous. Remember: rape and incest are about violation, not sexuality.

Aversion to Doctors, Especially Gynecologists, Dentists and Anesthesiologists

Many incest survivors remember feeling victimized and terrorized as children by having to undergo required medical procedures without any consideration for their fears or other feelings. Even the routine manipulations and explorations of the common childhood medical examination can feel like violations to the child if they are presented without sensitivity.

Many victims of abuses, including incest, experienced visits to doctors who they thought would see evidence of their abuse, or who actually did see this evidence but did nothing. The child could easily have felt as if the doctor didn't care or was part of the conspiracy. (The child may well have been right. Doctors may be sexual abuse perpetrators, too.) When her abuser is Doctor Sam, the man who has assisted the births of three generations in the town, whom will the townspeople believe? And of course, her powerlessness and entrapment are reinforced.

I have heard a number of stories of another type of victimization that incest survivors have experienced at the hands of doctors or dentists. More than one woman has told me that when, as an abused child, she turned to a doctor for help, or confessed her abuse to him as an adult, she was again molested—by the doctor.

Doctors are relative strangers who are routinely allowed to touch our bodies. They are also usually men (although the numbers are changing) whose social and professional training inclines them to view their role as detached scientists rather than nurturers. They are often described by patients as being either abrupt, patronizing, insensitive, unwilling to adequately explain to patients what is happening to their bodies, failing to treat patients as equals who are entitled to make their own decisions (for which they have been provided with adequate information by the practitioner). Worse, they often appear to be unwilling to end, or unable to comprehend, the damage that traditional medical practice has done to women.

Many women have more than one horror story of unwarranted medical procedures, unnecessary pain, emotional neglect or abuse, and even sexual abuse at the hands of their physicians, including their psychiatrists. While these problems are being addressed by concerned male and female physicians today, they continue to occur, both to survivors and nonsurvivors. However, some element of the victim mentality occurs for some survivors who take a passive role in their lives and then feel "done to." In some situations, where they complain that their needs were not heard, this may partly be due to their failure to say what then was not heard.

Small wonder, then, that so many incest survivors, who already feel violated, who are protecting their bodies so assiduously, avoid seeing doctors. The physical exam, which involves nakedness and touch, is a source of trauma for the incest survivor. Even worse is the gynecological exam, during which she is touched by someone, usually male, in the area of her greatest vulnerability, while required to lie in a position of total submission and passivity—one which most women find to be a challenge to their dignity. Similarly, the dental exam can be reminiscent of early abuses in a direct way. And, of course, the anesthesiologist renders us totally powerless!

When the incest survivor must go to one of these practitioners, she may insist on seeing a woman, although for some the experience is so fraught with horror that even this is not a solution. The incest survivor especially requires the sharing of the process wherein she is treated as an equal: the sharing of information, the sharing of power, the sharing of decision making. This attitude of partnership is of paramount importance because it helps reinforce that she owns her body. Yet it may not remedy the problem; it will take a lot of work to erase the prevailing social view of doctors as gods. Even if the incest survivor is treated as an equal initially, her self-esteem is so low that a doctor would have to practice humility to be at the same level as she perceives herself.

All of us can be said to benefit from such a relationship with our medical employees; in this issue, as in others, the concerns of the incest survivor are simply exaggerations of those that concern all of us every day. The empowerment and consideration that the incest survivor requires are entitlements that we all share and on which we should all insist.

SEX (Is Not Sex)

The context in which the child victim is first introduced to sex is responsible for numerous distortions in her later life. Sex is not sex for the incest survivor.

WHAT SOCIETY TEACHES ABOUT SEX AND THE SELF

Children are born with a natural sexual awareness and natural curiosity. They are capable of arousal from the start: male fetuses are known to have erections in utero. After birth, infants masturbate and feel pleasure, exploring their bodies' sexual responses just as they explore their other senses. The reactions of self-conscious adults give them messages of shame to accompany this pleasure. When they begin sexual experimentation with other children, which is a normal attempt to learn about the bodies of others and to experience touching and being touched by another person, they learn to shroud these activities in secrecy, for sex and guilt have already become fused.

Our society struggles with its attitudes toward this natural experience, teaching embarrassment, guilt, and shame along with sexuality. We can easily accept sex when it is done for certain reasons, which for women has generally come to mean sex as an obligation, or sex to make babies. But we do not easily accept sex for its own sake or for pleasure: masturbation, sex without reproduction, homosexuality, and sexual activities outside marriage. This has been called "erotophobia," which is a pathological fear of the erotic state of sexual enjoyment. In some states, this fear has been translated into an invasive statute, the sodomy law, whose existence the Supreme Court recently upheld in Georgia v. Hardwick. Rarely is such a law applied to heterosexuals; its intention is to criminalize homosexuality.

A baby girl touches her genitals because the touching *feels good.* She *chooses* whether, when, and how to touch her body. It is within her control. But for many women—not just incest survivors—this moment of sexual self-determination is soon eroded. In an ideal scenario, as the child begins sexual exploration, she chooses as her partners other children, whose bodies and personalities are like hers developmentally. She touches and is touched; she learns what gives pleasure and what does not. Later, her sexual experiments become more focused, progressing from the joys of holding hands to more overtly sexual activities. She learns to distinguish friendly kissing from sexual kissing, affectionate feelings from sexual desires. She experiences kissing, deep kissing, necking, petting, and finally intercourse or other intense, genitally based activities whose purpose is orgasm.

Step by step, she learns which sexual activities she enjoys and which she does not; she decides when she wants to pursue a certain sex act and with whom. And she decides when to lose her virginity. (In an ideal world, this decision is hers, and not the result of pressure or date rape.) She learns to value her body and its sexual expression, to engage in sexual activity for her own pleasure and (maybe) for bonding with a partner. And she learns that this is hers, this experience of sexuality, to do with as she wishes.

It is not only the incest survivor whose experience varies from this ideal. Women frequently do not engage in sex of their own free will. A recent Harris Poll (published in the *SIECUS Report,* which commissioned it) revealed that 17% of adolescent girls have sex because boys pressured them to; no boys reported having sex because of pressure from girls. Often women are deprived of their right to control when they have sex, whether they become pregnant, and how they deal with it if they do; our society has gone so far as to require women to undergo cesarean sections that save the fetus at the expense of the woman's own life. Thus we deprive a woman of her sexuality and treat her as an object whose sole function is reproduction—reproduction according to rules over which she has no control. This is worse then mere erotophobia; this is slavery.

Sex Exists in a Context

Sexuality has many aspects other than erotic function. It concerns *gender identity*, one's relationship with one's assigned gender (only one element of which is biological; much of gender identity has to do with socially assigned roles). Additionally, it concerns one's relationship with the sexual characteristics of one's body, the knowledge of how that body functions in the sexual realm, and what its feelings and reactions are. It also concerns self-esteem (regarding one's body, one's identity as a female or male, and general sense of self-worth). Sex has physical, emotional, mental, and, for some, spiritual components. It involves the entire person.

Sexuality also exists in the context of a person's relationships with herself and with others: strangers, friends, family, and intimates. Despite the assumption that our sexual urges underlie all the pleasures we feel, sex is only one part of our lives and relationships. It is not actively involved in every relationship we have. We must determine whether sexual interest for another person is present in each relationship.

In addition to social and legal issues, sexuality involves issues of trust, dependence and independence, and power. Sex is not about sex alone. It is about sex, relationships, society, and history. It is about life.

Life experience includes both feelings and behavior. Feelings may not be a choice, but behavior, for the most part, is.

Sexuality should be addressed throughout the child's life, in age-appropriate ways that answer the child's needs. The sexual climate in a family—whether the parents seem comfortable in their sexualities, whether comfort and openness prevail—teaches as much as talking about sexuality.

A child who is ignorant about her body does not own her sexuality. And a child who lives in a climate of tension and secrecy about sexuality will be that much less inclined to tell a trusted adult if someone molests her sexually.

WHAT INCEST TEACHES ABOUT SEXUALITY

Normally developing sexuality is of the child's choosing, and incestuous abuse is not. Therefore, the primary message incest sends is that the victim's sexual life is not her own.

Too Much Too Soon

Ideal sexual development involves different activities at different stages. As a person experiences each activity, she integrates it emotionally, physically, and intellectually in a context of equality and comfort. A 5-year-old's sexual interest is much different than that of a 13- or 19- or 30-year-old. An 8-year-old is not attracted to the musculature and body hair of a 40-year-old man. Even when children develop crushes on teachers or camp counselors, their fantasies are not of sexual intercourse, but of cuddling and kissing. But before the child victim has had the chance to go through the stages of feeling and experience that would bring her to adult sexuality, adult sexuality is imposed on her. Even though she has never held hands, someone is masturbating his frightening penis in front of her in an atmosphere of secretiveness and coercion. She has never gently kissed someone who excites her, and now her body has been forced to experience the stimulation of an adult's hand.

Do you remember what it was like when your friends told you about "doing it"? Did the activity sound alluring? Probably not. More likely, when you first heard the news, you thought, "Eeew. Daddy does that to mommy? YICH. My mommy would never do *that!*" But the incested child, even if she doesn't consciously make the connection, feels something quite different. She knows what it feels like to have "it" done to her. And that is how she experiences it, not as something she participates in, but as something done to her; even though she is powerless, she feels responsible. And so the socially imposed shame that she associates with her body is now exacerbated by the additional self-blame that accompanies sexual violation.

Sex can feel dirty and scary enough in this culture; children learn this by what they are told and not told, by the reactions of the adults around them when they are caught doing what comes naturally. Incest reinforces all these negative messages a hundredfold. To violate a child sexually is dirty, awful, shameful. But the child does not—cannot—understand who owns this negativity. So she thinks it is about sex, and she thinks it is about *her.*

Barbara describes the effects of premature sexuality:

I don't know what sex is to normal people. Before I had even gone on a date—before I had done *anything*—I had seen pornographic pictures, had read to my grandfather descriptions of people doing things that were so alien, so awful to me. I knew what sex was— what the *act* was—before I knew what it was to me. I *was never a virgin*, never got to build up to it. I've always been jaded. Sex isn't sex to me, I don't even know what it's like to have sexual desires, or enjoyment.

At the child's developmental level, the sexual activity associated with incest is alien: the child's feelings and understanding are not commensurate with what she is forced to endure. This is not experimentation. It is not education either, though perpetrators use this justification. One does not teach a 5-year-old about sex by raping her.

Sex as Rape

Incest is not only sex ahead of its time; it is sex against her will and, therefore, for her, not sex at all. No matter what physical form it takes, the violation the child experiences makes it rape.

Sometimes sex is the price that is exacted from her for warmth and attention. And if these sometimes wonderful moments of closeness must coexist with terrifying, confusing moments of abuse, she learns to see the two as parts of the same experience.

She grows to think she wanted the incest itself. Because they've become enmeshed, she doesn't know that it was love she wanted, not sex. Only it isn't sex—it is violence and dominance. She comes to believe that she allowed—wanted—to be abused sexually. These contradictory meanings and aspects of the sexual experience combine in the confusion of many adult incest survivors.

The incested child or adolescent also learns that the purpose of her sexuality is the gratification of the other person. She learns that she cannot control what sex acts she becomes involved in, that her body does not yield sexual pleasure, but shame, embarrassment, pain, entrapment, and betrayal: ultimately, she learns that sex is dirty and that it is the same as sacrifice.

Seductiveness and Power

She learns that the way to win approval is with her body—a body that has a strange power over men, but at the same time it is an entity over which she is powerless. She learns to use seductiveness to get what she wants.

Incest reinforces the social message that a woman's role is to be subservient to men, to satisfy them at her expense. She learns this through her experience of abuse, and, sometimes, from her mother's subjugation.

She learns that sex has nothing to do with trust, and certainly nothing to do with equality. Because sex invariably happens when she is unwilling, she learns that it is an obligation: sex becomes dominance.

Incestuous abuse is merely an extension of many women's experience in its distortion of power, imbalance in relationships, and the woman's sense that her body is not hers and sex is not for her gratification. Our society denies women the power of their adulthood; we call them "girls" until they're 90. Although we see women as children, we dress children like grown-ups: we dress 7-year-old models to look 15, and 15-year-olds to look 21. We sexualize children and expect women to look like children. It is not only the child victim of incest who is trained to be "Daddy's little girl."

And how is Daddy's little girl directed to act? We dress her in short skirts that show her ruffled underpants and train her to act "charming"—which means flirtatious and seductive. The pattern continues into adulthood. Daddy's little girl flirts to get Daddy's approval. Then she marries a man whom she calls "Daddy," whose power she defers to; she feels obligated to perform sex with him, and creates, as Phyllis Chesler points out in *Women and Madness,* a new "incest."

The most famous symbol of child seductiveness was little Shirley Temple. In *Shirley Temple: American Princess,* by Anne Edwards, the author describes one "Baby Burlesk" show that featured the child in a black lace bra, playing a "wealthy gold-digger." To "sparkle," a command often directed at her, meant to lick her lips so they looked wet. In a 1937 review of *Wee Willie Winkle,* Graham Greene said Temple had a "mature suggestiveness," and that her admirers—"middle-aged men and clergymen—responded to her dubious coquetry, to the sight of her well-shaped desirable little body"—while referring to her in terms like "a fancy little piece" and a "complete totsy"!

Indeed, as I now write this, there is on television a 5-year-old "beauty pageant" winner, who has been made to wear glistening lipstick and blonde curls, swing her hips and sing, "Hey, good lookin', what you got cookin'? How's about cookin' something up with me?"

As Sandra Butler points out in *Conspiracy of Silence,* "Our culture teaches young girls, implicitly and explicitly, that seductive behavior is the way to get what they want." We teach them also that they can expect to be victims, that they *deserve* to be victims.

It is not something we teach only our girl children; boys learn it as well. Butler cites this sad example: one young boy, after being sexually victimized, said "I felt dirty, disgusting, and nasty. Just like a girl."

Is the consequence of incest really that different from the consequence of being a woman in this society? Psychiatrist Judith Herman observes that women who were incestuously abused in childhood "grow up to be archetypically feminine women: sexy without enjoying sex, repeatedly victimized yet repeatedly seeking to lose themselves in the love of an overpowering man, contemptuous of themselves and other women [while overvaluing men], . . . hardworking, giving, self-sacrificing . . . (and) consumed with inner rage [that they cannot express]."

Marilyn Monroe: Quintessential Woman—Incest Survivor

Norma Jean Baker, the child who became sex symbol Marilyn Monroe, was molested by foster fathers in childhood; her mother was unable to care for her due to mental disability. She wanted to be an actress. She always was an actress. Early in her career, she posed nude for a calendar. Later, she dyed her hair and became the most famous sex symbol of all time. But what did she symbolize? What does it mean that we as a society so revered this symbol of woman-as-victim?

Monroe repeatedly married, or had relationships with, older or more powerful men. Her first marriage was at 16. One marriage was to playwright Arthur Miller, a man of status, power, seriousness. She is generally assumed to have had affairs with President John Kennedy and possibly his brother Robert. She had a breathy, soft voice. She made her fortune by exposing her body. She was what men wanted, and what women wished they could be, or thought they should be. But women also identified with her pain; they often felt protective of her.

She was the image of sex personified, but not for her own sexual fulfillment. Diana Trilling, in her *New York Times* review of Marilyn's recent biography by Gloria Steinem, summarizes it like this:

> She slept with men, and on occasion even with women, in order to please—perhaps also to make herself feel real by their desire for her. Apparently this ability to give rather than to receive pleasure in sex was the whole of her delight. Practiced in the arts of accommodation, she flattered many men into believing that they were the first to satisfy her.

Yet no one satisfied her. According to Jeanne Carmen, Marilyn's friend, Marilyn Monroe never had an orgasm. "She used to fake it." One musician who had a relationship with her said, "Marilyn must have been frustrated almost all of the time . . . I think she [thought] she was supposed to have sex with a man, because that was something she could do, that she could give."

Not surprisingly, Marilyn Monroe abused alcohol and drugs—a problem initially attributed to Hollywood, as in the film *Valley of the Dolls*. She had a lot of pain to anesthetize, not the least of which was her incest. Her chemical abuse persisted despite psychoanalysis. Eventually, it may have killed her. (I am aware of various conspiracy theories concerning her death although they are beyond the scope of this book. Notwithstanding that she may have been murdered, Marilyn had been dying for many years. If murdered, perhaps the consequences of her incest experience made her an easy target.) She was known to have attempted suicide at least nine times. Steinem's book tells us that early in her life she said:

> "Yes, there was something special about me, and I knew what it was. I was the kind of girl they found dead in a hall bedroom with an empty bottle of sleeping pills in her hand."

Trilling wrote of Marilyn:

She didn't die in a hall bedroom but the empty pill bottle is everywhere in Mr. Burris' pictures of her, perhaps especially when, below vacant eyes, she forces her famous smile, radiant and full of promise.

THE AFTEREFFECTS: CONFUSION OF SEX WITH AFFECTION, OBLIGATION, VIOLATION, VIOLENCE

The incest survivor often carries the confusions and lies of incest into her adult relationships.

Sex and Assault

For the incest survivor, affection is not affection; it is sex. And sex is an assault, not making love.

Due to this association, sex may always be equated with anger. Evelyn, an alcoholic incest survivor who struggled to achieve sobriety, could get angry only when she masturbated. Linda could masturbate only when she was already angry.

For many survivors, sex is equated with a posture of dominance or submission, or of abuse, as witnessed by the enormous number of survivors who have sado-masochistic fantasies or engage in S&M.

Generally, a survivor's sexuality bears the brunt of the damage of incest, but not always. One survivor, Nancy, says, "Everyone said the incest should have screwed me up sexually, but it didn't. And so I felt there was something wrong with me—because nothing was wrong with me!"

The incest survivor may experience great passion: she may be very sexual, enjoying sex a lot, and often. She may appear sexual in every pore, expressing her sexuality in how she dresses, moves, and talks. Even in adulthood, she may appear to be a paradoxical combination of sexual precociousness and naivete.

For many incest survivors, sex feels dirty and it always has. But because her image of herself was of a sinful person, she may not have noticed. She is likely, however, to have this negative association with her sexuality.

The child who is sexually abused is forced to be sexually involved before she has a fully developed sense of herself. The identity she develops as a person is inextricably entwined with training that she is a sexual object. At the same time, the image she develops of what it means to be a woman is impaired.

Her sexuality may be alien to her or riddled with guilt. She may struggle to accept herself as sexual and as a woman. However it occurs, her sexuality is almost never uncomplicated. It affects her relationship with herself, her partners, and, if she has them, her children; it affects what she teaches them about sex, about women, and about men. It can interfere with her relationship with her sons, because they are the same gender as her abuser. It can interfere with her relationship with her daughters, because when a woman hates her womanhood, she can impede her daughters' ability to love themselves as well.

Sexualizing Relationships

Generally, men sexualize relationships and women "affectionalize" them. Women are reluctant to be sexual when there is not the bond of relationship, while men are encouraged to bounce from one genital experience to another. However, a common aftereffect for incest survivors is the tendency to sexualize their relationships. Sexual contact makes a relationship real for many survivors, who often cannot make sense out of a relationship that contains no sexual activity. After all, doesn't closeness require sex?

But because sex is not sex, the survivor is often unable to clearly understand and distinguish sex from other areas of human interaction. When she wants affection, she may think she wants sex. This is due partly to the enmeshment of sex and nurturing at the time of the abuse; partly it may also result from the way the perpetrator eases into the incest, so that she can't tell where affection lets off and sexuality and abuse begin.

When she feels attracted to another person, she may define this attraction as sexual. All the possible levels of interest that one may feel for another—the desire for understanding or nurturing, intellectual stimulation, excitement over shared interests—she tends to reduce and misdefine as sexual. (In fact, many survivors "sexualize" much of human experience: affection is sexualized. Anger is sexualized. Fear, need, trust, touch, and insecurity are all laminated with sexual feelings.)

This characteristic exists, in a simpler form, in many who are not survivors. It is easy to confuse sex with love. Many times when people are lonely, they think they want to have sex. Sex also boosts our self-esteem, for we believe when someone wants sex with us, it is an affirmation of something. Really, however, it might mean little. For the incest survivor, these frequently crossed channels may be more thoroughly confused.

The survivor also misinterprets what is happening when another person shows interest in her. She is acclimated only to people wanting her sexually, and so, in many cases, that is what she sees in everyone.

Sex and Therapy   Because the incest survivor expects both dominance and sexuality, she is more vulnerable to sexual harassment by professionals who take advantage of their power or status.

Psychotherapists, who can become for an incest survivor the "perfect parent" in their caring, nonjudgmental posture with her, may elicit sexual feelings in her. The therapist might attach gleefully to this response as evidence of her oedipal transference: "Ah! You see! She wants me, just as she wanted her father!" And, indeed, the incest survivor herself might be swept with shame, feeling that yes, she must have wanted the abuse, because look what she's feeling now.

Sexual feelings may affect the therapy relationship in a variety of ways. The survivor may be driven from the therapy by the anxiety she experiences. She may feel as if she wants to act on these feelings with the therapist, and so may become "seductive" (a favorite word that male and some female therapists use to describe women clients). She may also feel as if she is *supposed* to be sexual with the therapist—isn't that what is expected when someone nurtures her? (Many therapists take advantage of this: in a recent anonymous American Psychiatric Association survey, a significant percentage of practitioners stated that they believed a sexual relationship between a therapist and a patient could be good for the patient's mental health). She may also reexperience the incest: she may feel trapped by her emotional needs. As Martha said to me, "I'm afraid you might want me sexually, and then I won't be able to turn you down."

"Promiscuity"   Valuing her sexual gifts more than her self and more than her own needs, the incest survivor may attempt to win attention and closeness by giving sex to friends and lovers. She is criticized for this. "Promiscuous" is a negative, judgmental word, used only to describe groups that we devalue (women and gay men). "Promiscuous" incest survivors are again victimized by being blamed for the damage that the incest has caused.

The survivor who manifests this extremely common aftereffect is also robbed. She is cheated of friendship in the purest, nondemanding sense. She simply does not understand what it means to have a relationship that does not have components of sexuality and demand. She is also deprived of the opportunity to develop trust, security, and self-esteem, for she can never really *trust* that she is cared about by someone whose attentions she has purchased with her body. Additionally, what hidden resentment there must be for anyone who takes advantage of what she has offered!

Seductiveness   Seductiveness may be the only language the incest survivor knows, but it may serve many purposes. It may be a way for her to win approval, to achieve power, or to express anger.

To the incest survivor, sexual arousal isn't necessarily what it seems. For the incest survivor who sexualizes her relationships, the experience often gives her no joy, no pleasure; she may not have been the least bit aroused, let alone satisfied. Often, she made love to the person but refused to permit that person to touch her.

What did she get out of it? She felt *wanted, accepted, important.* She felt closeness, perhaps, or at least what she has grown to see as closeness. And from all this came a sense of power. In fact, being wanted in that way is often the only power she knows. Or revenge. For while teasing men, while achieving power through arousing men, many of these women achieve a sense of "Now I've got you where I want you, you dirty little bastard." *This* partner may be a dirty little bastard, but he is not the original dirty little bastard, which is her perpetrator. Her anger is displaced onto another person.

Originally trained that sex was abuse, many incest survivors continue to affirm this association, whether they abuse others or, more likely, themselves. They gain only the semblance of power, and ultimately, more abuse. "I felt used and abused," Gladys said simply. "No one really wanted *me.* They wanted me for what they could *take* from me. My needs? Hah. Nobody ever asked what they were. And I didn't think I had the right to say what *I* needed."

In her twenties, before she remembered her incest, Jessica for several years routinely picked up men in bars, brought them to her car, and (using the jargon of the day) gave them "blow jobs." She received no emotional or sexual gratification in these experiences. But "I had control over the situation. And I knew they needed me. I knew I could dispose of them when it was over." And, perhaps most important:

"They couldn't take anything from me. Of me. They didn't"—she intended the double meaning here—"get inside me. *I kept all of me.*" Recognizing the illusion of power that covered what was really self-abusive behavior, she shakes her head. "Yick," she mumbles quietly, remembering.

Even the incest survivor who remembers being molested may not be aware of what she's doing or feeling. Judy came to therapy complaining that no matter what she did, how she acted, or what she wanted, "everyone always wants me. Wants me sexually. I'm so sick of it. They all say that I have this special quality. What does that mean? They don't know, they can't describe it." In the course of therapy, which ended a year later, unfinished, she was never able to connect that label to anything about herself, but it became increasingly obvious to me: she was seductive. In a previous therapy, she had devoted many sessions to graphically telling her therapist how much she desired him. She carefully—though not consciously—designed her behaviors to be exactly what would make the other person feel wanted. And we humans are often pretty insecure; we want who we feel wanted by.

Taking control of one's victimization is not taking power, but many female incest survivors settle for this illusion because they have not come to understand where true power lies.

S&M, or B&D (bondage and discipline), with their themes of abuse, dominance, humiliation, perhaps even pain, as necessary ingredients for arousal, are perfect expressions for these distortions of Post-Incest Syndrome.

Finally, many survivors find partners who abuse them sexually; for some, rough sex is a source of arousal—even the *only* source of arousal. For many other incest survivors, however, any pursuit or expression of interest from another, whether sexual or not, is experienced as a violation. These survivors feel threatened by what would perhaps flatter or satisfy or excite another person. They may, for instance, get furious at a lover's flattering attention. For others, sexual feelings may be overshadowed by shame and guilt or danger of abuse. The experience of sexuality may be so negative that it must be totally avoided.

Touch and Flashbacks

Touch is frequently misinterpreted by incest survivors, who are unable to experience touch as caring, affectionate, or neutral. The incest survivor may not tolerate being touched because of the sexual trauma it stimulates. Particular types of contact may trigger intensely negative flashes—not full visual flashbacks, but partial, traumatic associations. For instance, one incest survivor felt "tight inside, and like I have to get away," panicky, when her lover's hair brushed her face during sex. This touch was not *itself* a sexual exchange, but during sex it had connotations of sexual violation. Another could not tolerate the feel of a man's sweat. Many are disturbed by the feel of someone's breath on their face.

Strong Aversion to, or Need for, Certain Sexual Acts Many incest survivors cannot tolerate certain sex acts; others feel driven, compulsively, to perform particular acts. Usually the negative response is to oral sex or deep kissing. These are the acts of violation from her childhood. If she is touched in *that* way (a common or uncommon act, a part of the body, a type of touch) she relives the original abuse. On the other side, only a limited number of sexual acts work for some incest survivors, who may develop what are commonly called "fetishes" (a need, for instance, to be spanked to be aroused). This manifestation, however, is much more common in men than in women.

Rigidity of Role: Need to be Sexual Aggressor or Passive Recipient

Post-Incest Syndrome has previously been described as "life out of balance." Some incest survivors find themselves entrenched in one extremist stance, and some another. The significant factor is the rigidity of the stance.

Some incest survivors are comfortable only being the sexual agressor. They derive a sense of safety from being physically dominant while the partner is submissive, or from being clothed while the partner is naked. Thus she can satisfy her lover while she avoids being touched. This power (and protection from being vulnerable or exposed) is more desirable than her own arousal. Judy, who had that "special quality," and who reported sexualizing her relationships compulsively, took this stance; she made love to her partner but would never allow her partner to make love to her. Her satisfaction was not sexual.

The other expression of this aftereffect is the survivor who needs the passive position. There is safety in not having to take initiative in making love to someone else. To be sexually active stimulates feelings of discomfort—perhaps guilt.

Each of these dynamics protects the incest survivor against replaying the incest, against unexplained negative feelings that accompany certain stances. The survivor who experienced incest as being touched against her will may satisfy the need to take power back by being in control of the touching. For the incest survivor whose abuse represented having to touch and satisfy someone else, to take this active stance in later life may feel dirty and abusive.

For incest survivors who need to replay the incest rather than to protect themselves from its negative consequences, this rigid adherence to a particular role replicates the experience. If the survivor's sense of belonging and importance came at the expense of servicing someone's needs, she needs to repeat this, whether servicing is being active (e.g., performing oral sex on the other person) or being passive (e.g., allowing the other to touch her).

Guilt and Anxiety

Guilt and anxiety, common among incest survivors, are especially likely in the arena of sexual feelings and behavior. Survivors compelled to act in self-destructive ways and then feel guilty for it besides are doubly trapped.

Flashbacks with Arousal   When some incest survivors relive an episode of abuse, to their horror, they may be aroused. This is a manifestation of the confusion of sex and violence and may parallel the arousal that occurred at the time of the abuse. When they tell their therapists or peer group about the incest or another incident of abuse, their ability to relate the incident fully is frequently clouded by shame, even though their arousal is out of their control. But it is tremendously important that the survivor share this part of the experience; that way she can find out that she is not the only one to whom it happens and that it does not mean that she is bad or that she enjoyed the abuse. She is simply reacting as she was trained to react.

Fantasies of Rape   Sexual fantasies reveal a great deal about one's feelings and attitudes. They are internal psychodramas wherein issues and feelings are worked through. Because they aren't real, they are often viewed as harmless: it's "only a fantasy." What does it mean then when an incest survivor has rape fantasies?

In recent years, when rape was being redefined as an act of violation and violence rather than simply sex, and women revealed that they sometimes really did have rape fantasies, some confusion followed: Did women really want to be raped? Of course not. They did *not* want to be brutalized and humiliated. They wanted to be pursued and desired unequivocally. Being taken by a mysterious, beautiful, caring stranger, while surrounded by sand dunes, flowing chiffon, and violins, is not rape; it is a fantasy of adoration and submission without responsibility.

But incest survivors' fantasies are not scenes from Rudolph Valentino movies; these are not fantasies where, as Paula Grenot, clinical director, Middle Earth Crisis Center, Bellmore, New York, puts it, "Robert Redford won't take no for an answer." Incest survivors fantasize *rapes:* the excitement in the fantasy is derived not from being *wanted*, but from the humiliation, danger and brutality of rape.

The survivor pays for this with guilt, especially after she has received some treatment and has come to understand something of the nature of violation: she feels shame for being aroused by abuse, guilt over "wanting" to be hurt. Does this mean, she wonders, that she is somehow responsible for abuses done to her? Such fantasies greatly confuse her.

Sexual Addiction

Not everyone who is extremely active sexually is overdoing it; some are simply enjoying a full and active sex life. Sexual addiction has nothing to do with enjoying sex. It is sex as a compulsion, an activity over which the individual has little, if any, control. It brings not joy, but distress.

An incest survivor may have only this addiction, or she may suffer from a number of addictions. Many do not realize that they have sex or relationship addictions until they have achieved sobriety or abstinence in their other addictions. Sexual addiction (sometimes called "sex and love addiction") occurs when there is a compulsive urge to be sexual, which often involves going from one sex act to another; it is based on a craving for a high that is similar to drug-related highs. Like other addictions, sexual addiction is cyclical, self-perpetuating, and progressive.

In women, the addiction may manifest itself as an inability to go too long without a sexual encounter, especially in times of insecurity or emotional distress; this addiction, as others, serves to medicate pain, fill up emptiness that the person is trying to avoid, or meet other emotional needs.

It may also manifest as an obsession with pornography or telephone sex, but this phenomenon (like compulsive use of prostitutes) is almost entirely characteristic of the male sex addict. This is one dysfunction whose connection to incest is not overlooked; current researchers on this subject—including Boston psychotherapist Judith Marsh, and Patrick Carnes, author of *Out of Shadows*—cite childhood sexual abuse as the primary cause. Most of this work describes male behavior, although it's presented as general knowledge that applies to everyone.

Many suggest that rape, exhibitionism, child molesting, and other forms of sexual violence are addictions; they use this assessment to justify treatment rather than jail. Although addictions are explanations, they are not excuses. One is not responsible for having the addiction, but one *is* accountable. An alcoholic deserves treatment, but an alcoholic who drives drunk is responsible for the damage done. Likewise, if someone's sexual addiction leads him or her to molest others, then punishment—accountability—must be a part of society's response. At the same time, punishment is not enough; treatment must also be offered, for jail alone does not protect society or help the individual.

Sexual Abuse of Others

Some women incest survivors become sexual abusers themselves. While relatively rare, some research suggests this occurs more frequently than previously thought. Only now is the fact of this abuse "coming out of the closet," as survivors of abuse by women take the risk of sharing their histories.

Among the female incest survivors with whom I have worked, some do reveal that they abused a child sexually, but this event is still relatively rare, and seems to be relegated to an adolescent fondling of a younger child (while babysitting, usually). But the behavior differs from that of male abusers in that it is generally stopped after one or two events; the woman almost never rationalizes or justifies it, or blames the child or someone else in order to justify it. She is usually horrified at having hurt someone else, and does not continue to do so. When she finally confesses this to her therapist or support group, she is swathed in shame. Guilt and shame often keep her memory of her behavior blocked for many months in recovery.

Trouble Integrating Sex and Intimacy

At the same time that the incest survivor may be sexualizing virtually every aspect of her other relationships, she may feel great conflict when experiencing sexuality in an intimate relationship. As one incest survivor writing in the incest survivors' newsletter *For Crying Out Loud* described it, "sex and love are like oil and water."

As a distortion of intimacy, incest teaches many contradictions: to be cared about is to be taken from, to need someone puts one at risk of being taken advantage of, and to be given to leads to expected payback. For the incested child, intimacy equals danger and damage.

Intimacy, in this regard, can be more threatening than sex. The survivor is *used* to sex. She knows the rules and is detached from her body; she is used to "giving herself away." When she is sexual with strangers and friends (even people she's dating), she switches into automatic, as she has done ever since the incest, and feels nothing. And yet, at some point in a serious relationship, she may begin to feel as if something has gone wrong. She may feel threatened or abused (without seeing a connection to her incest, if she knows about it). She may suddenly feel that a relationship isn't working, doesn't feel fulfilling—*something* is just *wrong*. Or, for no apparent reason, she may lose interest in sex with her partner.

She has not learned to have healthy intimacy, and she is starved for it. She didn't experience it as a child, and she hasn't been able to develop it through a healthy friendship, because she doesn't know how to have a healthy friendship.

Many incest survivors in this circumstance desperately pursue intimate, sexual relationships, thinking that this will fill the emptiness. She comes to every new romance with enormous need and no inner resources or skills for relationship building. Often, this combination results in monumentally awful relationships. One after another, they fail.

When she finally finds herself in a relatively healthy relationship with a relatively safe, caring partner, irony of this aftereffect surfaces.

Because sex is not sex, and trust and caring and violation cannot co-exist, she may suddenly find that a door has slammed shut on her sexual interest, her emotional bond, or both. In the beginning she may appear to her partner to be a sexual free spirit, passionate and uninhibited. She herself may be surprised by how sexual she feels in this relationship; she might experience so many orgasms that they end only when she stops from exhaustion. This, she feels, must be *the* relationship. And when things start to change, it doesn't seem to make sense: this is, after all, the best relationship she has ever had—more trusting, more caring . . . and sexual!

And so the relationship progresses. But with increased trust and closeness, the basic conflict of incest is replicated: caring and sex cannot occur together, for sex means abuse, and abuse and caring are mutually exclusive. But since this new level of closeness replicates the original abuse situation, the climate is now right for the restimulation of old emotional themes, and flashbacks may begin to surface. Often, these flashbacks are the first she has ever experienced. This bewilders the incest survivor (and her partner as well).

The situation is more confusing if she does not remember her abuse. But, as with all the aftereffects, it is an expression of a healthy need and a clear direction for growth. (I know that many of you are reading this and saying, Oh, sure!) The next two chapters, on relationships, explain this conflict more thoroughly.

Crying after Orgasm   The incest survivor who develops intimacy with a partner may cry after orgasm. She may burst into tears immediately after climaxing. This reaction may seem to erupt from some deep secret part of her soul, bypassing her brain and surprising her as much as her partner.

At the moment this happens, she is flooded by feelings that she can't understand—confusion, fear, pain, or anger. Something feels *wrong*. A second after she has been in a state of blissful arousal and deep sharing, she is torn from comfort into the apocalypse.

She experiences this reaction in her gut, not in her brain. In her childhood, perhaps before she could even describe her life experience in words, events happened that contaminated sex and safety. These associations flood in on her in this moment that follows the experience of arousal, abandon, and surrender.

Shutdown and Splitting

Sex can trouble an incest survivor in many ways. Shutdown and splitting remove the incest survivor from the stressful experience, separating her from awareness, connection, or feelings but can occur so frequently that sex is ruined. She may pretend that these disruptions aren't happening. She does this because *she* doesn't want them to be happening or because she doesn't want to put her partner through these problems. (The incest survivor has an enormous problem seeing herself as a victim, damaged and struggling to heal; she can see only what she is doing to others, how she is not meeting their needs, especially sexually.) She may try to avoid this sexual problem because of the deeper, more disturbing problem it represents.

In any case, attempting to be sexual when all her systems are shutting down is self-destructive and useless. Not hearing her inner need to *remove* herself from the situation, she may have sex, but while her body is performing she is up in a corner of the ceiling, watching, detached.

Avoidance/Loss of Interest in Sex   One favorite talk show topic in 1987 was "inhibited sexual desire." *Newsweek* devoted a cover story to the subject, under the catchy title "Not Tonight, Dear." The authors interviewed a number of therapists and sex experts who suggested several theories that were reasonable and believable—the frantic yuppie lifestyle, failure to communicate, withheld anger. As usual, incest was overlooked.

Being invisible, incest can be responsible for all sorts of problems, but professionals don't even consider it as a possible cause. Incest may be *exactly* the reason for a certain problem, and it may be overlooked because none of the professionals brings it up. Incest may well be a primary cause of inhibited sexual desire.

For an incest survivor, sex is accompanied by confusion, complication, anxiety, guilt, anger. She may or may not associate these discomforts with their core issue. She knows she has sex, she knows she has pain, but she does not connect them. So she cannot choose to avoid the dangerous event. She may simply know that she does not feel sexual anymore, or that she has lost interest in sex.

The less aware she is of the effect of incest on her, the more "out of control" her avoidances are likely to feel. She feels as if they are happening to her out of the blue, for no reason. But her subconscious—her inner guide—is protecting her. She is taking control the best way she knows how. She should pay attention to the little kid inside her who is screaming as loud as she can, even though it's only coming out as a whisper: "Stop! I don't want to do this!"

But what are the risks of facing this feeling?

What would it have meant for the child not to give her abuser what he wanted? The answer, as has been discussed many times in this book, is abandonment or annihilation.

HOMOSEXUALITY—NOT AN AFTEREFFECT!

It is widely assumed—by professionals and others—that child sexual abuse leads to homosexuality.

One expresses prejudice by so insistently looking for a cause of homosexuality, by trying to explain "how it got to be that way." Prejudice against those who are different still exists, and bias against this sexual minority is condoned, if not encouraged, although other forms (such as racism and anti-Semitism) are condemned.

The theory that homosexuality results from a negative event in childhood supports the bias against it. But researchers have failed for generations to prove that homosexuals are less healthy or happy than heterosexuals. Virtually all the problems that are presumed to create this supposed disturbance have been carefully debunked in a book by Kinsey Institute researchers Alan P. Bell and Martin S. Weinberg, *Sexual Preference: Its Development Among Men and Women.*

Incest provides a safe haven for this bias, which is expressed, unchallenged, by many therapists who otherwise would describe themselves as unprejudiced. It may be subtle, but it is no less damaging. "Incest results in sexual identity confusion," the articles say. "When you resolve your incest issues, you will be free of this confusion" (happily heterosexual) the "unbiased" therapists say.

What logical conclusions can one draw from this assumption? Well, if a man molests a girl, wouldn't that turn her off to men forever? Even if this is so, and it does on one level make some sense, what about boys who are abused? (After all, men molest most boys as well.) Boys? Oh. Well, um, the boy becomes homosexual because he is over-identifying with the aggressor. Or maybe it's because of his naturally resulting castration anxiety. The urge to condemn homosexuality by associating it with a negative antecedent is so strong that these people shift their reasoning to suit the group at hand: they can come up with no clear and universal reason that incest causes homosexuality, it just does. But the fundamental inaccuracy of the argument is that one is not gay by default, that is, who one loves is not defined by who one hates. A woman who hates men because she was molested by a man does not gain the capacity to be aroused by women. One may, indeed, hate the very gender that one is attracted to. This occurs frequently among heterosexual men. We call the hatred of women misogyny, but have no equivalent word for the hatred of men.

This logic also breaks down in other ways. Many lesbians and gays know their orientation before any abuse occurs; many scientists suggest that *all* sexual orientation is fixed early in life, before age 5.

There is no evidence that homosexuality is caused by anything wrong in one's life. Girls who were not molested or harmed by anyone also grow up gay. Though society has held consistent assumptions about what bad things cause homosexuality, we know no more about the causes of homosexuality than the causes of heterosexuality.

For those who turn to research for the answer to this question, Judith Herman reports that her research "does not support the presumed connection between incest and homosexuality; the overwhelming vast majority of incest survivors" remained "steadfastly, even doggedly, heterosexual." In fact, incest survivors who reported being most seriously harmed, in Russell's study, were more likely to marry! Over and over, her heterosexual interviewees say that their incest made them distrustful of men, but they remained heterosexual.

Sadly, however, both authors reveal a limited understanding of homosexuality. Herman uses the term "become" lesbians, and describes it as a "choice"—a positive choice, perhaps, but, nonetheless, a choice. Homosexuality is no more a choice than heterosexuality. Russell's work is biased in a different way. Her heterosexual respondents may remain distrustful heterosexuals, but her book is devoid of identified lesbians. What impact does the apparent lack of lesbian women have on her research findings? And what statement does it make to readers, gay and straight, to not find the voices of any lesbian women in this sample of the population? Does it tell them that lesbians are not a part of society? (Wendy Maltz, in *Incest and Sexuality*, provides a much more inclusive view.)

Incest might indeed have an impact on the sexual orientation of survivors. It just isn't what you've been taught. It may make boys wonder if they are gay; it may make girls wish they were. For boys, incest is likely to cause a questioning of their sexuality, for a variety of reasons such as, "Why did he choose me? AM I gay?" But to posit that a boy would become gay because a man had violated him as a child doesn't make sense—and, the evidence shows, doesn't happen. Homosexuality and pedophilia (the desire for children) are not the same thing, and are not connected.

Incest survivors may go through a period of sexual experimentation, a common occurrence among women and men, whether gay or straight, incest survivor or nonincest survivor. The female incest survivor may purposefully *attempt* to live a lesbian lifestyle, feeling that this may protect her from Post-Incest Syndrome by removing her from the gender that represents her abusers. But trying something doesn't make one be that thing; otherwise (since almost everyone experiments in one way or another), almost all of us would be gay (and straight, at the same time).

We are who we are. For heterosexual women, sexual or romantic bonding with women feels as hollow as trying to go straight feels for the lesbian. Being healthy enables heterosexuals and lesbians to be comfortably what they are.

An incest survivor who experiences sexual identity confusion, is not necessarily deluded into thinking she's a lesbian before she comes to her senses. Sexual identity confusion is a confusion about, or an inhibited ability to understand and accept her feelings and preferences— whatever they are. She may not know whether she is gay or straight. She might be a heterosexual woman who wonders whether she is gay, or thinks she might be. She might also be a lesbian woman who wonders whether she is heterosexual, or thinks she is. Due to the many social pressures prohibiting homosexuality, a vast number of lesbians go through a period of this—sometimes a very long period, including marriage and the bearing of children. The survivor may shift back and forth between identities, her confusion reinforced by therapists who take a position on which identity is the right one.

There are many dangers in this type of "homophobic" or "heterosexist" bias. Lesbian incest survivors sometimes internalize this bias; they themselves say that they think they are gay because of what happened. When their therapists are biased, they may easily submit to this bias. Or the lesbian incest survivor seeking treatment may be afraid that she will be misjudged—that her homosexuality will be seen as an outgrowth of her abuse by her therapist. The fear of being doubly abused keeps many survivors from seeking the treatment they need.

Although incest does not create homosexuality, it does indeed have an effect on lesbians. In addition to possible self-doubt, self-hate, and confusion, the lesbian incest survivor re-experiences many themes of the incest. The lesbian lifestyle involves stigma and, for some, shame. It can elicit guilt over what one's sexual feelings or experiences are. By living in the closet (all but the most courageous and fortunate lesbians need to pass as heterosexual at least sometimes), the lesbian incest survivor adds yet another secret to her sexual life. Incest can (much to the surprise of some lesbians) complicate their relationship with, and respect for, women as well as men.

HEALING: RECLAIMING SEXUALITY AND SAYING NO

For many survivors, dealing with sexuality comes later than facing other issues; they may need to avoid this emotionally explosive subject. They are not necessarily avoiding sexual activity: they may be involved in uncontrolled, compulsive, self-destructive sex. The topic may be so threatening that their attitude about it may be casual, cavalier. Sex may be especially enjoyable for a survivor who has never faced her incest, only to have her efforts to uncover her abuse "rewarded" by the sudden development of problems she never had before!

The survivor should not attempt to fix sex before breaking the secret, facing the shame, repairing her self-esteem, and learning healthy friendship. Then she must deal with other areas of personal growth: healthy sexuality involves self-awareness, issues of power, and sophisticated interpersonal tasks.

Becoming Aware

The incest survivor who suffers from any type of aftereffect in this area should work to understand the real need that is being expressed by what she defines as sexuality.

The incest survivor who behaves "seductively" must become aware that seduction is the message she is projecting. She needs to look at the way people respond to her. Is it the response she wants? Is it the one she expects? How accurate is her judgment of what appropriate behavior should be?

She needs to consider for what emotional purposes she uses sexuality. If the goal is power, what does she need that power for? Is it replacing assertiveness? Forestalling abandonment? If she is seductive in therapy, for example, perhaps she is attempting to equalize the power imbalance in the relationship. Or maybe the goal is to protect *against* intimacy. (It may even be to test people who claim to be there for her: if they try to screw her, she knows where they're at. However, if by some chance they don't, she often doesn't know how to deal with them.)

Ruth, who knew that she had been molested in childhood, came to me to become "more sexual." Her husband, a therapist himself, had been urging her to see a psychologist for behavior modification (that would desensitize her to her pains and anxieties) and train her to become sexual again. Thinking this was what health meant and feeling that he must be right because he was a professional, she agreed. Besides, she wanted to give her husband what he wanted. She didn't stop to examine what she wanted.

It was clear, however, that she did not want to become more sexual. Being an incest survivor, however (and a woman, and an ACOA), she doubted her own feelings. She didn't feel she had the right to want something different from what her husband wanted. But after a couple of sessions, she was able to admit that she did not enjoy sex; it was contaminated by its associations with abuse. But she still went along with what her husband wanted to maintain the relationship. Consequently, she felt raped every time she had sex. Realizing what it was that *she* wanted put her on the right track for her recovery, for reclaiming her power.

Taking Care of Her Own Needs

After clarifying what she needs and feels, an incest survivor must learn that she has the right to say no and find the ability to do so. This assertiveness generally doesn't begin with sex, for that is too complicated a place to start; saying no under less important circumstances is first. She must work toward being able to do only what she wants, when she wants, because it meets her needs, not because she has no choice and not as the price she must pay to earn someone's attention.

Before a yes can be real, she must be able to say no. This is what the child had not the power to do.

This task is complicated for incest survivors who are involved with men who disregard their needs, or aren't willing to do the work necessary to hear them. Worse, but certainly not uncommon, many survivors are involved with men who victimize and abuse them, who take what they want from a woman in the same way that perpetrators of incest have taken what they wanted from the child. Rapes can and do happen on dates and in relationships with these men after women say no. Saying no effectively might be difficult, impossible, or dangerous. So here the task would be to help her see her partner clearly, to face reality about the limits of the relationship, and perhaps to learn to say no to the partner himself, not merely to a sexual act.

She may need to say no to the act of sex in part or in its entirety. Sex might be OK if she initiates it, so that she knows that she is in charge of when and whether sex occurs. The partner's feelings should be taken into consideration. If the survivor is comfortable with some intimate kissing that does not proceed to more intimate touching, is that also OK with the partner? Or is it too frustrating or arousing? If it is, the partner, too, needs to be assertive; he or she needs to say, "This is too difficult for me." This is not to be followed, however, by "you have to give me the rest of what I want" but rather, by "I don't think I'd better kiss in that way, because it's too frustrating for me." Assertiveness means taking charge of yourself, not controlling another person. The incest survivor needs to set this limit in a nonabusive way. She needs to work toward understanding when she is likely to have a problem, and she and her partner need to discuss it: "If we do this and that, and I am unable to continue, what will that be like for you?"

Limiting Sex

For many incest survivors, the only safety can be found in saying no to sex entirely. At the same time, she may or may not want to cuddle, be naked, or share affection in other, nonsexual ways.

Total refusal may be difficult, especially in the beginning. She may be unable to use words in that situation. She or her partner may have used "no, please don't" playfully. Or her partner may believe in the myth that when she says no, she really wants you to be more forceful.

So there needs to be a mutually agreed upon signal (say two short taps of her fingertips against her partner's skin) for nonnegotiable, undeniable, NO—a no that the partner absolutely respects, and respects her for.

The incest survivor may feel guilty (for not giving her partner what she feels he wants) or cheated (of her own sexual birthright) or angry (at men who want her to satisfy them). She may want closeness, though not sex, and may not see the difference. She may be afraid she must sacrifice closeness to say no to sex, or she may discover that there hasn't been any closeness except sex.

The partner also suffers from this aftereffect, especially the most caring partners. There may be self-doubt or blame ("Is it something I did? Am I no longer sexually appealing to her?"), or fear ("Doesn't she care anymore?"), or defensive distance ("Well, we're not close enough anymore; it's just not working"). The partner may be scared that the relationship is over. He or she may get angry over the perceived rejection or the actual deprivation. These feelings are no less important than the incest survivor's (but no more, either), and require attention as well. But the purpose of expressing them is not to make the incest survivor change. She is healing, and no one has the right to demand anything of her. (No one has the right to demand anything sexually from anyone; incest survivors just have a clearer case.) She may be struggling so mightily with what it means to say no that she cannot hear her partner's pain about it; this does not mean that the partner is any less entitled to feel and ask for a place to share that pain.

Choosing Celibacy   Once the incest survivor begins to say no directly, more frequent refusals to have sex may follow. An extensive period of celibacy may be necessary to regain a healthy sexuality. For many incest survivors, the old script of incest and its inherent distortions regarding sexuality cannot be edited; it must be erased. Total elimination of sexual involvement (even masturbation) may last a year, or two, or even more.

During this time, as the survivor begins to learn how to establish nonsexual relationships, and as she works on other aspects of her growth and the reclamation of power through her therapy and support group, changes take place in her relationship with sex. She distances herself from what she previously experienced as her sexuality, with its confusion with violation, abuse, powerlessness, obligation, compulsiveness. She effectively kills *that* set of meanings. At the same time, she heals the inner child and allows the child to grow toward adulthood, uncontaminated.

This incest survivor who was robbed of her sexuality so early in life is reclaiming her virginity, which she did not end by choice but was stolen from her. She has been deprived of the opportunity to develop her sexuality in stages ("I was never a virgin") or, indeed, to develop it at all ("sex never felt sexual to me; it always felt bad. I thought that that disgusting, horrible experience was what sex had to be"). Now, in choosing celibacy, she cleans the slate of its negative and, indeed, incorrect associations. She learns that she can have experiences and bondings with the world that have nothing to do with sex; she learns what childhood, pure childhood, should have been.

At the same time, the incest survivor can redefine her inner connections. She must not masturbate for the wrong reason, from anger and self-abusive S&M fantasies. The incest survivor needs to become clearly aware of what needs she is meeting by being sexual, whether alone or with a partner.

The survivor needs to develop a sense of herself as a woman, a woman who is not a sexual object, a woman who has worth and power. She may need to feel good within herself about what it means to be a woman before she finds the confidence and strength to demand to be treated respectfully. For many, the first step in this process is separating from misused and self-destructive sexuality.

Becoming Sexual Again   After she is free of sex (and violation), she can journey through the adolescent tasks of developing sexuality that she was robbed of by her early abuse. In stages, she can become sexual again, as she explores how to tell the difference between a friend and someone she's romantically interested in, and how far to go in a sexual encounter. She can learn what it's like to hold hands and nothing more. Holding hands can be an incredibly sensuous, exciting experience. But the deliciousness of that experience is often lost after we go all the way, which somehow becomes obligatory, a goal that compels us to lose the sensations of any lesser experience. The survivor needs to go "back to basics."

She can learn to kiss, and learn to set limits, and learn that she can do only what she wants to do, in climates of safety. She can learn to treasure an arousal that feels safe, one that feels like a gift rather than a betrayal. She can learn to reconnect her body and her mind, and to let go of the need to control. She can also learn that she can be swept away without being lost at sea; orgasms can be joyous, powerful, fully experienced, and without risk—from inside, or from others. She can learn that sex is taking for herself without taking from another. Finally, she can learn that healthy sex and caring are interdependent: to have sex can be to *make love*. Not to get raped, not to pay for attention, not to placate or merely satisfy the other. Not even just to have sex— though having sex is not in itself a bad thing if freely chosen. But, having done what she needed to do to gain control over this domain of choice, she can finally experience her potential to experience sex as a safe, intimate, life-enhancing sharing of pleasure. Thus she can reclaim sex for herself.

RELATIONSHIPS, PART 1— The Self, Then Others

A sequence of stages in our lives prepares us for healthy relationships. These stages cannot be reversed or skipped; each depends on preceding ones. The ability to sustain healthy company with lovers requires the ability to establish and maintain solid friendships. These relationships require the ability to know, accept, and love oneself.

Ideally, the child develops the first of these abilities as the recipient of the accepting, nurturing attentions of caretakers. Because the incest survivor did not receive these attentions, her relationship with herself, and subsequent ability to form relationships with others, can be impeded.

We do not grow up in a vacuum. Throughout life we respond to the people and experiences we encounter. We are influenced by our surroundings, and through our own acts we have impact on them, especially during our early years.

Developing one's sense of self is ongoing. It is a journey, not a destination. We never finish the task and we continue to respond to others along the way.

LEARNING TO TRUST: HEALTHY DEVELOPMENT

At the core of all healthy relationships is trust. The child learns to trust if her environment provides certain basics. Most important is nurturing: a climate of kindness and warmth that encourages growth. Research with babies in World War II and monkeys whose real mothers

were replaced with a kind of doll called a "wire mother" has reinforced the belief that the child requires more than attention to its physical needs in order to survive. She needs to be held, and talked to, and
bonded with through eye contact and a series of specific gestures and
exchanges. In these experiments, despite the fact that the babies and
monkeys were provided with life-sustaining necessities, the emotionally
neglected infants of both species died.

The child needs not a series of concerned strangers but familiarity,
for life, or a relationship, cannot be predictable when every experience
is new and carries no history. *Consistency* is necessary for trust. For if
a child can never know what to expect, she can never let down her
guard. She lives on edge, never even relaxing into nurturing when it is
offered, because those loving arms can go away, can slap her across the
room, can invade her body. Will the people and institutions that care
for her behave in a generally predictable way, or will a parent be caring in one moment, detached or abusive in another? Will her environment give total freedom one day, rigid, demanding perfectionism
another? Is life safe and relatively predictable, or chaotic?

With consistency is required *reliability:* that the trusted adults
around her can be counted on to do what they say they will do, to keep
promises, to pick her up from school when promised and not leave her
stranded, and to feed her when her body needs feeding. Reliability gives
her the security she needs to trust and grow. These behaviors represent
respectful treatment of the child. Consistently, reliably, those who care
for her must care about her feelings and needs, must have respect for
what she wants and doesn't want, for her boundaries, fears, and pain.
They must honor her natural dependency on them by giving her love
and power over her own experience rather than by taking from her
what they want because she is powerless to stop them. This treatment
will help her to believe that her feelings are valid, that she is entitled to
her needs, and is worthy for simply being herself.

Love is *behavior.* What can she expect of someone who claims to
love her? How does she know what it means to trust, and whom to
trust? These questions require some time to experiment, and reflect,
and review; there is no one answer to all situations for all people. The
child depends on her family and her wider environment to learn to
answer these questions for herself. She is being told she is lovable because she has been given a framework through which she can decide
what certain concepts mean to her. They can be answered only in a

climate of safety—of trust. Any other environment breeds answers born out of fear, self-hate, and desperation, and words like love lose their meaning.

Parental Responsibilities

The child's job is not to take care of the parent; the parent's job is to take care of the child, to put the child's physical and emotional needs first. The adult's own needs, fears, or desire for power must either be set aside for the benefit of the child or met with persons other than the child. If both parent and infant need attention, the infant cannot be left crying in her crib while the parent calls a friend. (I do not mean that parenting is a sacrifice of self; a parent must take care of his or her own needs, but not at the child's expense.) If one parent feels rejected by another, the child's job is not to fix or even to hear it. If a parent is drinking, the child's job is not to collect that parent at the tavern, or to bring the beer from the kitchen, or to call work. If a parent is lonely and sad, the child's job is not to comfort. If a parent is weighted down by fears and anxiety, that parent's responsibility is to take care of these crippling emotions so that the child is not made afraid to take risks, go to school, face the world. If a parent is emotionally impoverished, it is still a task of parenting to give to a child, and not take from a child.

A child's job is to be needy, demanding, questing, imperfect, and growing. The child's job is not to be perfect so that the world will like the parent. To learn and grow, the child must try new things and, inevitably, fail at some of them. The parents' job is to tolerate that imperfection—indeed, for what it represents, to applaud it. For only one who never takes risks can avoid making mistakes.

FORMING FRIENDSHIPS: HEALTHY BONDING WITH OTHERS

As the child grows, she can express her tastes, personality, and opinions. She can decide with whom to pursue a relationship and whom to avoid. With whom does she feel good, and with whom are her dealings painful or stressful? She can lean on a caring shoulder and she can be strong. She can tell her innermost secrets and know that they—and her feelings of vulnerability—are respected.

As she separates from her family, she can seek in these friendships allies against the dominance and greater power of parents and other caretakers. "My mother doesn't listen," she might complain. Or, "Dad won't let me stay out late!" (Generally, the more serious complaints, which she most needs to share, she most carefully keeps hidden.) In friends, we find someone who won't criticize us for our failures as if those failures are about them, who won't demand that rules be obeyed or chores be done a certain way. We choose and end our friendships; we are in control. Friends have a different role in our lives than parents: a friend's job is not to raise us, so friends won't tell us what to do or how to do it, or punish us if we do it wrong.

Eventually, friendship begins to take on a new dimension: crushes develop. As many junior high school girls express it, "Do you like him, or do you *like* him?" This dimension contains excitement, passion, and the question of first love. How do you know the difference? Whom do you *like,* and whom do you want only as a friend? Which gender elicits the intense bond, the romantic responses? How do you know how far to go sexually and with whom?

Having already begun to choose friends, the adolescent refines this skill as she decides what feelings she has toward individuals and what to do with those feelings. In stages, she pursues these desires. With each relationship of either kind, she learns about herself in relation to others.

THE SELF: WHAT INCEST TEACHES

Because the child victim of incest is trained to meet the needs of anyone who makes demands on her, stripped of power to affect her own life or her surroundings, and deprived of proper nurturing, her ability to establish relationships is corrupted. Contact with others should help us clarify our feelings, which can make reality more manageable. But in families where alcoholism or incest occurs we learn only confusion. If your childhood was spent being told you were not angry when you were, told not to be angry, told that what made you angry hadn't really happened, or shown that, for survival sake, you'd better not show anger, then you would have buried the awareness that this tension, this distressed excitement, this twisting in your stomach, was anger. The child who expresses feelings that her family cannot afford to face is the enemy in that family's view of what it needs to survive. They treat her as if it's "her or them," and she believes it.

Such a child cannot know herself, can hardly love herself. Sadly, the adult that she becomes often treats the child inside with the same disregard and repressive attitudes that the adults who surrounded her did. As Jackie* said, "I want that kid to *shut up*. She's too needy." If we do not wish to face the truth of our failures with children, we silence the child when she cries out in pain.

In the child within resides impulsiveness, play, imperfection (mistakes), rebelliousness, honesty without a social mask, and feelings such as fear and pain. The adult has learned to deny that child and all she represents. But the denied child has a tendency to tug at her skirt, to demand to be heard; accustomed to surviving in a hostile environment, the child is incredibly resilient and persistent. She will not be annihilated.

TRUST BROKEN: NO SAFETY

Incest sacrifices trust. How can you trust when you expect anyone you care about to rape you one way or another? The incest victim finds no consistency, only broken promises. The implied promise of the caretaker is, "I will take care of you," but the caretaker who is a molester abrogates this responsibility. The person who she feels should rescue her (usually the mother) is, in her eyes, also doing so (as she well might be, although perhaps for real reasons which the child cannot understand). The child learns not to depend on anything that seems to meet her needs. She is reluctant to let down her guard to begin with, for behind acts of caring lie monsters with big claws and razor teeth and mouths that suck her dry. Acts of kindness scare her. She may respond to the most loving companions with the most unreasonable anger.

Barbara had a dream that symbolically describes these implications of incest. In her dream, there were knives on her bed. To help her resolve the dream, I suggested a visualization exercise. As she closed her eyes, I expected this to be a fairly simple exercise: I would help her create a scenario through which we would dispose of the danger and replace it with safety. But to my surprise—and joy—Barbara was more creative with this imaging than I was. "Now, imagine two chests, like hope chests. I want you to pick up the knives and put them away." Eyes closed, she started to cry. "I can't." "Why not?" "Because someone won't let me." She was whining now, and sounded little—like a child. Following a hunch, I asked whether that "someone" was a man or a woman; as I suspected, it was a woman. "How won't she let you?" I asked. She replied, "She'll tell him, and he'll hurt me."

Here was her experience of her family: danger in her bed that she could not protect herself from and could not complain to her mother about. (Her mother, a weak and self-hating person, would send her to bathe or swim with her father, even after she knew of his touching and hurting her.)

And so I introduced myself into the scene to fill the void of protection. "Where are the windows and doors?" I asked her. She told me. "Can you let me in?" "I have to sneak you in," she said, "because if they catch us, they'll keep you out." "OK. I'll be quiet. Am I in? Good. Now I'm going to guard the door, while you take those horrible things off the bed and put them in that box. Don't worry, I'll protect you." She did as she was told. "OK. Now, on that other chest—over there—open it—see what's inside?" "A satiny, fluffy down-filled quilt. And pillows." She smiled. "Lots of pillows," she said, her voice still small, but stronger and no longer weepy. After she put the quilt and pillows on the bed and snuggled into this soft bed, her pain evaporated into serenity. "It's so soft," she told me, smiling now. In this safety and softness, she told me that she could go to sleep. Her bed reclaimed, we ended the fantasy and the session and, I thought, had reinforced her sense of safety in the world.

But I was wrong. We were not done. She began her next session by telling me that something felt oddly incomplete from the previous time. My efforts to protect her had not created for her a total sense of safety, but the danger no longer came from the man and woman in the other part of her house. It came from the safety that I had offered her. *She realized she was angry at me for being safe.* She had let her guard down and begun to depend on me to be as safe next time as I was this time. Now, I could fail her; she could be disappointed, for she counted on something. And if she needed me, then she was at risk, for whatever I wanted from her, she would have to give me; whatever I did to her, she would have to tolerate; whatever my whims made me do, she would have to endure. "What's the worst that could happen if you needed me?" I asked, as I often asked other clients. "The first word that comes to my mind," she said, "is rape." Not surprisingly, she experienced the danger, the threat, as sexual.

The daughter of a perpetrator who was also an alcoholic, she could never know from one minute to the next when her father's mood swings and abuse would victimize her. She could not turn to her mother, for her mother, having been molested as a child herself, and having become a timid woman married to a domineering man in an unfamiliar country, was too weak and isolated to take care of even herself. Barbara grew up with these lessons imprinted in her mind. When she finally found safety in therapy, it challenged the self-protective guard that she had maintained for 30 years, and it mightily confused her.

In *Man of LaMancha*, the musical play about Don Quixote, there is ongoing tension between Quixote and Aldonza, the whore at the inn at which he is staying. He wants to rename her "Dulcinea," a name for a lady, not a strumpet, but she angrily replies that she has lived her life the only way left to her, through prostitution and rage. His caring, respectful pursuit of her was extremely threatening. She rages at him: "Can't you see what your gentle insanities do to me, rob me of anger and give me despair; blows and abuse I can take and give back again, tenderness I cannot bear!"

After seeing this play again recently, I was struck by the likelihood that, among other tragedies that she had been forced to endure, Aldonza was almost certainly an incest survivor. I quote this song to my clients; it describes the conflicts with which so many of them wrestle. On the one hand, the survivor *needs* to keep her guard up and never need anyone. On the other, she is desperate to fill the awful void left by abuse and neglect (either real or perceived). In her childhood, the message was deceptive: she was not directly told, "C'mere, kid, I want to hurt you," but, "C'mere I love you," at which point the abuser, no longer seeing her at all, hurt her. Later, a warm, safe, nurturing environment is frightening; she has learned that behind the appearance of love is something different, and not safe at all.

THE CONSEQUENCES OF INCEST IN RELATIONSHIPS

With diminished self-worth, limited ability to trust, and the burden of shameful secrets she cannot express, the child victim's ability to develop necessary social contacts is inhibited. She is even more dependent on her caretakers—her nuclear or extended family, foster parents, or her surrogate family, babysitter, doctor or priest, in other words, her captors. She is encapsulated with her abuser. Once your protector has abused you, how can you trust anyone again?

There is no balance in her life. Neither between satisfaction and frustration, nor between her needs and the needs of others. Rather than developing an awareness of herself, she learns to deny herself. She knows that in life she will be expected to accommodate the other person's needs, and she often expects to be hurt. She cannot confide in outsiders, for that would jeopardize the secret. She cannot seek solace or ask for comfort. She cannot use social supports to fortify herself against the power of her caretakers. She dares not be vulnerable, because vulnerability results in her being taken advantage of. Her energies are devoted to learning the maneuvers necessary for survival. She has learned behaviors that mask and compensate for her missing self-esteem, she has learned to anticipate the needs and desires of others, so that they can be satisfied to forestall disapproval, abuse, or abandonment. In short, she has learned an entire repertoire of skills that sabotage intimacy. Hollowed out by the deprivations of her childhood, she has been able to develop neither the inner strength nor the external resources necessary to endure inevitable blows.

Needing Self-Acceptance

Her negative identity—the sense of being "soiled and spoiled"—is a serious component of the relationship problem. Judith Herman's research revealed that "with depressing regularity . . . [the incest survivors she interviewed] referred to themselves as bitches, witches, and whores. . . . Some women even embraced their identity as sinners with a kind of defiance and pride."

The incest survivor's intolerance of the child within, her inability to accept her needs and imperfection, damages her self-esteem and relationships with others. She does not feel entitled to complain about mistreatment or its consequences. Her self-blame and perfectionism deny her of compassion for the struggle that she lives with. And she expects and accepts the same mistreatment from others.

She often has much more compassion for others than for herself. When I hear a survivor be especially hard on herself I often ask her, "If you had a sister" (or a daughter, or a friend, depending on what she can most easily relate to) "who had been through what you have endured, and she said what you have just said about yourself, what would that make you feel? What would you say to her? What would you want to do to help?" Invariably, the incest survivor can see her imaginary twin's pain much more clearly than her own and, inevitably, she tells me that what she would like to give to this other incest survivor is a nonjudgmental, loving hug.

Needing Healthy Selfishness

In addition to self-acceptance, the incest survivor needs to develop healthy selfishness. This is difficult for women in general to do. Carol Gilligan, in *In a Different Voice,* explains the social influences that create this problem. Our society, which assigns women the role of family caretaker, establishes a value-system whereby a mother's job is to take care of everyone else and sacrifice herself. Mother inevitably takes the broken piece of pie. How many of you have heard mothers make statements such as, "Oh, I can't get a coat this year; the kids have to go to college?" Even when society finally acknowledged that women could be alcoholics, the educational posters didn't address the damage that this disease could do to the woman who suffers from it; instead the posters highlighted what alcohol could do to a fetus. These messages and rules are a morality: women should not put their needs ahead of others; it is immoral for a woman to take care of herself or to put herself first.

Incest compounds this training. The child is not entitled to love and is obligated to take care of others. Often when women are victimized, they grow up with an attitude not of revenge but of feeling unentitled. Whether a survivor is single or in a relationship, this feeling makes her less able to fill her private life with meaning and less able to tolerate her own company. Feeling unentitled sets her up to accept less satisfying, less respectful relationships. Because relationships are her only opportunity for fulfillment, an incest survivor can become dependent on the relationships that threaten her. She is terrified of being alone, for when she is alone it feels as if no one is there. When she is with herself, loneliness feels paralyzing, and feelings that she has never learned to manage, and cannot share, threaten to break through. She disowns her feelings, fighting to keep them down.

Fears of abandonment permeate the survivor's life. The incest survivor is terrified of losing what little she gets from human relationships. Deprivation has made her desperate. She cannot see how little her current relationships offer her, for it is all she's ever had. To let go of abusive relationships and rely on herself is not a choice: there is no self on which to rely. Hungrily, she goes from one relationship to another, never daring to be not attached.

She has not learned to make choices. She may let other people choose her, rather than selecting who she wants in her life. She is likely to tolerate whatever other people want or whatever she thinks they want.

She does not know the difference between liking someone and *liking* someone. Early on, her parent or caretaker inappropriately introduced a sexual component into their relationship, which robbed the child-victim of the natural pace and order of the introduction of sexuality into her relationships. This created, as Alice Miller says, "an interlocking of love and hate." The survivor is not able to follow the natural evolution from friendship into romance. Her view is that the two are synonymous, that relationships all become sexual. It simply never occurs to her, in many cases, to separate them. As numerous incest survivors have told me, relationships simply don't feel "real" without scx. For many of these women, the therapy relationship is the first one that did not include sex. She may interpret her feelings as sexual when they may in fact not be. Children are not born seeing adults in a sexual way. This is something her abuse teaches her to do. She learns to associate sexual meanings or physical responses with closeness or affection; it is the language through which she gives meaning to bonding experiences. When a client tells me that she "wants" or is "in love with" a parent, I wonder where she learned to define or experience relationships this way. At the other extreme, although I see it less frequently, are survivors who avoid any association with sexual feelings and who never react in a sexual way. These women may not see the sexual component of a relationship even if it is there and *never* sexualize *anything*.

None of these problems may be obvious to the outsider. To the survivor's friends, she may seem sensitive and concerned (but never about her own needs), crazy and fun (she's a high risk taker), strong and "take charge" (she never gets vulnerable), or brilliant and creative (intellectualizing is safer than feeling), seductive and sexy (she's been trained) or a little aloof. No one may notice her lack of relationship with herself, and her inability to attain the balance required of any healthy relationship.

Power Imbalances

The adult incest survivor is likely to become involved in sexual relationships with older or more powerful people, repeating her relationship with her older, more powerful abuser.

There is little room for intimacy, and much opportunity for abuse and sacrifice, in relationships that are so skewed. The survivor may continue to be "child," rather than an equal.

Power imbalances in relationships may take several forms. She expects to give more in a relationship. She may connect with men who resemble her abuser/caretaker, in that they are strong and controlling "protectors" who may never abuse her but with whom there is a basic power imbalance. She may also interpret a partner's possessive control as attention or caring. The incest survivor who manifests this pattern is likely to see commitment as suffocation; intimacy, for her, means having to give everything away. At the other extreme, she may avoid relationships out of fear she will be "sucked dry."

Trust: All or Nothing

The incest survivor has no framework for trust. She understands neither what it means nor how it develops.

If trust is defined as a feeling of safety, comfort, or security with a person, then the incest survivor can be said to be incapable of experiencing trust. She has in fact learned that words don't mean what they say, that things are not always what they seem, and that what appears safe is generally not to be believed. Because she has learned not to trust her own judgment, perceptions, or emotions, she can never feel comfortable making the decision about whether to trust.

In healthy development, trust evolves. How do we decide whether to trust? We share a feeling with someone and watch their reaction; if the response feels safe, if it is caring, noncritical, nonabusive, the first step of trust has developed. For trust to grow, this positive response must become part of a relatively reliable pattern. It need not—

cannot—be perfect. Because we are separate individuals with different personalities, we do not respond with unvarying perfection to each other's needs. But it need not be perfect. Trust develops with consistency over time.

The incest survivor may believe that she feels trust. But the development of this trust is not an active, evolving process for her. Trust, for her, does not discriminate among different people, is not in response to particular behaviors; she trusts despite overwhelming evidence that this investment is undeserved. She may trust from the first moment of the relationship without evaluating anything. She has not learned the judgment necessary to decide who and when to trust. She may trust everyone, in an attempt to have the relationship she never had. She may trust all the wrong people. Or she may trust no one.

When an incest survivor begins to trust (in therapy or in a self-help group), she may experience trust as an all-or-nothing state; or she may be unable to surrender to it, suspecting that the other shoe will fall any minute. Whether she decides to trust or not to trust, if something challenges this decision, she does not know what to do.

If she is totally unable to trust, even partially, even reluctantly, she may become paradoxically enraged when someone is too nice to her. If the incest survivor resists the urge to focus solely on the deficiencies of those she is attacking, a good friend or therapist may be able to see the pain behind the anger. If that person can help the incest survivor accept her need to protect herself and can show that her pain is heard, and if the survivor can then keep trying, she can work to focus on the issues that have interfered in her life. Over time, if the relationship can be sustained, the survivor may be able to see that most people do not want to take anything from her and that there is no danger.

SKEWED RELATIONSHIP PATTERNS

Relationships can at the same time be an incest survivor's biggest problem, greatest need, and best hope. If she can let them, caring, safe relationships can nourish her life, but she often experiences problematic relationships. In addition to abusive relationships, she often commonly becomes trapped in the distortions of the "pursuer" and the "withdrawer." Equally common is codependence, an addiction to relationships.

Abandonment and Engulfment: "The Pursuer and the Withdrawer"

The pursuer, in times of relationship crisis, demands to "work on it," with desperate urgency. Without the reassurance of verbal communication, the pursuer fills the empty space with doubts and fears. She is afraid her partner will stop liking her and go away. This fear forces her to try to control the actions and attitudes of the other person, demanding constant reassurance and contact.

The pursuer is terrified of abandonment. She cannot see this, however, as long as the focus of her attention is the other person's feelings or behavior. By dwelling on what the other person means by every word or gesture, she never sees that her fears are her own, not something caused by the other's unavailability. The situation is complicated by the fact that she often chooses a partner who is unavailable. The pursuer and the withdrawer always seem to find each other! Perhaps one reason for this is that two pursuers, together, would burn each other out.

The withdrawer, on the other hand, in times of stress, needs space. The withdrawer seeks isolation, finds the constant presence of another engulfing. The withdrawer's worst fear is that she or he will be swallowed up by another. This person needs to be in total control of his or her life and emotions. However, such control is reduced by involvement with another person, since others cannot be controlled. The withdrawer removes herself or himself in order to re-establish control. Control is experienced as lack of feeling, what has been referred to in this book as shutdown or numbing. For the withdrawer, commitment is entrapment. If two withdrawers got together, there would be so much distance that there would be no relationship!

Both pursuing and withdrawing are consequences of incest. Under each lies the theme of control or powerlessness. Abuse that engulfs the emotional and physical space of the victim can lead to withdrawal. If she is not able to control the treatment she receives from a partner, she can at least control whether she stays, physically or emotionally.

Abandonment leaves the dependent child defenseless and unable to manage. As the term "Adult Child" indicates, she may be an adult on the outside, but she is still a needy, fragile, undeveloped child in her soul. As an adult, she is unable to experience separation without feeling as if everything inside her has been hollowed out by the loss. Many incest survivors feel driven to "merge" with their partners; they cannot tolerate differences, disagreements, or separation. A therapist might find that she has a terrified or furious reaction to setting limits in the relationship (such as when phone calls may be made). People involved in her life may be met with rage or rejection if they put their needs first and are not available whenever she wants them. This incest survivor does not understand how someone can care about her and not owe her everything, because that is how she was taught to love her perpetrator.

The incest survivor learns that to maintain a relationship, she must give and be everything the other person wants—she must abandon herself if she expects to have anyone else in her life (as the song goes, "What she did for love!"). She is so terrified of being left that her message is this: "Hurt me if you must—do anything you want to me—just don't leave me."

From this, some have called her a masochist, but this is a misnomer. Although being abused may be more consistent with her poor self-image than respect, she does not like to be hurt. She tolerates being hurt because it is safer—better for her—than abandonment. She is really protecting herself by selecting the lesser of two evils. She is surviving life as she thinks it must be. If she felt she had a choice of less abusive behavior, she would take it. To imply that she likes to be hurt is, once again, to victimize her.

Caretakers and Codependency

The incest survivor is indoctrinated as a compulsive, extreme caretaker. A caretaker focuses on the needs and feelings of the other person instead of her own; she values being needed because she can't imagine being wanted. She obsesses on the other person's feelings and ignores her own. Becoming a caretaker is a hazard of the social training received by women; the sexually abused child learns it to the extreme.

The incest survivor is at risk to develop codependent or addicted relationships. She has a tendency to become involved with partners who, through their unavailability, drug dependency, or emotional instability, challenge her to change or rescue them. In focusing on fixing the partner, the "woman who loves too much," as Robin Norwood calls her, selects partners with whom she feels important or needed, but who really have nothing to give her other than pain. This pain then allows her to distract herself from the pain of her past that lives inside her.

Because the survivor needs to have partners who do not intimidate her (partners over whom she can have some sense of power), she tends to choose partners who are "lost puppies"—isolated people who need her help and are not happy in themselves. (These partners may abuse her as well.) This tendency is fed by the message given to women that their job is to take care of others, their job is to be the mother no matter how they are treated. The incest survivor is used to having a man be in control of her life, while simultaneously feeling that he needs her.

For this incest survivor, relationships follow the classic addiction pattern. As the addiction develops, other involvements, activities, and relationships are abandoned; the relationship (actual or desired) becomes an obsession with no correlation between the level of devotion and the degree of reward. Meanwhile, the obsession allows the survivor to concentrate on the deficiencies in the relationship. She spends her energy analyzing the intentions of the desired one, obsessing on every word and gesture. The challenges of the crisis-ridden relationship distract her from exploring and resolving personal problems, and give her a euphoria.

Relationship addiction can be more invisible than chemical dependencies, because what the relationship addict does is sometimes not much different from our popular image of falling in love. "Abstinence" in this framework means not starting new relationships while they work on themselves. A therapist who suggests this goal can be accused of being controlling ("How dare you tell me how to live?") or being cold and heartless ("How can you tell me to give this up? It's the best love I ever had!"). As with all addictions, abstinence is necessary to unmask the feelings, needs, and history that the addiction covers. The relationship addict feels enormous, overwhelming pain when she loses, or lets go of her relationships. She needs encouragement and help to feel her pain fully, for it makes her wise: it teaches her about herself, if she faces it and listens. It is the pain of a lifetime history of losses and abandonments, and it needs to be released.

A QUEST FOR MASTERY

The incest survivor may repeat patterns of her abused childhood, not because she wants an awful life, but because these patterns are familiar. They are also an attempt at mastery—an endeavor to correct the problem of the original relationship. From this perspective, the point of analysis of a relationship between an incest survivor and her emotionally unavailable partner, for instance, is not her troubled feelings over the ill effects of that person's distance. The goal is not to specifically alter or eliminate the partner's unwanted treatment of her. The issue is her sense of powerlessness, once again, in the face of the disturbing behavior of someone close to her.

As a child, she had no impact on her environment. No matter what she said, how perfectly she behaved, how she prayed or pleaded, her abuser remained unavailable to her, his humanity sacrificed to his relentless drive for sexual conquest, while her needs and feelings remained unaddressed. *There was nothing she could do.* Now, in adulthood, her lack of ability to master any aspect of such a relationship has stayed with her. Subconsciously, she resolves to *this* time make a needed person stop ignoring her, listen to her, care about her. She devotes endless energy to attempts to change the other person, not so much to affect their unavailability as to have her powerlessness redeemed by *having an effect* on this thing she cannot stand. *This* time, she will make him hear her. *This* time, she will make it different. It is not father's neglect per se that is most difficult to bear; it is her own powerlessness.

These relationship problems may address her attempt at mastery in other ways. She attempts to keep *this* needed person from leaving her by squelching her own needs (the needs that got her into trouble when they could not be denied in childhood). She may "willingly" submit to her abuse (against which she may have spontaneously protested as a child), becoming, if you will, a better victim. Or she may attempt to alter not how she is treated, but whether she lets it affect her, using the best means she knows—the aftereffects. For instance, she may not feel strong enough to be assertive, but she may try to cope by saying "this time, I won't be hurt by being raped if I 'split off' or if I 'control my feelings' so that it 'isn't really happening.' " Or, "this time, I'll 'just say no' (by being drunk and passing out)"; "this time, I'll fight back (by using my 'angry personality,' if I have split off into the 34 aspects of myself)." As self-destructive as many of the aftereffects of Post-Incest Syndrome may be, they are all attempts to stop repeating the past and to enable the survivor to get what she needs.

All these patterns provide the incest survivor with an opportunity to understand herself better. Barbara, after a final visit with an ex-lover, said:

I felt so very sad to understand that somewhere inside I hurt so much that I could (briefly) do what I had done: stay with someone who was no good for me, just to be comforted and distracted from pain that only I can take care of. Relationships have been a drug for me because I cave in when I don't have one, and expect my life to finally feel OK when I do have one. The sad thing is I allowed myself to be abused in hopes of feeling better. Ironic, huh? But now I'm facing my pain and learning that a relationship is not the place to be as long as I'm expecting it to fix something inside or keep something from hurting (the operative word being "expect"). As a matter of fact, I'd venture so far as to say that when you're feeling like that is exactly when to stay away from a relationship.

INTIMACY AND INCEST

Intimacy requires self-awareness, responsibility for one's feelings, and vulnerability—all of which are very difficult for the incest survivor.

Self-Awareness

Intimacy with another person requires a deep, honest, loving, aware relationship with oneself. These overused terms are rarely fully explained. What do they mean, and how do they apply to an incest survivor's relationships? Self-awareness means being aware of her feelings instead of "acting out," acknowledging that she is angry, needy, afraid, rather than abusing, demanding, or running. Such awareness works through levels, closer and closer to a core; many times, one feeling covers other feelings, and only courageous, honest exploration reveals the layers. For instance, an incest survivor may get angry if someone is late meeting her for a date, but that anger may cover jealousy, which itself covers a history of loss or abuse and a resulting sense of worthlessness.

Such exploration is often frightening and reveals deeply painful feelings. It is easier to focus on a partner's unreliability than one's own fears. But without such understanding of oneself, it is impossible to be aware of one's emotional reaction and the motivations behind one's responses and behaviors.

Taking Responsibility

Intimacy also requires the ability to take responsibility for one's feelings. "Taking responsibility" is the individual's willingness to understand that her reactions come from inside her and that an interpersonal conflict is an opportunity not to describe what is wrong with the other person, but to explore more thoroughly her weaknesses, strengths, associations, history, and problem areas. (In cases of real abuse, the purpose of such exploration—the desired change—would be to see that she is being treated abusively and examine how she could escape or protect herself while understanding that the abuser is totally responsible for the abuse.) For instance, if she is vulnerable to abandonment, she may be easily scared or angered by the behavior of others. However, they may have not intended to hurt her; they often have no idea that they are hurtful. Another person may experience these same behaviors as warm, loving, or neutral (without emotional content, either good or bad). If I am insecure when I am with you, that does not mean that you reject me; it means that things that you do trigger in me an insecurity. These things touch the part of the iceberg that is above the surface, while the greater part, the reason for my reaction, resides under the surface. It is inside me, and is for me to uncover and resolve.

In this view, interpersonal problems are an opportunity to explore the self and grow. No matter what happens in a relationship, one's personal growth is the primary goal.

Being Vulnerable

Intimacy requires vulnerability. Vulnerability is confused with weakness, because it means that one can be hurt. However, vulnerability is the antithesis of weakness, for it requires strength and courage to risk openness. To be vulnerable is to be open to the impact of our environment and responsive to others. It leaves you able to be touched by human contact, and capable of feeling all that it brings—joy and pain, sorrow and excitement.

In intimacy, contact with the other is fully felt. Rather than focusing on external things, each participant uses the opportunity of the bond to fully experience her or his own reactions and reflect deeply. In the intimate relationship, partners communicate openly and freely; they are physically and emotionally available to each other. This requires that they be open to themselves as well, to their own thoughts and feelings, problems, tensions, angers, conflicts, needs, and wants. They uncover and welcome these parts of themselves with patience and caring, and without expecting anyone else to correct the past. Intimacy requires that each person have sufficient self-confidence to allow for differences, separations, and mistakes. When one trusts, one does not need a perfect partner.

Incest-Related Blocks to Intimacy

None of the relationship patterns described in this chapter represent intimacy. Each blocks intimacy by preventing closeness and distracting from one's feelings. Each is an extreme skewing of intimate involvement and a compulsion. For example, the pursuer and the withdrawer are joined in a dance at arm's length; when the pursuer moves forward, the withdrawer steps back. Each uses her reaction to the other person as a distraction from facing her own issues with abandonment or engulfment. The pursuer focuses on her partner's feelings more than her own, and the withdrawer focuses on no feelings at all! Similarly, the caretaker does not take responsibility for herself and her needs; she gives to others what she really wishes for herself.

The codependent person works hard to correct what cannot be changed, her past, by changing what she cannot change—another person. (This time, someone will do better by her than someone did then.) The relationship addict creates excitement in lieu of intimacy.

These patterns are protective reactions to the abuse and neglect of incest—protecting, ironically, against intimacy, which is not, in the context of Post-Incest Syndrome, safe. She finds relationships that reflect her weakened self-esteem and that continue to diminish it. She creates distance and conflict in a left-handed pursuit of power. The incest survivor feels that if she does not allow herself to be vulnerable, she is safer. If she never depends on anyone, she cannot be expected to trade away her ownership of her self; if she never gets close, it won't matter if she is left. If she never needs someone, she can accomplish in an adult relationship what was never an option for the child: she can leave. If she is in a victimizing relationship, she can continue playing out the only pattern she has known; if she gets involved in a conflict-ridden relationship, she can re-experience the familiar theme of love and hate at the same time.

These attitudes arise from the fact that in all of her relationships, she re-experiences some aspect of the incest experience, especially the basic conflict: that relationships mean loss of self, giving away what you don't want to give, and being powerless to say no or make choices. In maintaining problematic relationships she is protected from the temptation to lower her guard, for her guard is all she thinks she has.

Occasionally it may enter the mind of an incest survivor who is not in recovery to do things differently, to say no, to do what she wants, or to ask for help. To take this risk fills her with fear. The fear alone can interfere so severely with her adult functioning that it supersedes whatever consequences result from the feared act. The fear alone can stop her. This leaves her entrenched in these "protective" patterns of relationship, taking care of herself at the expense of intimacy.

The irony is that when she finds a relatively healthy relationship—one in which she is truly cared about, that offers consistency, respectful treatment, and a safety into which she can relax—her incest issues are especially likely to surface. Of course, this is not what most people would expect. The next chapter explains why this occurs and why it may not be as destructive as it sounds.

RELATIONSHIPS, PART 2—
Intimacy: Replaying the Incest

Many incest survivors eventually find their way out of the cycle of entrapments discussed in Chapter 14. Frequently an incest survivor escapes after seeking help for the incest or for related problems such as alcoholism and low self-esteem. She reaches out for support and grows stronger. These changes provide the safety she needs to stop fighting intimacy and to begin expecting, even demanding, respectful treatment. The partners she chooses now are safer and much less likely to abandon or abuse her.

At the beginning of her journey, she will encounter problems and complications, but the old way becomes unacceptable. She becomes aware that when she masks her pain, disappointment, or anger over the way things are, she loses her capacity for pleasure, warmth, or joy. One cannot dispose of only one feeling; the baby gets cast out with the bath water. She may see how much her previous existence was numbed and brittle, made worse by the unresolved pains. She may realize that pleasure has been contaminated, instantly and inextricably associated with pain.

Even healthier relationships are bound to be complicated and problem ridden. The incest survivor may see abuse where none exists, or react in an exaggerated way to the most harmless of transgressions; she takes out on her partner the unspoken rages of her childhood. This pattern could easily apply to the themes of boundary violations, perceived or actual abuse, the possibility of the other person's selfishness (her feeling of being used), and a variety of trust and sexual issues. She may see issues from her past only in her present, whether they are there or not. Inevitably, they interfere with intimacy. Although her relationship problems are confusing if she blocks her awareness of her abuse, she has substantial problems if she remembers it as well. For instance, one characteristic of an incest survivor who remembers her abuse is that she is likely to enter relationships armed and ready—emotionally invulnerable.

In one way, the incest survivor is likely to follow this "you can't get to me" approach whether she remembers the incest or not. The difference may be one of attitude: if she remembers, there may be arrogance, hardness, or careful remoteness. If she does not remember, this fighting stance might be supplanted by a quieter, more timid, more inner-directed control: emotionally she is simply not there. Not angry, necessarily, just not present. In this regard, remembering may make her anger more available or her behavior more calculated.

Sexual abuse is confusing. Because it is mislabeled love, because it is what results when love is sought, or because it is connected to other experiences that *are* wanted, sexual abuse is not a purely bad experience; it is mixed. The victim believes she must have sought it because she "went back for more." She concludes that the only way to protect herself is to stop asking, stop needing, stop expecting. Thus the survivor learns that needing makes her bad.

A safer or more caring relationship can replicate the conditions the child was wishing for when she got abuse instead, and can have a down side. To admit that good conditions are possible, she has to face that what happened to her was not caring but abuse. Vulnerability, intimacy, even some dependence, combined with sexuality, restimulate the incest conflict, even though no abuse or significant imbalance of power is present. Needing the other person immediately jeopardizes her sense of power. Trusting the other person paradoxically creates a sense of lack of safety. Closeness and sexuality together recreate the violation.

Caring, vulnerable intimacy in a context of sexuality can result in intense conflict for her, an intolerable combination of mutually exclusive opposites. For by definition, violation and trust cannot coexist. It is at this juncture in an intimacy that some of the most troublesome feelings are likely to surface.

HOPEFUL BEGINNINGS TURNED SOUR

In the beginning these relationships progress nicely, without obvious problems. The joy of the new bond seems pure; the incest survivor feels great relief and hope. "Finally. Finally, a safe relationship, a good one. Finally, my troubles are behind me. Maybe this is the one I've been looking for." (Finally, the magic cure!) The relationship might be much calmer than she has ever known, yet it can be the passionate, long-awaited combination of love and desire that the incest survivor has longed to find. She sinks into the safety and joy of it, letting her apprehension fall away, letting her guard down, looking forward to a future free of the confusion and trauma she has known. She may, if she remembers her incest, tell her partner, or she may not, thinking, "Well, maybe that's all behind me now."

Then, to her great surprise and indescribable disappointment, all hell might break loose. When this happens, it may be her bewildered partner who bears the brunt of the emotion meant for events of long ago, whether shock, anger, rebellion, loss, or terror. In this way, while one may survive incest, one's relationship might not. The relationship becomes the incest "victim," even as one—or both—partners are incest "survivors".

If the incest survivor was abused by a male and her partner is a woman, that partner might be especially confounded. Lesbians generally do not expect the consequences of abuse by a man to interfere with their relationships. "Why would she have a problem with me?" the partner might wonder. "How could I possibly remind her of him?" But this question fails to recognize that the incest survivor's problem is not her partner—it is her struggle with what a relationship means and her conflict with her own sexuality. Lesbian partners should also be forewarned that lesbian incest survivors who are only beginning to deal with their incest may retreat from their homosexuality, in a manifestation of the sexual identity confusion described earlier.

The incest survivor is likely to be no less bewildered by these events. She feels the shock of confronting the horror of her long-buried past, combined with the paradox that the awfulness should erupt in the safety and happiness of the current relationship. If the relationship elicits her first awareness of an incest history, she faces also the seemingly endless ramifications of this newly uncovered aspect of her life. Some times, emotional flashbacks occur before any actual awareness of incest surfaces; this can lead to even more confusion. Flashbacks are likely to occur during the incest survivor's first involvement with a healing relationship (e.g., therapy or support group). In fact, therapy and a respectful relationship often coincide. Therefore, the probability of flashbacks occurring is much greater, and the flashbacks are less easily attributable to either factor exclusively.

The incest survivor may suddenly lose her emotional attachment for her partner. Or she may shut down completely, her emotions fading until she feels detached from her life. She may fall into a serious depression. Or she may find herself suddenly, unreasonably angry at her partner, for nothing and for everything. (Sometimes for the best that the partner had to offer: safety and love.) She may feel overwhelmed and confused by what intimacy feels like, what it reminds her of.

Effect on Sexual Relations and Intimacy

Sexual activity is directly affected. The survivor may suddenly find sex terrifying, or may feel unable to go on. She may return to, or may experience for the first time, shutdown or splitting off during sex. She may for the first time cry after orgasm (for no previous orgasm may have been so fraught with intensity and confusion). This may appear paradoxical because at this point many of these women experience their first, or their most potent, orgasm.

Ultimately, sex may become such a struggle that she loses interest in it. Indeed, ironic though it is, this may be the time that she chooses, or needs, celibacy.

Immediately the pro-survivor, as partners are called by many survivors' groups, feels the shock of contending with this. Something new has come crashing into their routine, and it has changed all the rules. Closeness has become distance; the closeness they once shared is now transformed into steady tension, or tension that unpredictably, erratically erupts between them. Passionate sex is now a disaster. The sexual activity that the incest survivor once joyously pursued now elicits rage or shutdown. In fact, much to her partner's surprise, she may now reveal that all along there had been times when she hadn't really wanted to participate. It was just impossible for her to say no. Half the time, she sees now, she felt raped. For this, she may become blaming, even if she was not aware of her own feelings.

Suddenly she may have a great need for distance. In some cases, the revelation of an incest history explains the puzzling periodic quests for distance that she had manifested. As the old script surfaces, the incest survivor often sees or expects to see her partner recreating (or attempts to provoke her partner into recreating) the original context in which the incest took place. Suddenly, the partner who was embraced as the savior, the perfect parent who rescued her from all her troubles, is attacked for selfishnesses, impositions, neglects, and abuses. These seemingly irrational responses cause great confusion and disruption.

The pro-survivor is faced with his or her own problems, and a difficult balancing act.

Many pro-survivors take the incest survivor's reactions personally: they feel personally rejected, self-doubting, unworthy. For some, this turns into retreat. Others turn it outward, attacking the incest survivor for what she is no longer able to give sexually, or what she is not able to deal with. The partner with whom the survivor has developed this new ability to say no feels singled out. He or she may become impatient with the painful slowness of the incest survivor's recovery, or may abuse the incest survivor verbally, physically, or sexually. (The fragile incest survivor may experience *any* assertion of the pro-survivor's needs as violation, demand, or abuse, even where none was intended or exhibited.)

The Pro-Survivor's Needs

But the pro-survivor is a person, too, another innocent victim of this distant conflict between the child and her caretaker. The partners of incest survivors are invisible: their needs are addressed neither by most books on incest nor by many therapists or programs that work with child abuse. There are few therapy groups for partners of incest survivors and even fewer self-help groups for them. Partners of incest survivors are hidden victims of incest.

Partners are in a particularly helpless position. They cannot speed up, or in any way affect, the recovery of the incest survivor. Nor can they meet their needs at the expense of the incest survivor, for that would perpetuate the abuse. One must take charge of one's own life but may never control another in the process.

While healing is possible, the consequences of incest are not negotiable; they are not choices that the survivor makes, any more than the immobility that follows a broken leg is a choice. The incest survivor is a broken child. She must be healed, rehabilitated, strengthened before she can be expected to take on the tasks of an adult. Like a child, she must be nurtured, even catered to before she can be expected to give to others in a healthy way. (She has given to others her whole life, but the gifts of servitude and the gifts of freedom are worlds apart.) The partner of the incest survivor must ask: If you loved someone who suddenly became incapacitated, what would you do? The question is complex and the answer depends on many particulars. There is no right answer. Partners must find their own.

If there is genuine love and commitment in the relationship, commitment may keep the pro-survivor in the relationship and allow the required concern for the trauma that the incest survivor is forced to endure. In that case, the pro-survivor must become like a LaMaze coach, putting the incest survivor's needs first while assisting in, and focusing on, the survivor's struggle for rebirth.

Reciprocally, the incest survivor's job, if she wants to preserve the relationship, is to work on healing. The incest survivor cannot expect her partner to be everything to her with absolute disregard for self, or to put his or her own needs on hold and wait for her forever while she does nothing. The incest survivor's daily job is to remember that it was not *this* person who molested her; the pro-survivor is neither the cause nor the cure for her problems; she, the survivor, must save herself.

Who is the Pro-Survivor?

What type of person is likely to get involved with an incest survivor? Pro-survivors span a continuum. At one end is the abusive partner; then, one who is extremely controlling. Next would be a "caretaker type" who spots the survivor's wounded soul and swoops right in to help out. At the other end is a caring, careful person who is extremely sensitive to and aware of the survivor's issues.

Finally, incest survivors often find each other. I hear from therapists who work with pro-survivors that ultimately their clients' own incest histories are uncovered. It may also be true that other children of trauma, such as adult children of alcoholics, are likely to find a soulmate in the survivor. One adult child of an alcoholic says this of his relationship with his survivor-lover:

Although I didn't know it consciously when I first fell in love with her, I'm still with her in large part because I realize that everything I've ever been though, she's been through, and more. If I'm falling apart at 4:00 in the morning, she's who I want to be there. She has a peculiar kind of spiritual honesty that all the acknowledged, recovering incest survivors I know have (whether they want to or not). Her particular needs make my particular skills (the special ones I learned growing up in an alcoholic family) and experience (the stuff I might otherwise wish I hadn't lived through) valuable in a way that they would not be for a total civilian. The same goes for her skills and experience and my needs. Last but most, we both have plenty of respect for pain, we know what loneliness and spiritual hunger feel like, and we care about other people besides just ourselves. We are both living for the same reason and we don't ever take that life or that reason for granted.

Awareness of the Self and the Other

Self-awareness is necessary for the partner as well as for the survivor. The pro-survivor must continually examine his or her own feelings, asking these questions: Why am I with this person? Why with an incest survivor? How did I come to choose her? Does this choice reflect a savior fantasy, a need for power, or other dynamic in myself that I need to explore? If I choose to stay, why do I do so? Which needs of mine are being met, and which sacrificed?

In the relationship, the pro-survivor needs also to ask a question that is important for anyone who cares about someone in need: Whose needs am I meeting when I do or say something that I claim is to help the survivor? For whose needs do I want her to talk, cry, confront her feelings, get mad at her perpetrator, recover? Do I want her to change in ways I want, or in ways that she chooses? It may be much easier for the pro-survivor to be angry at the perpetrator than it is for the survivor. For the pro-survivor to push the survivor toward yelling at her abuser, or to demand that she confront him, is selfish and damaging. It is certainly understandable that the pro-survivor is angry, but he or she needs to find a personal outlet for this emotion.

And sex. The incest survivor's well-being depends on her never having sex against her will. Do not push her. Do not attempt to force her (or any woman) to be sexual when she does not want to be (or even when she would like to be but feels that she cannot). It would help if you could go a step further: Be sensitive to her tendency to think sex is always expected of her, and that she is obligated to give you what you want. Create the safest climate you can for her to say no, and try to hear a no when she cannot voice it.

Both partners must talk openly about the effects of the incest on their lives and on the relationship, and both must continually evaluate the consequences of maintaining the relationship. The pro-survivor may encourage the incest survivor to discuss the details of the incest but should never push; the survivor has been pushed more than enough already. The partner needs to express interest with delicate care. Also, the partner needs to remember the incest survivor's tendency to take care of others.

Eleanor, with great caution and sensitivity, told her lover Cajean, "I don't want to pry—I've always been afraid to ask, but would like to know—do you want to tell me about what happened?" Cajean was willing to tell her partner what her grandfather had done and did so in classic survivor fashion, with matter-of-fact detachment. But Eleanor was upset by this discussion. This had happened to this woman whom she cared for so much. She broke down crying. And Cajean ended up taking care of her.

Sometimes it's fine for this to happen. But couples need to remain aware of what is going on, what the emotional issues are, and to whom they belong. Both must work hard to allow for the honest expression of anger and resentment. Each must avoid blame, maintaining responsibility for their own feelings and lives. And both must develop their ability to empathize with another. Empathy, the ability to understand the world as the other person does, is perhaps the most important skill in any relationship.

The challenge of a relationship is to understand and accept how different other people are. One partner may want closeness in a crisis, and the other, distance. Whose needs would you be meeting if you insisted on staying close to the person who had a great loss and needed to be alone?

In life, patience is a virtue; in a relationship tainted by childhood sexual abuse, patience is a necessity. So are tolerance and some sacrifice of one's own needs. But each must avoid becoming sacrificial. As always, the needs of the relationship must be balanced with the needs of the individuals. No one should give oneself away.

The partner needs to be aware that many, if not most, incest survivors tend to blame themselves for any imperfection, failure, or dissatisfaction felt by a partner. A feeling of not being entitled to their own happiness often accompanies this self-blame. When the pro-survivor expresses dissatisfaction, both partners should be on the alert for this reaction. And both should remember that many of their problems are not something the survivor is doing, but something that is happening *to* her.

The incest survivor needs to give her partner the space for his or her own issues, without swooping in to take the problem away through self-blame or defensiveness.

STRUGGLING TO GROW

The more intimate the relationship, the more likely are swings of emotion—stormy periods, chilly periods. Surviving these requires a mutual commitment to healthy behaviors, and probably outside support.

Because we must respect the survivor's privacy and autonomy, she should not be required to report what went on in her therapy or recovery group. However, sharing what she learns in these forums may help her partner trust that she is working on her issues. The partner who shows an interest in learning about incest—through reading, attending workshops, and the like—helps the survivor feel cared about, and helps himself or herself as well!

Unfortunately, one cannot predict whether these efforts will sustain a relationship. Indeed, the goal of this work is not a sustained relationship; it is the growth of the individual. Staying together might be impossible; it might require too great a sacrifice for either or both. They might fight all the time, or one partner might feel constantly disappointed, unfulfilled, or abused. How easy it is at those moments to think, "Things would be perfect if only the *other* person would change." But they are who they are, and it is up to the dissatisfied partner to take responsibility for his or her own happiness even if that means leaving the relationship, however reluctantly. You cannot change anyone else; you can change only yourself. If you do so, the other person may well change in response, but not necessarily in the direction you wanted! One can control, as a goal, only self-change—and even then, only sometimes.

It is an irony—a sad one for the pro-survivor—that health, for an incest survivor, starts with saying no—with taking back power, setting limits, no longer giving the other person everything asked for. The pro-survivor must remember that it is a tribute to the quality of the relationship—and its only hope for survival—that the incest survivor no longer is a victim, giving away what she does not want to give away, able to take the risk of taking care of herself, able finally to proclaim "I'm entitled!" No relationship can survive in a healthy state through the unhealthy sacrifice of either partner.

This relationship might be a training ground—a place to learn new, healthier ways of conducting an intimacy. The lessons that are available here would be of value to any couple. There is an opportunity for both partners to abandon a genitally based pattern of sexuality for one where touching is fully appreciated. Toward this end, there are exercises (called "sensate focus exercises") commonly used in sex therapy that teach partners to touch again. (These exercises and others can also be found in some sexuality self-help books.) These exercises begin with partners giving each other back rubs or exploring each other's faces with the fingertips, so that they can experience the intimacy of touch without erotic intent. These evolve to exercises that have an erotic, but not genital, focus, so that partners learn the erotic potential of touching that is leisurely and not goal-oriented. The value of the lessons contained in these exercises is not limited to survivors and their partners; they can benefit everyone.

Both the survivor and pro-survivor also have an opportunity to develop their communication skills; all relationships can be made or broken by communication, and individuals in partnerships can grow emotionally if they learn to explore properly the inevitable problems that intimacies bring. To do this, one should ask: What does this problem in this circumstance make me feel? What does it remind me of? What issue could I be struggling with that makes this situation a problem for me, or what pattern of mine might this be about? If the survivor and her partner can keep the focus on themselves in this way, they can learn a lot.

Finally, the couple has the opportunity to understand that there are many ways of expressing feelings or needs other than through sex, and that there are many ways to achieve closeness other than making love.

WHEN A RELATIONSHIP ENDS

We often do not choose our relationships for the right reasons; we are attracted by the other person's sense of humor, intelligence, interest, looks, sexual skills. How the person functions is much more important. Our partners should handle crisis, pain, communication in ways that make us feel safe and cared about. Both partners must feel good about themselves in the relationship. Relationships are a choice; one can and should choose to start or continue a relationship based on whether it is good for one's growth. For many people who are growing, each relationship is a better choice than the preceding one, yet not as fully developed as the one to follow.

The first relationship in recovery (whether from abuse, alcoholism, or the like) is one stage of the journey, not the arrival point. The temptation to see the first good relationship as "the answer," and the reluctance to let it go are strong. But from the incest survivor's first steps to where she becomes "strong in the broken places" may be a journey of many years and many stages. Like a snake, she may have many skins to shed along the way; from each molting, a brighter, stronger self emerges.

HOPE, HEALING, AND BEYOND

*I*n knowledge there is power, and empowerment is necessary for the incest survivor to overcome the effects of her victimization. I hope that my description and analysis of the consequences of incest have helped you know yourself, your loved one, your client, and other women. I hope I have helped you understand sexuality, relationships, and power. I hope that this book has moved you to ask questions and think in new ways, not only about incest, but also about other human experiences.

Merely reading a book cannot change a person's life. And no problem as traumatic, as comprehensive in its effects, as deeply wounding as incest can be resolved through intellectual analysis alone. The survivor can pursue this painful and challenging journey in many ways. Some involve working with a therapist; some do not. Many survivors find that psychotherapy in combination with a self-help group is more productive than either one individually. Other activities may also enhance her recovery program. And the journey does not end there.

WHO MAY NEED HELP FOR INCEST?

Because a history of incest is often not remembered, what red flags indicate that it has occurred?

Although research shows that all women are at risk, women who are especially likely to have experienced incest are those who suffer from addictions, eating disorders, phobias, obsessive-compulsive behaviors, multiple-personality disorder, sexual dysfunction, chronic anxiety, or depression. Also likely are battered women, runaways, prostitutes, rape survivors, women from alcoholic homes, women whose mothers died from or suffered from a chronic illness, women who lived in foster homes, and women who lived with stepfathers.

Certain aftereffects virtually always indicate incest or another serious trauma or abuse:

- Blocking out some period of early years, or a person, place, or event (indicates serious trauma).
- Night terrors (indicates serious trauma)
- Alienation from body (indicates battering or incest)
- Intolerance to being touched (indicates battering or incest)
- Self-injuring behavior (highly associated with incest)
- A history of sexual acting out, promiscuity, or inhibited sexual desire (highly associated with incest)
- Difficulty with water hitting the face (specific to incest)
- Desire to change name (specific to incest)
- Gag reflex (specific to incest)
- Inappropriate clothing (too much for season, much high-necked clothing, baggy clothing) (specific to incest)
- Discomfort using public bathrooms (specific to incest)
- A pattern of relationships with older or more powerful partners, or (in adolescence) much older teenagers or adults (highly associated with incest)

Clusters of items from the Aftereffects Checklist are significant in predicting an incest history; the more there are, the more likely there is incest.

If you find out about one incident, or one perpetrator, there may be others. You remember less close abusers before those who were more important to you. If you remember an experience of stranger abuse or acquaintance abuse in childhood or adolescence, you might also have suffered abuse from someone known and trusted.

THERAPEUTIC HELP

If you are troubled by the aftereffects that you have read about here; if you think that something may have happened in your childhood (whether you remember it or not); or if this information applies to someone you know, there is help in the form of therapeutic intervention, intensive workshops, and other activities. Recovery services help survivors change destructive behaviors and heal from the pain of a violated childhood. Such help is available in groups (either self-help or led by a therapist) and individual therapy.

Self-Help Groups

Self-help or mutual support groups for incest have become increasingly available, although in many areas they are still limited.

Advantages and Disadvantages Self-help groups offer support, encouragement, the benefit of shared experience—a good family to replace the old one. They also offer a wonderful opportunity for ending isolation and self-hate ("Hey, she was molested, and she's an OK person—maybe I'm not so bad!"), and an opportunity to develop trust and to function socially. They are needed for incest survivors, (male and female), their partners, and their mothers (in families where there was paternal incest). Slowly, these groups are being developed. They rely on incest survivors' taking initiative for their own recovery. Some take a step beyond "recovery" into "social action."

Usually run by incest survivors, this invaluable resource requires no fee and lacks the stigma associated with being a psychotherapy client. However, because they lack official or professional leadership, self-help groups must rely on some structure to govern the sharing in the group. One such rule concerns no crosstalk or no feedback: participants share but no one responds to what they have said. Many women feel protected by this policy from unwanted responses, criticism, advice, or distractions from their feelings. Others, however, feel that sharing in a group where no response is offered feels like talking in a vacuum. Some structure is necessary, however, to ensure order in the emotionally charged atmosphere of incest discussions.

Group Leadership Whoever guides the group—the person who founded the group, an elected "chair," or a rotation of all participants—may not be a good leader because of her relationship with power, where she is in her recovery, or her personality. The guide may be over-controlling or too timid to maintain order; she may be more interested in performing or getting attention than in helping group members get what they need from the group; she may attempt to impose her views or feelings on other people.

To lead any group is difficult. To lead an incest group requires extreme patience, firmness, openness, and an enormous ability to hear other people's pain (an incest survivor who can't yet face her own pain may feel unable to tolerate others'). All participants need a healthy understanding of boundaries, limit setting, and safety. These groups are especially vulnerable to their leader, and in some self-help groups leaders have been known to abuse their power, or abuse the groups through their incompetence.

Sometimes, to protect against a power imbalance in the group, self-help groups are led or co-led by volunteer professionals who serve as advisors. Members can benefit from the involvement of a professional while maintaining power over themselves and their recovery.

Group Members An extremely important consideration is whether the group is mixed or women only. I strongly advocate the latter, at least in the early stages of recovery. Many women incest survivors are not comfortable enough or strong enough around men until far into their recovery. Some feel threatened; some find it impossible to be assertive, to discuss sexuality, or to express anger. Others defer to the men in the group, needing their approval so much that they sacrifice their own needs.

One issue that many incest survivors address in their recovery groups is the violence that all women are at risk for at the hands of men; this discussion would be inhibited in a mixed group. Also, there is a reasonable possibility that a male who was molested may become a perpetrator of violence against others; that is why many resources for men often stipulate that they are for nonoffending males. I know of one mixed group that apparently did not screen its members, and had at its meetings an incest perpetrator and also a multiple murderer! The necessity for adequate screening for these groups cannot be overemphasized.

Groups for men have been slow in developing. Men are not trained to network or nurture in the ways necessary to start a group. Often, men rely on women to take care of them, and this includes expecting women to develop resources. These women, however, are taking care of themselves, and that is what the men need to do as well. One male survivor who was molested by both female and male relatives wrote to pursuade me that this is a problem not primarily of women but of everyone being victimized. He was, he said, surrounded by women who helped and nurtured him. I wondered, reading his letter, where were the networks of men, surrounding and nurturing victimized women? In more advanced groups, the presence of men can offer each gender the opportunity to work out issues about the other.

Types of Groups   Once you have decided to consider a self-help group, you must consider the type of group (where you have a choice). One common format for incest groups is the same as for AA, OA, and Al-Anon. They are called twelve-step groups because of the steps or tasks they share. The national twelve-step incest network is Survivors of Incest Anonymous (SIA), formerly Sex Abuse Anonymous (SAA). These groups are based on a well-proven program, a 50-year tradition that has helped millions of addicted persons throughout the world. Although many supporters have benefited enormously from this program, some object to using this model for incest survivors on several grounds. Some survivors complain that incest is not a sickness, not a behavioral problem that requires admitting that one is sick. They do not feel they need to make amends, as the anonymous programs require, because it was they who were victimized. On the other hand, some incest survivors interpret this task as the need to make amends to themselves for their self-blame, self-abuse, low self-esteem. Also, the damage incest does sometimes has led them to blame others for their own inability to be assertive; being victimized causes them to treat others badly, and amends are in order.

A major focus of the "A" programs is spiritual—the belief that one should "turn things over" to a "higher power." Although they state the program is not religious, many meetings end with the Lord's Prayer. The Serenity Prayer, earlier cited in this book and used in all meetings, begins with a more generic, but still religious (though non-denominational), "God grant me. . . ." Some incest survivors are relieved to find a view of a caring, safe Higher Power who does not blame them in the way they blame themselves. They need and welcome a spiritual focus in their lives. But others are alienated by what they consider to be pressure to have certain beliefs, or by the idea of turning their power over to an all-powerful "Father." SIA has addressed this concern by redefining the Higher Power as a "she or a he," and broadening the view to better reflect the needs of women incest survivors. Yet a kind of a creed remains, and some believe that incest survivors have been robbed of so much that nothing, no structure, no value system, no orientation, should be imposed on them. Still, the benefits of this fellowship have been time-tested and many people of all creeds have felt helped by it; you, as an incest survivor, must evaluate whether it's for you. Many other types of groups exist as well, though they generally do not have a national structure or as long a history.

For the names of groups in your community, look under self help or incest in the phone book. Call your local rape crisis or women's center. Check around in related groups (many members of ACOA know of incest groups, for instance). Call the Self Help Clearing House nearest you. Begin networking through the national survivors' groups listed in the appendix.

Therapist-Run Groups

Therapy groups are interactive: participants share and work on their emotional responses to the interactions they have with each other. Therapist-run groups can offer a sense of protection, with the expertise of someone trained in helping people uncover and work through their feelings. They can offer exercises such as role-playing that can help you identify and work on relationship and communication problems. A therapist can help members who need guidance in their recovery and can make sure no one gets out of control. These groups generally cost money, though usually they are much less expensive than individual therapy; sometimes health insurance helps pay their cost, and some are available through public facilities at a sliding scale.

However, some survivors find the presence of a therapist—a power figure—invasive, and feel that any attempt to question or guide them intrusive. They want only to be free to say whatever they wish, without any external intervention.

Additionally, just because someone is a professional doesn't mean that he or she is capable or knows about incest. And just because an agency or mental health clinic advertises itself as offering services for incest survivors doesn't mean that it understands incest or offers good therapy. Incest survivors have called me with some pretty frightening stories about the incompetence and unprofessionalism of therapists who lead well-publicized groups at mental health agencies that are known for their incest services. As usual, the incest survivor seeking this kind of help must be careful.

Individual Psychotherapists

An incest survivor can be involved in psychotherapy alone or in conjunction with group involvement. Because individual therapy is a private relationship without the input of other incest survivors, the therapist's role is important—a therapist can be extremely helpful, virtually no help at all, or even damaging to a client. Incest survivors not only have the basic concerns of a consumer (yes, the therapist is your employee, although it is easy to feel that they are in charge and you are powerless), but also need to make sure that the therapist is knowledgeable about incest and the needs of incest survivors.

For those requiring therapist-run services at a public clinic (rather than practitioners in private practice), I usually recommend family service agencies rather than mental health clinics. I like less focus on diagnosis and more on interpersonal functioning.

Couples Therapy, Sex Therapy, Assertiveness Training

Although these therapies can be extremely helpful, an incest survivor should not begin any of them if she is so internally demolished that she can't deal with her life or her past. Some inner rebuilding may be a good idea before these refinements are addressed. The survivor in couples therapy, for instance, needs to be strong enough not to take all the blame for the problems in the relationship and not to allow herself to be persuaded that her needs are invalid and she should change to meet her partner's needs. Sex therapy is helpful only after other recovery tasks have been achieved.

How To Choose a Therapist

You should address some general and incest-related questions when interviewing a potential psychotherapist. The following are meant as guidelines. The assertiveness required to ask a psychotherapist these questions is more than most of us can muster! These questions can also offer a basis for continuing evaluation of the therapy relationship.

1. Where did you get the referral? If you asked for a name from your doctor or minister, you are not necessarily getting advice

from anyone who understands what makes a good therapist, and often you are given the names of psychiatrists. Doctors rarely recommend social workers. Good referrals often come from people you trust who have good relationships with their shrinks (and who are making progress). Ask members of your self-help group for the therapists they trust. Get a few names—just because someone else likes a therapist doesn't mean you have to (and it's OK not to).

2. Are you more comfortable with a therapist who is energetic, warm and nurturing, or laid back? Do you want feedback, or would you prefer someone who only reflects back what you've said? Will she answer your questions, or respond to all of them with, "What do you think that means?" (When I was 19, I had a therapist who responded that way, refusing to give me the definition of "sibling," as if the meaning I gave it were significant to my emotional functioning!) The pace of the therapist is important: do you work fast or do you need to go slowly? Does the therapist need to have a sense of humor? Are you political—do you want to address the power imbalances in society and other gender-related issues?

3. The gender of the therapist can be important. I believe that women can best serve women, because women and men are raised differently. It is hard for a man to understand the life experience of a woman. However, since I have become involved with the issue of sexual violence, I have met some excellent, sensitive male therapists—caring men who work hard to understand how power issues affect women.

4. Do you feel the therapist respects your decision to screen her/him? Is the therapist willing to answer your questions?

5. Does the therapist believe in "therapeutic touch"? How does he or she define that? What do *you* think of it? Does she understand that a touch or a hug should always be up to you?

6. What does the therapist believe are the boundaries around the relationship? Will it be OK to call her outside office hours? Under what circumstances? What does she feel about socializing with clients? (It's not a good idea to confuse the therapy relationship by socializing with a therapist, who is a person of power and authority to a client.)

7. Does the therapist think that sexual activity between therapist and client is *ever* OK? If so—RUN. And tell everyone you know to stay away too. (It would be wonderful to have a registry of therapists who have been convicted of sexual abuse of clients and other forms of malpractice.)

8. Does the therapist believe in recommending reading? I know a therapist who feels this interferes with therapy, but I think that it enhances it, as long as the client doesn't hide behind intellectual answers in lieu of emotional work. Most survivors I know are thirsty for knowledge and use reading well. What is the therapist's level of awareness of current books?

9. What does the therapist know about your areas of concern (not only incest, but eating disorders, phobias, etc.)? Ask open ended questions, not questions such as "Do you know about incest?" I recommend asking, "What experience do you have working with incest survivors?" "What training have you had," and "What do you think incest survivors need to work on in therapy?"

10. Does the therapist know of and refer to recovery groups (for addiction) and self-help groups (for incest)? For some problems, one or two hours of outpatient psychotherapy a week are not enough. A good therapist knows his or her limits, and does not need to be the only important or helpful person in your life.

11. A trick question I use when evaluating therapists is "What percent of your clients are incest survivors?" Therapists who are aware of incest give a high percentage, even if the clients have not remembered yet.

    Perhaps the best trick question is, "When is incest the fault of the child?" (Yes, ask it just like that). Any answer other than "NEVER!" should send you runnin' and hollerin'.

12. Does the therapist use special therapy exercises such as role playing, letter writing, or sex therapy through behavior modification? The therapist need not be everything you want, so if she does not do these things, you can evaluate how important they are, and whether you can go somewhere else, too, for them.

13. How important does the therapist think memories are to recovery? If you don't remember much, what will she do with that? Does she know what else to work on?

14. Ask specific questions based on what you've learned, such as "How do you define incest?"

15. How do you feel talking with the therapist? Do you feel accepted and listened to? Is power shared? Do you feel that the therapist has expertise? Or do you feel judged, dominated, dismissed, distant?

Review these questions continually as you work together. But understand that tension or discomfort in the therapy relationship, as with all your relationships, may be an outgrowth of the problems that brought you to therapy—your issues, rather than the therapist's. So for your own sake—if you have a problem with a therapist who generally meets your needs, your first step is to look inside yourself. Blaming the therapist can be a convenient way to define all your problems as belonging to the other person, never looking at what you need to work on. If you are unhappy with the therapist's responses, try to discuss it. In intimate or power relationships such as therapy, such conflict is virtually inevitable and is an opportunity to grow. You can still decide to leave as soon as you've faced it, but you may decide not to.

However, if you feel abused, get out. Many incest survivors have a distorted perception about abuse, either missing it when it's there or seeing it when it's not, so check with other incest survivors in recovery when you feel this.

Leave if the therapist belittles your experience by saying, for instance, "It couldn't have been that bad, he really only loved you, are you sure?"—or "That doesn't happen in this kind of family," or "Didn't you want it to happen? Maybe you imagined it."

Don't feel bad if you can't ask all or any of these questions, but keep them in mind. Like any other relationship, the therapy bond is a choice. You have the right to leave if the partnership does not help you.

UNBLOCKING MEMORIES

Considerable growth and recovery can occur without memories being revealed to the survivor; all of the items on the Aftereffects Checklist can serve as topics to be addressed in recovery. Yet many survivors feel the need to unlock their repressed pasts and to know what happened to them. Two techniques are especially helpful for this: hypnosis and body work.

Hypnosis: Uses and Cautions

Hypnosis appeals to some survivors because it seems to be a way to "get it over with." A survivor who is interested in hypnosis should explore her expectations. Does she hope that hypnosis can help her avoid dealing with the pain? Is she ready for the memories and feelings that hypnosis may unlock? One of the few stories I ever heard of an incest survivor being damaged by unblocking occurred because a hypnotist let her remember everything she had blocked. As incest imposes premature sexuality, hypnosis can impose premature remembering. An incest survivor should consider only a hypnotist who understands incest, therapy, and the value of the inner guide, who should be invoked during the hypnosis to allow the incest survivor to remember only what she can handle.

Body Work

The body stores the memories of incest, and I have heard of dramatic uncovering and recovery of feelings and experiences through body work. This type of therapy includes massage therapy and other traditional forms of body work, as well as newer types or adaptations specifically designed to unlock memories of such childhood traumas as incest. One such type of "body memory work" has been adapted by Wendy Hoffman, founder of Human Healing Arts, for incest survivors. Other types of body work are being created every day. This therapy has been around for a long time but never taken seriously by talk therapists. It should be. It can release memories and feelings that talk therapy cannot touch.

MIND AND BODY TOGETHER IN RECOVERY

Much information has come to light in recent years about the effects of trauma on brain chemistry and the relationship between brain function and mental illness. Nutritional or biochemical treatments use foods, vitamins, enzymes, and other nutritional substances to improve emotional or mental functioning through changes in the organic functioning of the brain. Many incest survivors have been able to change dramatically through these treatments.

The buyer should beware in this new field. Although professionals—psychiatrists, doctors, nutritionists, and chiropractors—are involved in this field, traditional credentials bear no correlation to an ability to do this work. Some give basically the same answers and treatment to everyone, while some tailor specific programs to each individual. I've seen it make a big difference for some people. I've seen others waste a lot of money.

SPECIAL ISSUES, SPECIAL APPROACHES

A variety of other approaches provide intensive, time-limited intervention which is a catalyst for incest recovery.

Workshops for Incest

Around the country, many women's therapy centers and other programs offer day, weekend, and week long retreats and workshops that address sharing the secret, healing the inner child, dealing with anger, and other aspects of recovery. Many incest survivors report these to be powerful experiences. Some programs screen their applicants, some do not; some suggest or require that applicants be in ongoing therapy, some do not. Those that do not screen their applicants risk overwhelming or harming some participants. Some workshops can be extremely expensive, while others respond to survivors' needs for flexibility.

Releasing Anger

Talk therapy alone fails to unlock the repressed rage of many incest survivors. Anger workshops, limited or extended residential treatment, role playing, guided physical ventings of anger, and other forums may be necessary to strip the protective covers off the anger while providing the frightened child with the safety of a controlled environment. For some, however, this experience would be too frightening and intense, jeopardizing the fragile controls they have struggled to develop.

Witnessing the anger that may arise in these settings can also upset incest survivors; for this reason I recommend that self-help groups for which members are not screened and professional supervision is not provided, *not* engage in activities to dramatize anger.

However, support groups can serve as a safe space for the expressing of anger among people who do not judge. They are great for giving permission. At an incest survivors conference, an initially soft-spoken woman speaker's anger began to build and build, and her strength grew as it did, until she was shouting her mighty protests about the injustice that had been done to her. Finally she ran out of steam, her tears and rage vented, and there was a moment of stunned silence, at which point the room full of survivors burst into applause!

Therapy—especially if anger arises in response to the therapy itself—can guide the incest survivor toward focusing on and identifying her anger, venting it, and learning the awareness and communication skills necessary to manage it in relationships. If a therapist is not anger phobic, welcoming the healthy expression of a client's anger is helpful to the therapy. The incest survivor can learn that anger doesn't kill her, nor does it kill a healthy intimacy. She can learn that she is entitled to her anger, and the power of her anger, and the power of her life, if she acts on this anger to work for social change.

Empowerment Without Therapy

Women can overcome feeling vulnerable and powerless in ways other than psychotherapy or recovery groups.

Self-Defense Training Many women—not only women who were molested as children—need to discover their power and eliminate their fear. Self-defense courses (including the martial arts) are one way to do so. A good program combines teaching confidence and survival skills with genuine attention to the particular needs of women. One outstanding program is "Model Mugging." In situations designed to resemble real attacks, men who portray muggers "attack" women; applying newly learned skills, the women beat them up while other women cheer them on. The men feel a commitment to the empowerment of women because of abuses suffered by a woman close to them. Participants—women and "muggers" alike—share a deeply felt and moving experience. The only problem is that the cost (around $500) is prohibitive for many women. But this appears to be an ideal model for programs of this sort.

Personal Challenge: Wilderness Retreats Another empowering experience for survivors is a wilderness challenge such as those pioneered by the program Outward Bound. Participants learn to rely on themselves and trust others as they scale mountains, raft in rapids, cross ravines. Currently, Looking Up, a survivors group in Maine, and The Incest Awareness Project in North Dakota, offers these challenges. (See the appendix for addresses).

Used by cancer patients, troubled adolescents, Vietnam vets (it is being recognized as a recovery tool for post-traumatic stress disorder), it provides the participant with an opportunity to believe in herself and others again—all in a natural setting. Such trips can be genuinely dangerous (there are varying levels of challenge, some for beginners, some for the more rugged), but the reward can tap something real inside the adventurer, something that, in today's society, is often unrealized. As with some other resources, it can be extremely expensive. But for the same money, one can go on a purely recreational trip that does not yield the same positive outcome.

ISSUES IN RECOVERY

Certain questions commonly need to be addressed in recovery from incest.

What To Do About the Perpetrator

Incest involves at least two people: the victim and her abuser or abusers. The adult incest survivor has much work to do on herself, but she also has a ghost to deal with: the perpetrator, his crimes against her, and her relationship with him. Even if he is dead, or if she has had no contact with him for many years, the abuser can be a strong presence in her life. What should she do about him? What type of relationship, if any, should she have with him, and what about protecting others? The incest survivor must resolve these questions for herself.

"Keeping Families Together": Whose Needs?

Some argue for keeping families together or reuniting them. A primary proponent of this view is a national group called Parents United, whose founder, Dr. Henry Giaretto, runs a treatment program for "incest families." He appeared on a "Geraldo" show to debate this question, along with a family who had gone through his program. Both he and the family strongly asserted that punishment and separation of abusers from their families was not the solution. Treatment could— and should—keep families together.

What about the protection of the victim? Giaretto responded that his program was so successful at changing abusive behavior that there is less than 1% recidivism, and that parents aren't allowed to return to their families until they're sure at the program that the abuse won't occur again. However, the very family he brought to the show was evidence of their inability to provide any such guarantee: the father had re-molested his daughter. Concerning this, both the daughter and Giaretto protested that this took place in the beginning of treatment. But why was the father in the home considering Giaretto's insistence that abusers are not returned until the problem is arrested for sure? What does it mean that the daughter says that "right away they *returned*" to treatment?

The father himself said that he believed in jail first for incest: treatment too, but after punishment. And, indeed, he served some time for violation of his daughter. He served ten days.

David Finkelhor points out serious limitations to such treatment programs. Current projections of recidivism are inaccurately low. Recidivism rates go up when followup takes place over an extended period of time. In the first year, or two, or three, incest perpetrators are still more connected to the messages of their intensive program and still on their best behavior. Finkelhor goes as far as to recommend that before we believe any program's claims, their patients should be followed up for 10 to 20 years. His comprehensive review of research supports his claim.

Judith Herman highlights another factor: recidivism rates are based on self-reporting. That is, the victim, other family members, or the perpetrator himself must reveal that incest has again taken place. But for problems that involve denial—such as alcoholism and incest— self-reporting is notoriously unreliable. Herman presents research that provides frightening proof of this: more than two times as many parents said they were likely to conceal an incident at the completion of treatment than at its beginning. That is, having gone through treatment, they are more inclined to lie.

Finkelhor states powerfully: "It cannot be said that [anyone's re-cidivism studies] provide strong evidence in favor of the positive effects of treatment."

Still, there is hope: Finkelhor assures us that "[t]his does not . . . mean that treatment is ineffective." We should not give up on its po-tential. Prison-based treatment programs should continue to attempt to change the behavior of perpetrators while they are punished for their crime, before they are released back into society. But to risk our chil-dren's lives on Giaretto's claim—which strikes me as outrageous—of virtually 100% success is foolish. And we cannot underestimate the power of these claims, these biases, on the part of program directors. Herman found that in programs where reconciling families is the goal, families do just that: in one such program, three-quarters of the fami-lies were reconciled. But in programs where it is not set up as a goal, most, in fact, separate.

Giaretto's approach, perhaps clearly revealed in the name Parents United, does not seem to me to be victim-centered. The safety of the powerless child is again sacrificed for the sake of the father's place in the family. But maybe Giaretto's own words—a slip of the tongue, per-haps, but a very revealing slip—can help put the attitude behind this philosophy in its place. Early in the show he said that he wanted to be clear how disgusting he felt it was that a man would "make love" to his daughter. The audience reaction was immediate. *Make love!?!* they protested. "This has nothing to do with me!" "I never said that," Gia-retto said. Twice he tried to deny his words. But he had, indeed, said just that.

What basis should be used for reuniting families? Many research-ers and specialists have come to the same conclusion. Studies performed in five different treatment centers all agreed that in families with pater-nal incest the excessive power of the father must be reduced, the mother must be empowered, and the mother-daughter bond must be strengthened.

One justification used for reuniting families is the assumption that most daughters don't want their fathers to go to jail. This is a half-truth. Most children do not want to be responsible for a parent being sent to prison (or sent away from the family); this is one of the success-ful threats used by abusers! The child victim wants safety, nurturing, and the presence of others who can take care of her. She wants only *good* Daddy to stay, and bad Daddy to leave, but she cannot have only the Daddy she wants. Difficult as it might be to do, we must protect her, even if it appears we are not giving her what she wants.

Even in adulthood, her secret desire often stays the same: she still wants daddy. This ambivalence makes it difficult for many incest survivors to face their anger at their fathers directly. But their anger is clear: many, if not most, of my incest survivor clients, when hearing that Cheryl Pierson killed her father, responded with, "Good for her!"

Confronting: Some Considerations

Many survivors agree on the value of confronting the perpetrator, but some therapists have taken an unrealistic position on confrontation. One author of an early incest book, for instance, stated that if only the survivor would just do this, then she could heal quickly from her incest. Other therapists virtually require a face-to-face confrontation of their clients. Such therapists urge the survivor to confront her abuser much too early in her recovery, overlooking what is required for a victim to face this person to whom she may have strong emotional ties.

Confrontation does not start the process of recovery; a survivor *may* do it, *if* she wants to, *when* she is ready. It often needs to wait until she feels strong in her recovery.

Often, in the case of paternal abuse, family systems therapists pull everyone together to talk about the incest right in the beginning. "You must work with the family system as a whole," they say. "But what if the incest survivor is too fragile, too intimidated, too overwhelmed, to face her abuser?" I ask. "Then, you see, a family session is the perfect place for her to work on that, and get stronger," they respond.

I could not disagree more. In any therapy involving a victim, the needs of the victim should be the primary therapeutic concern. Victims should never be forced into therapy with their victimizers while there is any fear or a psychological power imbalance. That is therapeutically supervised abuse. The child victim within the adult is often timid and easily conquered. I have heard too many stories of fathers who apologize too quickly, without believing that they did anything wrong; of daughters too scared or weak to resist the therapists' pressure to work it out, giving in and letting go of their anger long before they are ready (or never finding their anger at all!). The goal of treatment for an incest survivor—whether child or adult—is the recovery of the victim.

The perpetrator must recognize his accountability for his abusive and illegal acts. Other children must be protected. The perpetrator is not on equal footing with nonabusive or victimized family members. Strengthening bonds among nonabusing family members—siblings, mother—is, however, important.

Confronting the abuser can, however, offer many benefits. It is an opportunity to face him with the consequences of his acts, to vent the rage and pain that the child has been forced to endure in silence. It is a forum for the adult to ally herself with the child and declare to the abuser, "I will not protect you any more!" It is the ultimate reclaiming of power for the survivor; it declares that she is not silenced, is not controlled. To confront is an opportunity to declare, "*I know what you did*, and you had no right."

But the incest survivor may not wish to, or be able to, face the abuser in person. Because most women pursue their recovery in adulthood, their perpetrators may have died. She may not feel strong enough. She may doubt the benefits of confronting an old, pathetic alcoholic who does not remember abusing her, who does not even resemble the aggressive, violent man he once was.

It is not necessary to face the abuser in person. Confrontations can take place through a letter, whether mailed or not. They can be played out through role playing in therapy or monologues in a recovery group. Catharsis can come through psychodramas or even actual plays, or written scenarios.

If you are considering confronting your abuser in person, here are some things to keep in mind:

1. Do it only because you want to, when you want to. Only you can decide when you're ready. And there is no shame in not doing it; after all, whose life is it, anyway?

2. Do it from a position of strength. Generally, you do not get a heartfelt acknowledgement and apology from the abuser. Most likely, he does what he has always done—protect himself. You may be challenged, blamed, laughed at, told you're crazy. He may rage at you or respond with such earnest bewilderment that you (again) doubt your own experience.

   Confrontation itself is your goal, rather than some wished-for response. Herman states that the survivor should not expect her family to absolve her of guilt; "rather, she absolves herself in their presence." If family members respond with denial, panic, hostility, or threats, through her response she can better identify with the inner child's early struggle.

3. Do it to honor your own feelings.

4. Although recall of details is not necessary for healing, it helps in confrontation, especially if your belief in yourself wavers. I know women who have said, "I know what you did" so convincingly that the accused never dared say, "Yeah? What?"

5. Do not let him apologize too quickly, too easily. Fast apologies shorten a process that is awkward for him; they end *his* pain. If he is concerned with your feelings, hard as it might be for him, he accepts your right to complain; he listens, cares, and feels his own pain at what he did to you. *Then* he apologizes for what he did. This may take time and may require therapeutic guidance, but he should at least try.

6. If there are other sexually abused children in the family, it might strengthen your position if the siblings confront him together. However, no sibling should be pressured into anything.

7. Thoroughly review your expectations and all the possible outcomes. The more prepared you are, the stronger you will be before, during, and after any confrontation.

8. Most of all, get the emotional support you need, both for preparing for the confrontation and for when it's over. Let people know when you're doing the confrontation and line up some supports for right after, if you should want to talk then.

9. Do it for you. I know I said it before. It bears repeating.

(One of the national incest support groups, VOICES in Action, Inc., has a useful flyer available to members called "How to Confront Your Perpetrator, Dead or Alive." Their address is in the appendix.)

Confronting a nonabusing parent is also helpful, but it is a separate task, with a separate goal. A mother-daughter confrontation is for the mother to hear her daughter's pain, and for the daughter to realize her mother's possible victimization. The mother's job is to strengthen herself so that she can finally become the ally that her daughter wants and deserves.

Forgiving: Who is it For?

Much is made—by churches, therapists, and many Anonymous-type groups—of the need to forgive parents. Incest survivors are told, "You will feel so much better if you forgive him." Adult children of alcoholics are told, "He had a sickness." Children with complaints about unhappy childhoods are told, "They did the best they could."

Is it in the incest survivor's best interest to forgive her abuser? Alice Miller claims that this attitude expresses the therapeutic and social bias in favor of the parents' needs at the expense of the child's. Will we make it, again, the job of the child to take care of the parents?

Is it true that the abuser did the best he could? No person who violates or victimizes another is doing the best he can. This is not a well-meaning but fallible parent, struggling with his own doubts and history. This is an adult with a sacred trust who violated another human being—a child, sometimes his own child—again, and again and again.

Would we argue that an adult survivor of a sexual assault by a stranger should forgive him? Although the law—and other segments of society—treats incest as less a crime than rape by a stranger, the ultimate moral horror lies in the abuser's violation of his responsibility to protect the child who is in his care.

Society's job is to understand that, as author/attorney Andrew Vachss says, "We cannot continue to reward a certain class of criminals simply because they may have biologically produced their victims." It is time to stop excusing the abuses of incest perpetrators and others who abuse family members.

Should the victim forgive? Only if she truly wants to. Only if it's for herself. And only if she understands that she has another option: as Bass and Davis suggest in *The Courage to Heal,* she can *let go.* She would not benefit from carrying resentment around for the rest of her life. To do so would further victimize her and continue to give power to her abuser. By letting go, she can shed the unnecessary burden of stored hostility, freeing that energy for better purposes.

It's your choice, but I feel that before you forgive or let go, you should make sure that you know what happened and that you have honored your anger fully. And if you want to forgive your abuser, I feel that he should earn that forgiveness by facing what he has done, and letting you tell him what he has done to you, for as long and in as much detail as you need.

Suing Perpetrators

Incest survivors can be clever and resourceful. Even though criminal prosecution is in many cases impossible (due to factors such as the statute of limitations and lack of evidence), they have still pursued justice for the crimes against them. Like other victims of the misconduct of trusted "professionals", survivors of incest have initiated civil lawsuits to compensate for damages.

Often these survivors are challenged. "Why are you doing this?" a talk-show audience member demands, "Is it just for the money?" "No," they answer. "The money can hardly replace my fractured sense of myself; nothing can give me back my childhood. The money is a symbol. He should pay for what he did to that child."

Alan Rosenfeld, a Vermont attorney who helped pioneer this litigation, routinely asks the reason for the lawsuit on a questionnaire he sends women who contact him. Most say that their desire to sue comes from an "overwhelming need for justice." The suit offers them an opportunity for some validation from the system that abandoned them; a positive outcome is the system's acknowledgement that yes, something happened, and yes, he had no right.

There are also practical reasons for suing: incest often results in large medical and psychotherapy expenses for women whose earning ability (low because of their gender) is reduced by the damage done by the abuse.

But these survivors are faced with a Catch-22. The statute of limitations—the time allotted by law during which criminal or civil action may be initiated—is limited. Although it varies state to state, one example of a liberal law imposes a limit of 3 years after the date of discovery of a crime (which would be when the abuse is remembered). However, many states do not take into consideration the blocking often done by survivors. In New York State, for instance, a survivor has only 3 years from the last incident, or from the age of majority, whichever is later. And even those states with "date of discovery" statutes do not take into consideration that many incest survivors within 3 years of remembering their abuse are not emotionally ready to pursue a lawsuit because of the damage done to them by the crime.

The basis upon which Rosenfeld, and other lawyers country-wide, as well as the National Organization for Women (NOW), are challenging the statute is called equitable estoppel. According to Rosenfeld, equitable estoppel asks that the court prevent the abuser from using the damages he caused as a shield from liability. Why should the incest perpetrator be protected by the fact that he has emotionally incapacitated his victim?

I saw Rosenfeld argue this point before the U.S. Court of Appeals in 1988. But the justices were not persuaded. Perhaps their concern is reflected in their statement that, if the statute were lifted, perpetrators of incest would have to look over their shoulders for the rest of their lives in fear of legal action. Somehow that possibility struck me as eminently fair.

Around the time of this case, a tragic event occurred that brings this legal concept clearly to light. In the spring of 1987, a client of Rosenfeld's, Cynthia Gustafson, committed suicide. Newspaper accounts reported that when she was 32, and her father, Philip Weis, wrote her a letter saying that her niece reminded him of Cindy, suddenly her awareness of her abuse was released. First she called her brother to warn him about the father. And then she attempted suicide. But she survived and initiated legal proceedings against her father. She began suffering flashbacks and nightmares. According to Rosenfeld, her suicide "graphically demonstrates" the way in which incest damages prevent the survivor from initiating civil action "and shows that statements in court about life-threatening consequences are all too real." "If you take on a suit before you are ready," he says, "it will kill you." Like other lawyers who understand incest, he requires incest survivors who are pursuing legal action to be involved in therapy. But sometimes therapy isn't enough. Sometimes there is too much pain.

In the letter he wrote to the Barre, Vermont, *Times Argus* memorializing his courageous client, Alan Rosenfeld said of her, "Cynthia Gustafson, the adult survivor, is no longer with us. Cindy, the still-trusting, ever-hopeful little girl, is finally at peace."

In June 1988, a Massachusetts Superior Court granted an incest survivor's request to suspend the statute of limitations. The court said that she could not possibly have known the damage done by the abuse until a nervous breakdown that she suffered more than a decade after the abuse ended. "Often," declared Judge Herbert Abrams, "it is not until adulthood that a child victim of incest abuse will begin to exhibit signs of incest trauma. Although the victim may know that she is injured, until such time as she is able to place the blame for the incestuous abuse upon her abuser, it will be impossible for her to realize that her abuser's behavior caused her psychological disorders."

Because this is the lowest court in Massachusetts, the decision is not precedent-setting, in that it affects no other courts. This is only a partial victory in other ways as well: it allows the moment of discovery to be when the survivor understands that incest is the source of her problems, but still fails to take into account how emotionally incapable a survivor might be of pursuing a lawsuit within the time stipulated. At this writing, Vermont will soon reconsider a bill to make equitable estoppel law in these cases.

TECHNIQUES AND METHODS FOR HEALING

A number of exercises facilitate getting in touch with—and working through—feelings. The reader is referred to the Appendix for books that discuss these. What follows are two activities that I have found helpful for survivors.

Reunion Therapy: The Child Within

"The child," the saying goes, "is father of the man." Your childhood gave birth to who you are today. Finding, allying with, and healing that child within are necessary tasks for adults whose childhoods were damaged by incest or other abuses, alcoholism—any childhood loss, unhappiness, or trauma. The child's needs, feelings, and thoughts have been so long silenced that many of us struggle to hear her, to acknowledge those parts of ourselves that are hers. When we intellectualize, or suppress our feelings, we silence the child. When we forget how to play, we negate the child within us.

To help my clients meet and learn from the child within, I have them do an exercise that I call "reunion therapy." First, we define who the adult is and who the child. The *adult* might stuff feelings, be guarded, block memories, think things through instead of feel them through, be capable and responsible, try to be in control, or take care of other people. The child might be spontaneous, impulsive, feel her feelings immediately and in their raw form, be aware of the damage that has been done to her—and she hurts. She is vulnerable, she needs people, she can be selfish; she is awkward, she makes mistakes; she is imperfect; she has no secrets; she can be demanding, honest, loyal, and needy. (It is her job to be needy.) She can play and laugh and be alive. She can also be a pain in the neck, tugging at your sleeve to make you pay attention to her—to your own feelings and needs.

The client sits in one chair to be the adult and switches to another to be the child. They talk to each other about how they feel about each other, what they want from each other, or their feelings about the situation. The experience is often powerful and informative. Often, the adult learns more from the child than vice versa. Pretty smart, that child she's worked so hard not to hear. The child usually has the strength to feel her pain; the adult usually resorts to defenses to manage her feelings. The child often tells the adult to stop ignoring her when she expresses that pain. The adult—the mother to the child within—often realizes that it is so hard to watch the child's pain that she often responds with, "It's not that bad," or "Try not to think about it." Her anxiety over not being able to fix the kid's pain, or her own pain, are so overpowering that she cannot acknowledge the child's feelings; she is too weak within herself to be a strong parent. Many realize that this is like the responses that many survivors got from their mothers, many of whom were battered, married to alcoholics, or untreated incest survivors themselves. Now, they have a clearer understanding of why their mothers failed them.

To parent the child well is to never minimize her pain, discount her, or ignore her. The survivor often thinks she should get rid of the child's pain, but all the child wants is to be listened to. She's afraid to share that pain with the adult because she's scared she'll be rejected or abandoned. They need to re-connect and learn to trust each other. Each has things of value to offer the other. Each needs to work on accepting her own limits and the other's. But the child is rightfully impatient. After all, it's been so long, and she's been so alone.

Letter Writing

Many incest survivors have found writing to be extremely helpful. Letters to important persons—parents, abuser, siblings—are an especially effective way to face and unload feelings. But letters don't have to be to persons: recently, I had a client write a letter to "sex." She had always felt obligated to have sex with any man she needed. Her letter began, "You don't know me, and I don't know you." Some letters you mail, some you don't. The ones you don't mail can often express feelings more honestly, for the other person's response is not a factor. Here is part of a letter that survivor Lilly Artemis* wrote to her abusing father:

> Your anger and abuse of me must have been sheer panic for a little girl to deal with. But I was a very smart little girl; I knew that I couldn't go anywhere—I needed my parents to take care of me—so I made up a father! I forgot the sexual molestation, I don't remember your not talking to me, I instead remember a loving, caring, protective father. I think back on my life with you and I feel sadness. I loved you so very much and you ruined it. Your irresponsible actions ruined our relationship forever.
>
> You know something—it's your loss. I know that for you I am dead. I figure that is your way of gaining some control and not hurting. Well guess what: I am not dead, I am very much alive and I have a big mouth, I tell anyone I can that you are a child molester. . . . I am always scared after I say those things, because I figure that you're going to come and kill me after I fall asleep. You damaged my ability to trust myself, but after a little while the fear passes and I feel so good that I don't carry the secret—that I am no longer the receptacle for your disease. I will not die carrying your secret.
>
> You tried to destroy me and at times you almost succeeded, but you know, "Darth Vader," you're beginning to win less and less.

This letter by another survivor expresses another approach to reclaiming power:

> I will not be a part of that big untruth that we've all tried to call a family . . . I have resigned from the job of trying to make a family of us. All of my soul went into that job, trying to fill in all those voids for all of you. . . . [As a child] I knew I would die for you, without a moment's thought or hesitation. That would have been easy because there really was no "me" that I'd be losing, then, by dying.

But I would not die for you today.

THY SISTER'S KEEPER

I strongly recommend that an incest survivor break the secrecy that surrounds and protects incest because openness is a healing act. Likewise, what she chooses to do about her perpetrator should be based on her own recovery needs. After a lifetime of training that she is unimportant, the incest survivor is more than entitled to focus on her own needs.

The survivor is in a unique position in terms of experience and special interest, with regard to the welfare of future generations of vulnerable children. What role, if any, should an incest survivor have in protecting potential victims, in changing society?

She can strip the protective cloak of secrecy off the perpetrator, so that he can at least be kept away from current or potential child victims. In breaking the secret, she provides a role model for others whose fear of coming forward had prevented them from getting support. Among the survivors I have heard of who took a "public" stand within their families, many were approached, at least in some tentative way, by young relations. On a broader level, victims or survivors who reveal abuse by, for instance, a minister or teacher can sound an alarm that reaches even strangers who were also in contact with the perpetrator.

When joined with the voices of other incest survivors, hers can become a part of an awesome force for change—increasing social awareness, political support, economic resource development, and, potentially, inspiring adjustments in therapeutic, legal, religious, and other institutions. She can bear witness, forcing us to face reality about our elected, appointed, or cherished "emperors." She can add her truth to the stories of countless other survivors, to assure that researchers finally obtain accurate information about the rate of occurrence of incest. These statistics can then help all of us who care to join incest survivors to end the horrors of incest and its surrounding conspiracy. As a brochure distributed by the Incest Awareness Project of Fargo, North Dakota (the address is in the appendix), instructs survivors, "Refuse to be silent: Break the NO TALK rule. Call the crime of incest a crime."

Survivors can put pressure where it needs to be put; educate, fundraise, lobby, and, perhaps most, shatter the lies such as "Incest doesn't happen here!" and "Dr. Jones would never do THAT!"

Ultimately, activities of incest survivors can help people understand and face the importance of changing some deep-rooted attitudes and fundamental beliefs in society; only then can we begin to address the power issues that encourage and preserve the power imbalances in the nuclear family. In *Father-Daughter Incest,* Herman says:

> Preventing sexual abuse will ultimately require a radical transformation of the family. The rule of the father will have to yield to the cooperative rule of both parents, and the sexual division of labor will have to be altered so that fathers and mothers share equally in the care of the children. . . . These ambitious, even visionary changes will not be the work of one lifetime.

It is time to begin, and we have begun. The voices of many courageous, even defiant incest survivors have smashed our denial and forced into conscious awareness the fact that many of our children, sisters, friends, lovers, mothers, and grandmothers were victims of childhood incest.

But the incest survivor is wounded, and she is healing. And it is she, and only she, who has the power and the right to decide what action she can take in the greater problem. She may simply have the strength to do no more than survive; if she is fortunate, she has the strength to take on the task of her recovery as well.

THE JOB WE ALL MUST DO

But while the incest survivor heals, we do not have to wait for change. There are quiet things that all of us must do. Protecting the innocent is not a job for only the survivor. It is a job for all of us.

As long as those who are directly charged with their care are abusing that trust, if the rest of us do not take on the job, these children are being sacrificed.

Each of us must consider this commitment. That is the extent of our obligation: to evaluate the need and decide our own course of action. The outcome of that decision is our choice.

With all my soul and heart I challenge everyone to join together to end sexual abuse. But I know that each person must decide whether, and how much, to get involved. I also know that the incest survivor is not in the same place with this as the rest of us.

We can educate our children, but not merely by telling them to say no to strangers. To expect a child to say no to someone she needs or to a person with authority over her, to expect her to know how and when, to expect her to have the *ability* to do this, is unreasonable. And unfair. Certainly we should empower our children with support for their ownership of their bodies and lives. But let us beware of the message that this gives. First, it is not up to the child to stop incest. Second, she may run away from a stranger, but she cannot run away from Daddy. Indeed, as Joan Retsinas pointed out in "Don't Speak to Strangers," her 1988 *Newsweek* article, warning kids about strangers may make them suspicious of *just* the wrong people: "We end up with a schizophrenic nightmare: surrounded by potentially friendly strangers, we live with people who may actually be dangerous."

When we provide sex education for our children, we have to do the complete job, without illusions. Finkelhor's research revealed that when parents discuss sex and sexual abuse with kids, less than a quarter mentioned the possibility of abuse by a family member.

And fathers must involve themselves in this aspect of the parenting role: men must take a stand with their children, that no man has the right to impose anything on them. They must model gentleness while they take a stand firmly on the side of the powerless. Men have abrogated this aspect of their responsibility as parents and citizens. Finkelhor states that "educators in the field of prevention report that their classes consist almost exclusively of women."

Further, we must start sooner. Most parents think discussions about sex should start when a child is 9. By age 9, many, if not most, incest survivors I know were already abused.

Women need to be realistic about the possibility that men of their acquaintance might harm their children. Citing the disproportionately high rate of incest by stepfathers, Russell recommends that women "seriously evaluate the interest of these men in their daughters, observe the way they relate to them, avoid placing their daughters in vulnerable situations, warn the daughters about the dangers of incestuous abuse," and create a climate where "daughters will come to them if abused. . . . This is a much more effective means of protecting daughters than remaining in destructive marriages with the concomitantly destructive role model [they] provide."

We must change far more than just sex. We must rethink touch, affection, family, and the distribution of power. As Russell points out, restructuring society is a lofty goal, but is can begin on a smaller scale, with the empowering of women, the gentling of men, and the balancing of relationships. These changes would benefit everyone. As Herman says, "When men no longer rule their families, they may learn for the first time what it means to belong to one." In the end this is hardly an individual problem, not even a family problem: it is a problem so vast, so entwined with what it means to be a woman or a man, that it has become a social norm.

If one believes the statistics that 25% or 38% of all women were molested by an adult or much older child, and if we then add the 8-year-old child whose abuser was 11, or the daughter whose uncle regularly exposed himself to her, or the many who do not remember and so cannot report, then the number of women who were sexually abused as children may easily exceed 50%. More than half of all women were violated as children, most by someone they loved. Sixty million women (and many, many men as well).

What we consider normal behavior in women may in large part be the distorted life experience of Post-Incest Syndrome: the passivity, the seductiveness, the inability to accept her body, the dependency, the sense of duty and resignation regarding men's sexual needs, the perpetual victimization, the compulsion to deaden her feelings, the life-long pattern of sacrifice, the sense of obligation. If incest is the heritage of so many women, then its pathology comes to be seen as normal. This pathology bleeds down through the generations. It affects survivors' loves, their relationships, and the way they raise their children.

GUERRILLA TACTICS

Drastic changes are necessary. In desperate times, desperate measures are called for. But the system ignores the needs of survivors and the cries of children. As a result, many women have become, indeed, mothers of invention.

The Underground Railroad

In the late 1980's, a number of women responded to the problem of a judicial system unresponsive to their children's abuse.

There are many kinds of mothers. Although the stereotype is that the mother of an incest victim is weak, cold, needy, or abandoning, many mothers try to rescue their molested children from their husbands (only to be met by a court system whose reaction is just short of a Fellini movie.) When they attempt to seek court protection for their children, the courts often give full custody to the perpetrating father. The courts claim that the mother is a trouble maker or that she is brainwashing her children.

The tape recordings of these children's screams as they are carried away for unsupervised visits with men who raped them are horrible to hear. The medical documentation of their internal injuries and sexually transmitted diseases is indisputable. Some judges admit that there is clear and convincing evidence of abuse but permit visitation anyway. Courts continue to disregard the mothers' pleas and children's cries, again and again delivering the victim to her rapist. Some mothers have resorted to protecting their children the only way they know how: by hiding them and refusing to reveal their whereabouts. For violating the court order, the mothers are jailed. For violating their daughters, the fathers are not.

There has developed a network of homes whose doors are open to these women (and some men) and their children. Often it is comprised of women who were themselves molested as children, or mothers who, in earlier times, were unable to rescue their children because no one listened and no one cared.

The courage and strength expressed by these mothers, and some of their loved ones, who give everything up to protect their children, is matched only by the kindness of strangers. The women who open their homes to these refugees, risking their own welfare, are vindicating their pasts and helping save a future generation.

Until recently in New York State, the law prevented a perpetrator from being convicted only on a child victim's complaint. In Washington, D.C., at this writing, that is still the case.

It will be many years before the courts respond properly to this crisis, if they ever do, and many will pay the price. Rosenfeld's advice to mothers dramatically reflects our times. If your child indicates to you that she has been sexually abused, do not surrender to the impulse to take her in your arms and urge her to tell you about the pain she has experienced. Instead, take her immediately—immediately—to the most socially credible expert you can find, and have her tell her story to that stranger. If you talk to her, the perpetrator, or the courts, can accuse you of brainwashing her, and if that happens, not only may her claim not ever be believed, but also you might lose custody of your daughter.

Judith Herman puts it this way:

> As in the case of other crimes against women and children, for too long the power of the justice system has protected the men who victimized them. . . . As long as the justice system remains a male preserve, it can hardly be expected to reform itself. . . . The initiative for those reforms that have already been carried out has come almost entirely from women: from the rape counselor, the child advocate, and the small minority of women who work within the system—we look forward to a time when women, who are so frequently the victims and rarely the offenders, adjudicate the majority of domestic and sexual crimes.

Until then, we have the underground railroad. And mothers like Elizabeth Morgan, M.D., released after a two-year jail tenure in Washington, D.C., whose case brought national, and legislative, attention to this outrage. And we have incest survivors who fight back in creative ways.

Suzanne's father died when she was 18, before she had the opportunity to confront him. The unveiling, a Jewish ceremony about one year after burial, was about to take place, and Suzanne could not let the ceremony pass without making a statement. How could she tolerate the rabbi's saying nice things about this man who had victimized her and others? We talked about her options. Some of our ideas were pretty outrageous. She considered, for instance, putting something on the grass to kill it and spell out a message, or a sign on the grave, under his name, to tell the world, "Norman is a child molester!" But she decided against this out of concern for the family, who deserved, she felt, a less shocking way of finding out. Some other ideas, like simply turning her back and walking away through the mourners after Norman's name was read, seemed too tame (like many survivors, Suzanne did not—could not—call her rapist "father"). I suggested she check her motives: Did she want to make a scene or a statement? The next session, she brought me the note that she had written and given to the rabbi. Her expectations about its effectiveness were limited: she had recently discovered that the rabbi had known Norman since childhood.

> Dear Rabbi Z———,
>
> Before you say anything about Norman. I urge you to consider the following:
>
> While driving drunk, Norman killed someone.
>
> By threat of death, Norman made me lie about this "accident" under oath in court.
>
> Norman was a child abuser. Over the years I've ended up in the emergency room more than once because of him.
>
> Norman was a child molester. He molested me.
>
> For my sake, for Lisa Steinberg, [the New York City child whose father, Joel, was convicted of beating her to death] and all the others who have suffered at the hands of their parents, and especially for the many children still being abused now—the many who will come after us—I implore you, please don't ignore the ugly reality. Please, in some small way, acknowledge Norman as he really was.
>
> Only by admitting that a problem exists are we free to look for solutions, and offer hope to the silent, innocent victims who have gone without help for so long.
>
> —Suzanne Cardinal* (nee Shubinsky)

There were two unveilings that day. Norman's was first. For the second person, the rabbi said the customary nice words. But for Norman, he said *nothing*. After everyone else left, Suzanne put a black rose and a bunch of dead flowers on the grave and "stamped them into the ground," wiping the mud from her shoes onto the gravestone. Then, "I told Norman he was a bastard and not fit to live and I was glad he was finally dead." She had had her confrontation, and the secret was no longer.

HEALING IS ENOUGH

Even by "merely" healing, survivors such as Suzanne are doing a great deal to affect the greater problem. When she heals, one more story is told, one more voice is heard, one more woman finds her power.

Only one, you say? But it is hardly only one. The incest victim or survivor is usually a part of a cycle of abuse; various studies estimate that between 30% and 80% of children who were molested had a parent who was as well. And, as Herman points out, the chain expands geometrically: because most perpetrators abuse more than one child, each generation of abusers multiplies the problem until, in the end, one perpetrator may have, without exaggeration, spawned thousands of victims—and new abusers. And that addresses only one aspect of the problem, for incest also affects what partners women survivors choose (many marry abusers) and how well they parent their children. Incest recovery can break this chain: it is, in that sense, primary prevention. Given the questionable success rate of current offender treatment programs, prevention (whether at the individual or social level) is our best hope for reducing the abuse of children.

There is an overwhelming power for social change contained in the one, plus one, plus one, in voices that combine to comprise 38% or 50% or 60%.

Ultimately, healing is a personal experience. Survivors who undertake the journey of recovery deserve support and need time to grow strong in the broken places, to make friends with her physical self, to reunite her mind and body, to feel safe in her own skin, to develop social skills, and to let go of being seductive. Slowly, the incest survivor who is healing learns to trust. First, she learns how to know *whether* to trust; she learns to let a little of her vulnerability show, or to share an important thing about herself, and to see how it is received. Then, if the coast is clear, she lets another thing out, and another, one step at a time, measuring the impact of the sharing or her safety in the relationship. She learns to trust her perceptions, to trust her guts, to trust her self. To rely on herself, but to sometimes lean on others, too.

The incest survivor inevitably asks, "Why me?" Although this is a reasonable thing for her to wonder, she learns that she needs to let go of this question and accept her history. She also learns that a little self-pity makes sense for the wounds she has suffered (and that nobody else has the right to judge how much is too much and that her training is to say that any amount is too much). Not pity as in, "Oh, poor me, now I can give up on myself and expect everyone to take care of me," but, as in, "Oh, that poor little girl that I was, I feel so bad for her." Like a hug for herself. Like honoring her experience.

The incest survivor has a childhood to mourn. She mourns the losses of expectations and needs that are a child's birthright. Think of an 8-year-old kid. Think of an 8-year-old kid with sad eyes. *She cries for her, for the child inside.* She's had nowhere to share her pain, but now someone affirms it: she does.

The incest survivor's greatest struggle may be in validating her feelings. It is so hard for her to feel entitled to complain about what happened to her, entitled to be given to instead of taken from. Finally, in the safety of her group, her therapist's office, the arms of a friend or lover, she finds her pain.

There is so much pain. "Every time I tell about it, I hurt in a new place," says a woman in *Father-Daughter Incest.*

Understandably, she wants it over. She wants to be rid of it. But in her pain lie the wisdom and understanding that will help her grow. I tell my clients who are trying not to cry but to "figure it out" that if they let themselves sit with it and fully experience it, the pain will show them, teach them.

The pain isn't entirely hers. It's the pain of the little girl that she was long ago. It's her that he silenced. It's her cry that deserves to be heard.

This journey of recovery can be slow, fascinating, tortuous, exhilarating, overwhelming, frightening, empowering, devastating, and freeing. But it is her journey.

Once the secret is broken, the story may come rushing out whenever she talks to anyone. So long held down, the pain may pour out as all of her senses and nerve endings come back to life. Dealing with incest can fill her every moment and every pore with anguish, but also offers many opportunities for victory as well.

In this period she almost certainly needs support 24 hours a day, although it may be difficult for her to reach out and ask for help. The support of other incest survivors who are at different phases of healing is invaluable.

This is not a treatment manual; see books such as Bass and Davis' *The Courage to Heal* and others in the recommended list for step-by-step, task-by-task analysis of this process.

Readers might find help in the following guide, which, after its initial distribution by *Voices in Action*, was expanded into *Reclaiming Our Lives*, by Carol Poston and Karen Lison. It is reprinted with permission.

14 STAGES OF GROWTH FOR SURVIVORS OF INCEST

by Karen Lison, MA

1. I cannot manage my pain alone. I must seek help.

2. I acknowledge that something terrible happened. I know it is not my imagination; I was a victim of childhood sexual assault.

3. I begin to recognize my feelings. There may be sadness, anger, fear, guilt, and shame. I allow myself to experience them all.

4. I discuss the abuse thoroughly with my therapist. I completely re-experience and begin to deal with feelings appropriate for each incident of abuse that I can recall. I share feelings of shame with my survivors group.

5. I begin to realize that I was probably acting *appropriately* at the time the abuse occurred. (That is, my reactions were appropriate; the abuse was not!)

6. If there was a part of the molestation that was pleasurable to me, I am coming to terms with the fact of that pleasure and I am dealing with the guilt surrounding it.

7. I perceive the connection between my molestation and my current behavioral patterns and relationships. I am beginning to develop some control over that connection.

8. I recognize that I have a choice as to whether or not I confront my perpetrator(s).

9. I am beginning to understand what I desire from relationships, as I learn to trust my perceptions.

10. I am able to enjoy intimacy.

11. I develop a sense of self and my self-esteem has increased.

12. My resistance to talking about the abuse (although not necessarily the details of it) has diminished.

13. I realize that I have a choice as to whether or not I forgive my perpetrator. I *have* forgiven *myself*.

14. I am in touch with past anger, but detached from it so that it is not a constant part of my feelings and a negative influence on my other feelings, my functioning, and my relationships with others. I no longer live in the past. I live in the present and welcome the future will all its fears, imperfections, and unpredictabilities.

This book follows the order not of recovery tasks, but of the aftereffects of incest: starting with perception and thought distortions, through guilt, fear, and anger, to related disorders such as alcoholism, and finally, to the incest survivor's relationship with her body; only then, with the fundamentals of the survivor's relationship with herself being addressed, did we arrive at sexuality and intimacy.

None of these guides is absolute: The course of recovery is never linear and follows no absolute order. Although you might want to compare your process to one of these lists (and feel inadequate!), these topics are a general framework, offered to help clarify the general course of events. Be gentle with yourself. You are following the course that is right for you. Always compare yourself to where you've been, not to where you're going, and eventually, you may find yourself where Barbara, whose story has been told often in this book, did.

Barbara had been in therapy 4 years. Finally she risked leaving an unchallenging job for a position in a neonatal unit. She was very excited; there was so much to learn, and so much opportunity to screw up! But she didn't. In fact, she had three crises in a row and met them all head-on, with confidence and wisdom. After spending a session excitedly telling me of all her victories, she said, "What a week! But I'm fine. In fact, in all the commotion, I forgot to be a survivor!"

Facing a problem is a rebirth. Frequently, I am struck by the perfection of this symbolism with regard to many types of clients, but none more than the woman who is working to resolve the aftereffects of incest. Purifying a sin that was not hers, she becomes her own parent. How can we fail to celebrate the incest survivor? Through healing and finding her power, she is, like the phoenix, reborn.

The incest survivor faces a struggle every day. With undeniable resilience, she endures a childhood of horror. Persistently, she "keeps on keeping on," hoping to one day find the strength and the help she needs to face what has happened to her in some therapeutic way.

While she struggles, those of us who are strong enough must do the work of declaring that our emperors are naked, of breaking secrets, smashing lies, and working toward change wherever we can. As for the incest survivor, we must support her right to do what she can, when she is able, by her choice, not by our command. In the meantime, while we work for change, we create a climate in which it is safe for her to do the work she must.

Resources

*T*his section organizes the names of groups, books, and other resources according to the chapter to which they relate.

Unless otherwise specified, send a business-size, stamped, self-addressed envelope to the group for information on membership and services.

Some groups have meetings or offices throughout the country but may not have a national contact address listed. You can probably find them in the phone book in your area. Additionally, two organizations are helpful in finding specific resources for a variety of needs. (Note: Resources specific to incest can be found in the appendices at the end of this section.)

- *Self Help Clearinghouse.* This national organization is an excellent resource for names of groups or individuals that support emotional and physical needs, support groups for special populations, and concrete services regarding poverty, education, unwed mothers, and so forth. Many local affiliates publish a directory of community services.

  For information on starting or finding self help groups, and for listings of many local affiliates, a guidebook called *The Self Help Sourcebook* is available. Write to Self Help Clearinghouse, Attention: *Sourcebook,* St. Clares-Riverside Medical Center, Pocono Road, Denville, New Jersey 07834.

  Self Help Clearinghouse affiliates exist in most areas but may be hard to find because their name often starts with the name of the area—for instance, "Michigan Self Help Clearinghouse" (which doesn't list a town name!) and "Long Island Self Help Clearinghouse." Call (212) 642-2944 for local referral.

• *National Council on Alcoholism (NCA).* This organization has a national phone number: 1-800-622-2255. Call for your local affiliate, which may be listed in your local phone book under NCA or the name of the region. Local chapters can give you information about a variety of resources for alcoholism and other addictive problems.

There are national hotlines for incest that offer local treatment and self help information, but I have not listed them, because they generally do not screen their resources and refer mainly to public agencies, which may or may not do the job best. (The skills necessary to win government funding are different from those required to deal with incest.)

CHAPTER 5: AM I CRAZY? NO, YOU'RE COPING

Multiple-Personality Disorder

International Society for the Study of Multiple Personality and Dissociation (ISSMP&D), 5700 Old Orchard Road, Skokie, Il 60077, (708) 965-2776. This group will respond both to professionals and sufferers of MPD.

Newsletter: Many Voices, P.O. Box 2639, Cincinnati, Ohio 45201-2639.

Post-Traumatic Stress Disorder

Society for Traumatic Stress Studies, P. O. Box 1564, Lancaster, Pennsylvania 17603-1564. This group is developing task forces to research the implications of childhood incest and develop training tools. Addresses needs of professionals only.

CHAPTER 8: ANGER AND RAGE

Bach, Dr. George and Peter Wyden. *The Intimate Enemy.* Avon, 1968. Although this book says there is no difference between women and men regarding anger, it offers a comprehensive analysis of how to fight productively.

Rubin, M.D., Theodore Isaac. *The Angry Book*. Collier Books, 1969. This book (by the author of *Lisa and David*) may be hard to find, but it's worth looking for. It discusses what we do to avoid anger and how these avoidance tactics hurt us.

Lerner, Ph.D., Harriet Goldhor. *The Dance of Anger*. Perennial/ Harper and Row, 1989.

CHAPTER 9: FEAR, TERROR, AND PHOBIAS

Phobias and Panic Attacks

Phobia Society of America, P. O. Box 42514, Washington, D. C. 20015. Literature, research updates, resource directory and self help information. Many communities have self help and peer-based treatment available, as well as professional services.

Many people who suffer from anxiety and panic disorders report being helped enormously by two books by Claire Weekes: *Peace from Nervous Suffering* (Bantam, 1972) and *Hope and Help for Your Nerves*, (Bantam, 1981).

CHAPTER 10: ADDICTIONS AND COMPULSIONS

For information on self help and treatment for all addictions, contact your local chapter of the National Council on Alcoholism. The Anonymous programs (12-Step Programs) are available nationwide for all addictive problems, including the following: Debtors Anonymous, Narcotics Anonymous, Pills Anonymous, Cocaine Anonymous, and Gamblers Anonymous. Check your phone book or newspaper, or call NCA.

Groups are available also for loved ones. For those involved with alcoholics, there is Al-Anon; with Gamblers, Gam-Anon; with Overeaters, OA-Anon (not available in all areas).

Alcoholism

Look in phone book for Alcoholics Anonymous. Contact Women for Sobriety (a woman-only group not affiliated with AA) by writing to WFS, Quakertown, Pennsylvania 18951, (215) 536-8026, 24 hours.

Al-Anon national numbers (through which you can also obtain information on Adult Children of Alcoholics groups) in New York, 800-245-4656; outside New York, 800-334-2666.

Christopher, James. *How to Stay Sober: Recovery Without Religion*. Prometheus Books (1988), 700 E. Amherst St., Buffalo, New York 14212.

Johnson, Vernon E. *I'll Quit Tomorrow*. Harper and Row, 1973. The basics of alcoholism.

Sandmaier, Marian. *The Invisible Alcoholics: Women and Alcohol Abuse in America*. McGraw-Hill, 1980. Ground-breaking, comprehensive discussion of the alcoholics whom we have ignored: women!

Swollow, Jean, ed. *Out From Under: Sober Dykes and Our Friends*. Spinsters, Ink, 1983. Another invisible population: lesbian women.

Wholey, Dennis. *The Courage to Change*. Warner Books, 1984. Interviews with famous people who are alcoholics. Informational and inspirational.

Sex Addiction

Sex Addicts Anonymous, Box 3038, Minneapolis, Minnesota 55403. Mixed meetings.

Sex and Love Addicts Anonymous, P. O. Box 119, New Town Branch, Boston, Massachusetts 02258. (Offenders may seek help at these groups.)

Carnes, Ph.D., Patrick. *Out of the Shadows*. CompCare, 1983. Comprehensive (though primarily male identified). Second half addresses partners.

Relationship Addiction
See resources for Chapter 14.

Eating Disorders

ANAD (National Association of Anorexia Nervosa and Associated Disorders), P. O. Box 7, Highland Park, Illinois 60611.

ANRED (Anorexia Nervosa and Related Eating Disorders), P. O. Box 5102, Eugene, Oregon 97405.

National Anorexic Aid Society, 550 S. Cleveland Avenue, Suite F, Wasterville, Ohio 43081.

American Anorexia/Bulimia Association, 133 Cedar Lane, Teaneck, New Jersey 07666.

Overeaters Anonymous (check your phone book).

Kano, Susan. *Making Peace with Food.* Harper and Row, 1989.

Kaplan, Jane Rachel. *A Woman's Conflict: The Special Relationship Between Women and Food.* Prentice-Hall, 1980.

Bass and Davis in *The Courage to Heal* offer additional resources on eating disorders.

Adult Children of Alcoholics

National Association of Children of Alcoholics (NACoA), 31582 Coast Highway, Suite B, S. Laguna, California 92677. Information on all resources for ACOA's.

Adult Children of Alcoholics (ACOA). Some groups have broadened their focus to be "Adult Children of Alcoholics and Dysfunctional Families.": call NCA.

Black, Claudia. *It Will Never Happen to Me!* MAC Publishing, 1981.

Heckler, Jonellen. *A Fragile Peace.* Pocket Books, 1986. Fiction.

Woititz, Janet Geringer, Ed.D. *Adult Children of Alcoholics.* Health Communications, Inc., 1983.

Changes, a magazine published by The U. S. Journal of Drug and Alcohol Dependence, Inc. and Health Communications, Inc., 1721 Blount Rd. Suite 1, Pompano Beach, Florida 33069. Full of resources, but also illustrates what "big business" the addictions has become.

Obsessive-Compulsive Disorder

Obsessive-Compulsive Disorder Foundation, P. O. Box 9573, New Haven, Connecticut 06535. Information, "finder-friends" (linkage for people with OCD). Guidelines for support group development.

CHAPTER 11: VICTIMIZATION AND SELF-DESTRUCTIVENESS

Self-Injury Behavior Consultant: Karen Conterio, P. O. Box 267810, Chicago, Illinois 60626.

CHAPTER 12: THE BODY

Westurland, Ph.D., Elaine. *Body and Movement*. Cambridge Women's Center, 46 Pleasant Street, Cambridge, Massachusetts 02139.

————"Inside Out: Therapeutic Body Work for Women with Incest Histories." 45-minute tape (available from the same address as above).

CHAPTER 13: SEX (IS NOT SEX)

SIECUS (Sex Information and Education Council of the United States) offers information on research, education, and resources. It is affiliated with New York University. A bimonthly journal, *The SIECUS Report*, is available from SIECUS, 32 Washington Place, New York, New York 10003. At the same address is the Mary S. Calderone Library, also called the Resource Center. Write for a topic-related bibliography.

See *The Courage to Heal*, by Bass and Davis for a further listing of resources on body awareness and function, as well as sexuality.

CHAPTER 14: RELATIONSHIPS, PART 1

Co-dependents Anonymous, Box 33577, Phoenix, Arizona 85067-3577; Relationships Anonymous: Check your local Self Help Clearinghouse or newspaper. Look for women-only meetings: "cruising" often goes on at mixed meetings.

Beattie, Melody. *Codependent No More*. Hazelden, 1987.

Dowling, Charlotte. *The Cinderella Complex*. Pocket Books, 1981. Criticized for overlooking social issues and blaming the victim, nevertheless this book offers valuable insight.

Halpern, Howard. *How to Break Your Addiction to a Person*. Bantam, 1983.

Hoffman, Susanna. *Men Who Are Good for You and Men Who Are Bad*. Ten Speed Press, 1987.

Norwood, Robin. *Women Who Love Too Much*. Pocket Books, 1985. This book hit a nerve in many readers, but it overlooks issues of women's socialization.

Russianoff, Penelope. *Why Do I Think I Am Nothing Without a Man?* Bantam, 1983.

Books specifically on codependence may be found listed in *Courage to Heal.*

CHAPTER 16: HOPE, HEALING, AND BEYOND

Model Mugging, P. O. Box 921, Monterey, California 93942-0921.

Human Healing Arts, Inc: Wendy Hoffman, P. O. Box 1898, New York, New York 10025. Recovery and education through the performing and visual arts.

Appendix A
Groups and Newsletters
for Incest Survivors

These groups offer programs, resources, book reviews, and linking for survivors, and pro-survivors. Some are for women only, some are predominantly made up of women, some focus equally on women and men. Membership opens the door to an outstanding networking opportunity; with every newsletter comes notice of additional resources for incest and related issues.

Many of these organizations operate on a shoestring and are grateful for your donation.

VOICES (Victims of Incest Can Emerge Survivors) IN ACTION, INC., P. O. Box 148309, Chicago, Illinois 60614. Individual membership $45 (may have to follow up on correspondence). Literature, conference, local groups and "special interest groups" that link people by mail and phone nationwide (for example, survivors who are male, and survivors who experienced cult abuse).

The Incest Awareness Project, *Breaking the Silence* (newsletter), P. O. Box 8122, Fargo, North Dakota 58109. $12 for membership and 6 issues of newsletter.

Survivors Newsletter Collective, *For Crying Out Loud* (newsletter 4 times a year), Women's Center, 46 Pleasant Street, Cambridge, Massachusetts 02139. $10. Also available from Survivors Newsletter Collective: *Incest Resources* (one-time only resource handbook). $3.

The Looking Up Times (written by survivors) and *The Survivor Resource Chronicle* (information, resources). $15. Wilderness trips, retreats, referrals, consultation and training of professionals. Serves m/f survivors. Looking Up, Box K, Augusta, Maine 04332-0470.

Incest Survivor's Information Exchange, P. O. Box 3399, New Haven, Connecticut 06515. $10 for quarterly newsletter. Issues follow particular themes.

Survivors of Incest Anonymous (SIA), now merged with the former Sex Abuse Anon (SAA). 12-Step "spiritually based" (focus on a "higher power") recovery program that follows the model used by AA and Al-Anon. Meetings in most cities. Offers extensive literature list—send self-addressed stamped envelope. World Service Office (headquarters), P. O. Box 21817, Baltimore, Maryland 21222-6817. No newsletter.

Adults Molested as Children, 605 SE 39th, Portland, Oregon 97214.

FOR GROUPS IN YOUR AREA

Some of these groups (such as VOICES and SIA) may offer local group meetings in your area. Calendar sections of newspapers, Rape Crisis Centers, Victims Services, and knowledgeable therapists may also be able to provide you with information on local self help groups for incest.

Appendix B
Resources for Special Populations

FOR PARTNERS

Sections on pro-survivors are included in some of the recommended incest books in Appendix C.

FOR MOTHERS

Advocacy groups for children and the mothers who are trying to help them:

- National Child Rights Alliance, P. O. Box 17005, Durham, North Carolina 27705-0005. Voting membership consists of victims and survivors of child abuse (all kinds).
- MARC (Mothers Against Raping Children) P.O. Box 783, Charleston, South Carolina 29402. Helps mothers who are trying to rescue their children.
- Children's Freedom Project, P.O. Box 1540, Montpelier, Vermont 05601.

Byerly, Carolyn M. *The Mother's Book: How to Survive the Incest of Your Child*. Dubuque, Iowa: Kendall/Hunt, 1985. Available for $5.95 plus $1 postage from Washington Coalition of Sexual Assault Programs, 110 E. 5th St., Room 214, Olympia, Washington 98501. Focus is on mothers of young victims, but much applies to mothers of adult survivors as well.

FOR MALE SURVIVORS

PLEA, Box 59045, Norwalk, California 90652-0045. For nonoffending males.

Some of the groups listed in Appendix A include or provide subgroups for men.

Lew, Mike. *Victims No Longer: Men Recovering from Incest.* Ruby Street Press. A sensitive, aware book for all survivors.

See also *Adults Molested As Children* in Appendix C (books).

FOR RITUAL ABUSE SURVIVORS
(and their CARETAKERS)

Believe the Children, P.O. Box 1358, Manhattan Beach, California 90266.

The Cult Hotline, 1651 3rd Ave., New York, New York 10028.

VOICES IN ACTION has a "Special Interest Group" (SIG) on Ritual Abuse. See Appendix A.

Healing Hearts, P.O. Box 6274, Albany, California 94706.

Somerset County Chaplaincy Council, Executive Director, Rev. Kathleen Roney-Wilson, 100 W. Main St., Somerville, New Jersey 08876.

The Cult Awareness Network, 2421 W. Pratt Blvd., Chicago, Illinois 60645.

Appendix C
Books for Adult Survivors of Child Sexual Abuse

STORIES

Bass, Ellen, and Louise Thornton, eds. *I Never Told Anyone: Writing by Women Survivors of Child Sexual Abuse*. Harper and Row, 1983. Personal, intense stories.

McNaron, Toni A., and Yarrow Morgan, eds. *Voices in the Night: Women Speaking About Incest*. Cleis Press, 1982. Stories in their own voices.

WHAT INCEST IS (INCLUDES POLITICAL ANALYSIS)

Butler, Sandra. *Conspiracy of Silence: The Trauma of Incest*. Revised edition. Volcano Press, 1986. Comprehensive analysis of the social attitudes and circumstances (the politics and the sex roles) that contribute to the family dynamics and other situations in which incest occurs.

Herman, M.D., Judith. *Father-Daughter Incest*. Harvard University Press, 1987. A wonderful overview of feelings and issues, very political.

Rush, Florence. *The Best Kept Secret: Sexual Abuse of Children*. Prentice-Hall, 1980. The original challenge to Freud's—and society's—betrayal of women.

Ward, Elizabeth. *Father-Daughter Rape*. Grove Press, 1985. Political analysis of the relationship between women, men, power, and sex.

TECHNICAL AND PROFESSIONAL

Finkelhor, David. *Child Sexual Abuse: New Theory and Research*. Free Press, 1984. Research findings on all aspects, including aftereffects, of child sexual abuse.

Miller, Alice. *Thou Shalt Not Be Aware*. Meridian, 1984. A psychoanalyst puts Freud and his "drive theory" in their place. Mostly for professionals and serious readers.

Masson, Jeffrey Moussaieff. *The Assault on Truth: Freud's Suppression of the Seduction Theory*. Ferrar, Strauss & Giroux, 1984. Challenges Freud's abandonment of incest survivors; its accuracy has been questioned by some scholars.

Russell, Diana. *The Secret Trauma: Incest in the Lives of Women and Girls*. Basic Books, 1986. Research findings and analysis, but an easy read.

RECOVERY AND TREATMENT

Bass, Ellen, and Laura Davis. *The Courage to Heal*. Harper and Row, 1988. A comprehensive and sensitive review of what the survivor feels and what she can do about it, stages of recovery, exercises, therapy issues, and resources on *every* topic; including body awareness, sexuality, sexual violence, and others.

Bear, E., and P. Dimrock. *Adults Molested As Children: A Survivors' Manual for Women and Men*. First Society Press, 1988. Order through The Safer Society Program, RR#1, Box 24 B, Orwell, Vermont 05760-9756. $12.95 (includes postage). Short book, but full of resources.

Gil, Iliana. *Outgrowing the Pain*. Launch Press, 1983. The perfect introductory book—it's gentle, easy, and comprehensive. Addresses what the survivor will experience.

Lison, Karen, and Carol Poston. *Reclaiming Our Lives*. Little, Brown and Co., 1989. How to conquer negative aftereffects.

Loulan, JoAnn. *Lesbian Sex*. Spinsters, Ink, 1984. Not just about sex and not just for lesbians, this very wise book discusses relationships, communication, self-esteem, body image. Gives exercises to address the consequences of incest.

Maltz, Wendy, and Beverly Holman. *Incest and Sexuality: A Guide to Understanding and Healing*. Lexington Books, 1987. Includes information for partners. The authors' work was originally with teenage incest survivors, and much of the book is taken from that.

Index

DATE DUE

2? '98		
8·11-98		
ILL		
734161		
3/24/00		
JA 01 '02		
JA 30 '02		
AP 10 '03		

GAYLORD